Feel the Grass Grow

FEEL THE GRASS GROW

Ecologies of Slow Peace in Colombia

Angela Jill Lederach

Stanford University Press
Stanford, California

Stanford University Press
Stanford, California

Printed in the United States of America on acid-free, archival-quality paper

Library of Congress Cataloging-in-Publication Data

Names: Lederach, Angela Jill, author.
Title: Feel the grass grow : ecologies of slow peace in Colombia / Angela Jill Lederach.
Description: Stanford, California : Stanford University Press, 2023. | Includes bibliographical references and index.
Identifiers: LCCN 2022039165 (print) | LCCN 2022039166 (ebook) | ISBN 9781503634640 (cloth) | ISBN 9781503635685 (paperback) | ISBN 9781503635692 (ebook)
Subjects: LCSH: Peace-building—Colombia. | Peasants—Political activity—Colombia. | Political violence—Colombia.
Classification: LCC JZ5584.C7 L44 2023 (print) | LCC JZ5584.C7 (ebook) | DDC 303.6/609861—dc23/eng/20220923
LC record available at https://lccn.loc.gov/2022039165
LC ebook record available at https://lccn.loc.gov/2022039166

Cover design: David Fassett / Notch Design
Cover photograph: Claudia Verenice Flores Escolero, *Sanctuary of Peace*, view of Montes de María from the Villa Barbara Sembrandopaz Farm
Typeset by Elliott Beard in Adobe Garamond Pro 10.5/15

Dedicated to Sembrandopaz
Gracias por posibilitar mi proyecto de vida—
Que sigamos soñando juntxs

CONTENTS

PART III
Paz sin Prisa—Slow Peace

ACKNOWLEDGMENTS

MANY VOICES HAVE CONTRIBUTED TO this ethnography. I am especially indebted to my friends and colleagues in Montes de María who have accompanied me from the beginning of this process, providing invaluable reflections, analyses, critiques, and support over nearly a decade of partnership. My research questions, lines of inquiry, and field of vision for this project would have been profoundly diminished without close accompaniment from Sembrandopaz, the Proceso Pacífico de Reconciliación e Integración de la Alta Montaña, the Jóvenes Provocadores de Paz de la Alta Montaña, and the Espacio Regional de Construcción de Paz de los Montes de María. Thank you for the many ways you all invited me in, oriented my research, and engaged in the co-construction of this work. I have often reflected on the immense privilege it has been to learn from your social processes, community organizing approaches, and daily engagement in peacebuilding, all of which have fundamentally contributed to my own political formation—for which I am deeply grateful.

I am especially thankful for the formation that I have received in participatory action research and grassroots peacebuilding from Rosa Jiménez Ahumada, Ana Verónica Montaño Chamorro, Ricardo Esquivia Ballestas, Lillian Hall, Yésica Blanco, Etel Salas, Wilton Ortíz, Oscar Vergara, Narciso Díaz, Manuela Emperatriz Buelvas Anaya, Stella Ramos, Daris Padilla, Osmar Ortega, Leidy Ballesta Ríos, América Vaquerano Romero, Rosa del Carmen

Argueta, Ana Milena Ballesta, Claudia Verenice Flores, Lani Gomez Pickard, Pablo Abitbol, Chucho Pérez, Jose Francisco Restrepo, Jose Macareno, Catalina Pérez, Pedro Vasquez, Amilcar Rocha, Víctor Negrete, Eduardo Porras, Camilo Rey, Dionisio Alarcón, Luz Mery Valdez, Hernando González Meléndez, Yolyz Correa, Claudia Cueto, Juana Alicia Ruiz and family, Gabriel Pulido, Soraya Bayuelo, Julia Cagollo, Rosember Barón Berrio, Jorge Montes, Miledys Vásquez Navarro, Lenis Navarro de Vásquez, Jocabeth Canoles, Aroldo Canoles, Truby Canoles, Ciro Canoles, William Jaraba—and the whole Jaraba family, Jose Arrieta, the Mendoza family, Omar Rodriguez, Elisa Judith Buelvas Garcia, Deiver Canoles, Julio Parra Arrieta, Domingo Rafael Deavila Buelvas and family, Reinaldo Ovalle Olivero and family, Irina Junieles, Ivonne Díaz, Arturo Zea, Judith Pinedo Flórez, Angelina González Jiménez, Naún Álvarez González, Geovaldis González Jiménez, and Ignacia González Jiménez. I want to extend my deep sense of gratitude to the many members of the Proceso Pacífico de Reconciliación e Integración de la Alta Montaña, the Jovenes Provocadores de Paz, the Comité de Mujeres de la Alta Montaña, Mampuján Mujeres Tejiendo Sueños y Sabores de Paz, Afro-Música, Sembrandopaz, the Zona de Reserva Campesina, the Mesa de Interlocución y Concertación, and the Espacio Regional de Construcción de Paz de los Montes de María who made this project possible. In addition to professional support, the moral and emotional support that I have received from Naún, Jocabeth, Elmer Arrieta Herrerra, Jose Ortega, Jose Niño, Darlis Hernandez, Ronald Mendoza, Glenda Jaraba, and the Vigías Ecológicas—who were central participants in the research and writing process—has sustained me across many years of friendship. Thank you for evenings of *echando cuentos*, walks through the campo, moments of rest in the sway of the hammocks, and companionship. The videos of the birdsongs and landscapes of the Alta Montaña in the final months of writing were especially significant for my own sense of rootedness. Larisa Zehr, in particular, played a significant supporting role throughout the research process. Lari, thank you for orienting my research and walking alongside me from the beginning—our evening conversations, many adventures, and your critical questions are present throughout this ethnography.

I would have been lost without the transcription and research support that I received from Paola Benavides and Silvia Lozano. Silvia Lozano also contributed significantly to the translation of written materials. I also want to acknowledge the skills of Elkin, Rafael, and Yair who always provided me with safe passage and companionship along the many journeys in the Alta Montaña. Borja Palidini, Josefina Echavarría Alvarez, and the Barometro/ PAM team provided important spaces for sharing early iterations of this work. Anna Vogt, Sarah Richardson, Becca Méndez, Carolina Serrano, Luis Felipe Botero, Elise Ditta, Gwen Burnyeat, Saskia Nauenberg Dunkell, Alex Diamond, and Daniel Ruiz Serna all contributed to the analyses and theories present in this book by creating spaces for sharing scholarly work while I was living in Colombia and after I returned to the United States. I am especially indebted to my dear colleagues Manuel Salamanca, Mery Rodriguez, Martha Márquez, María Lucía Zapata, Wendy Kroeker, and Cécile Mouly for creating a supportive, generative, and caring community of scholar-practitioners that has deeply shaped this work. I received immense support and companionship through writing retreats and writing accountability groups shared with Danae Yankoski, Stefanie Israel de Sousa, Lucía Tiscornia, and Janna Hunter-Bowman—thank you for helping me to find joy in the writing process. The caretakers at GilChrist Retreat Center created a space where—in the rush of deadlines—I could tap into a slower rhythm of life that enabled me to immerse myself in the creative process—for which I am grateful. A number of coffee shops—across states and countries—also sustained me while writing this book. Thanks to Cerro Maco in El Carmen, Época Café in Cartagena, The General in South Bend, Red Buffalo in Silverthorne, and Archetype in Omaha for skilled baristas and community spaces.

The New Research from Women Studying Violence working group provided key spaces for collaboration and scholarly engagement throughout multiple iterations of this project. I am grateful for Lucía Tiscornia and Abby Córdova's thoughtful organization and planning—and to all of the members of that community who have shown me what building scholarly communities of care and support can look like, may we keep cultivating such spaces together. I want to especially thank Janice Gallagher and Angélica Durán-Martínez for insightful comments that improved and deepened the analysis found across the pages to follow. The Communications Team of the Alta Montaña provided rich visual images found throughout this book—I am especially grateful for the artistic support from Elmer Arrieta Herrerra and

Omar Rodriguez. I want to thank Julio E. Cortés for the detailed maps used throughout this book. I am also thankful for the writing support I received from Justin de Leon, Nicole Gerring, Cat Standfield, Kate Paarlberg-Kvam, Dan Fahey, Garrett Fitzgerald, and Elena B. Stavrevska. And, I would have been lost without the constant care extended to me by Roxani Krystalli— thank you for generative conversations, poetic morsels, and notes of encour- agement— all of which have deeply informed the chapters that follow.

The research for this book would not have been possible without funding support from Fulbright Colombia, the United States Institute of Peace Jen- nings Randolph Peace Scholarship, USAID Global Development Fellowship, the Kellogg Institute for International Studies, and the Kroc Institute for In- ternational Peace Studies. Parts of chapter 2 appeared in an article published by *American Anthropologist*: "'The Campesino Was Born for the Campo': A Multispecies Approach to Territorial Peace in Colombia," *American Anthro- pologist* 119, no. 4 (2017): 589–602. Sections of the discussion on youth iden- tity formation, found in chapters 2 and 7, appeared in an article published by *Peacebuilding*: "Youth Provoking Peace: An Intersectional Approach to Ter- ritorial Peacebuilding in Colombia," *Peacebuilding* 8, no. 2 (2019): 198–217. I am grateful for the ways those publications—and comments from thoughtful reviewers—led me to deepen and clarify the arguments further developed in this book. I also want to thank my editor, Dylan Kyung-lim White, assistant editor, Sunna Juhn, and the editorial team at Stanford University Press for thoughtful feedback, attention to detail, and support for the vision and eth- ical commitments expressed in this book—it has been an immense pleasure to work with and learn from you all.

Early iterations of several chapters received insightful comments from Caroline Hughes, Emily Maiden, George Lopez, Siobhan McEvoy-Levy, Roddy Brett, Jeff Peterson, Emily de Wet, Todd Marek, Amanda Cortez, Rieti Gengo, Sara Morrow, Heather Dubois, Kyle Lambelet, Laura Weiss, Janna Hunter-Bowman, and Francis Bonenfant. And, to Leo Guardado, Leslie MacColman, Dana Townsend, Jesse James, Katy-Marie Lance, and Chris Haw: Your voices are present throughout this book—thank you for walking alongside me from beginning to end. Joanne Rappaport and María Clemencia Ramírez provided invaluable feedback that led to significant im- provements in the organization and flow of the final manuscript—thank you for your time, care, and generative engagement with this project. Finally, the suggestions, questions, and feedback that I received from members of the Espacio Regional, the Proceso Pacífico, Sembrandopaz, and the Jóvenes Provocadores de Paz on an early draft of this manuscript were critical for deepening and clarifying the arguments made throughout this book.

I'm grateful for my scholarly communities at Creighton University and the University of Notre Dame. The Kroc Institute for International Peace Studies, the Department of Anthropology, and the Kellogg Institute at the University of Notre Dame all created formative spaces of learning and intellectual collaboration. The support that I received from my colleagues in the Department of Cultural and Social Studies at Creighton University sustained me amid the pandemic and in the final stages of the writing process—with special thanks to Laura Heinemann, Renzo Rosales, Cristina Pop, Erin Blackenship-Sefczek, and Alex Roedlach. I also want to thank Carolyn Nordstrom, whose scholarly work and personal support across the years has deeply shaped my own trajectory as an anthropologist—and whose feedback at early stages of the research significantly contributed to the final project. I lack adequate words to express my gratitude for the seemingly unending reserves of time, care, and feedback that I received from Catherine Bolten, Agustín Fuentes, and Ann Mische over the course of the entire research process, which brought this ethnography into being. Cat, I think you have read more drafts of this book than anyone else mentioned in these pages. I am so grateful for your time, care, and engagement with this project; Ann, thank you for reading deeply and helping me forge generative connections across disciplinary silos; and Agustín, I am thankful for your exuberant support, guidance, and ethical commitment to the wider vision in which this project is situated. I am deeply grateful for the ways in which you all model intellectual curiosity and ethical commitment to public scholarship.

The continuous support—meals, conversations, spaces of rest—that my parents-in-law, Jack and Ruth Yoder, as well as my grandparents, Naomi and John Lederach, provided were much needed over the course of many years. And while my grandma Naomi will not see these pages between two covers, I know her spirit is celebrating.

Writing brings me great joy, apprehension, energy—and doubt. Whether I needed to take a break, rekindle confidence, or celebrate milestones, my mom, Wendy, was there every step of the way. Thank you, mom, for getting me through and helping me have fun along the way. My dad, John Paul, has shaped the pages of this book in more ways than I realize—long before the first questions that animate this text came into being. Mom and dad, I am immensely grateful for your care, patience, listening ears, and guidance—all of which have fundamentally shaped my sense of self and *proyecto de vida*. To my brother, Josh, thanks for keeping me grounded—our conversations over dinners, drinks, walks in the woods, and long bike rides helped these pages materialize.

To my life partner, Jeff, words fail to express my gratitude for your companionship throughout this process. Your joy, love for Colombia, long walks, endless conversations, translation support, and constant presence throughout the research and writing process made this book possible. To Isa, thank you for reminding me to play, walk slowly, and find wonder in life's smallest and most remarkable gifts. This book would not have been possible without the love, care, and joy that my family brings. You both (and the growing *relevo generacional*) constantly remind me that we are always more than ourselves.

In the process of writing this book, my dear mentor, colleague, and friend, Rosa Jiménez Ahumada, passed from this world. Rosa's enduring commitment to peace animates these pages—and it is my hope that her life lives on through them, *siempre caminando*.

LIST OF ACRONYMS

ACCU: Campesino Self-Defense Forces of Córdoba and Urabá (Autodefensas Campesinas de Córdoba y Urabá)

ADR: Rural Development Agency (Agencia de Desarrollo Rural)

Alta Consejería: The Office of the High Advisory to the President on the Regions (Alta Consejería Presidencial para las Regiones)

ANT: National Land Agency (Agencia Nacional de Tierras)

ANUC: The National Association of Campesino Users (Asociación Nacional de Usuarios Campesinos)

ART: Territorial Renovation Agency (Agencia de Renovación del Territorio)

AUC: United Self-Defense Forces of Colombia, or the paramilitaries (Autodefensas Unidas de Colombia)

BACRIM: Illicit Criminal Networks (Bandas Criminales)

CCAI: Center for the Coordination of Integrated Action

CEV: The Commission for the Clarification of Truth, Coexistence, and Non-Repetition, or the Colombian Truth Commission (La Comisión para el Esclarecimiento de la Verdad, la Convivencia y la No Repetición)

Citizen's Commission: Citizen's Commission for Reconciliation and Peace in the Caribbean (Comisión Ciudadana de Reconciliación y Paz del Caribe)

CNMH: National Center for Historical Memory (Centro Nacional de Memoria Histórica)

CORPOICA: Colombian Corporation for Agricultural Research (Corporación Colombiana de Investigación Agropecuaria)

CTC: Colombian Confederation of Workers (Confederación de Trabajadores de Colombia)

CRS: Socialist Renewal Movement (Corriente de Renovación Socialista)

CSPP: Committee for Solidarity with Political Prisoners (Fundación Comité de Solidaridad con los Presos Políticos)

ELN: National Liberation Army (Ejército de Liberación Nacional)

EPL: Popular Liberation Army (Ejército Popular de Liberación)

Espacio Regional: Montes de María Regional Space for Peacebuilding (Espacio Regional de Construcción de Paz de los Montes de María)

FARC-EP: Revolutionary Armed Forces of Colombia-People's Army (Fuerzas Armadas Revolucionarias de Colombia-Ejército del Pueblo)

Forgotten Communities: Association of Forgotten Communities of Montes de María (Asociación de Comunidades Olvidadas de los Montes de María)

ICA: Colombian Agricultural Institute (Instituto Colombiano Agropecuaria)

INCORA: Agrarian Reform Institute (Instituto Colombiano de la Reforma Agraria)

INGO: International Nongovernmental Organization

JAC: Community Action Council (Junta Acción Comunal)

JEP: Special Jurisdiction for Peace (Jurisdicción Especial para la Paz)

JOPPAZ: Youth Peace Provokers of the Alta Montaña (Jóvenes Provocadores de Paz de la Alta Montaña)

M-19: 19th of April Movement (Movimiento 19 de Abril)

MIC: Roundtable for Dialogue and Coordination (Mesa de Interlocución y Concertación)

MOVICE: Movement of Victims of State-Sponsored Crimes (Movimiento Nacional de Víctimas de Crímenes de Estado)

OACP: Office of the High Commissioner for Peace (Oficina del Alto Comisionado para la Paz)

PAM: Peace Accords Matrix

PAR: Participatory Action Research (Investigación-Acción Participativa)

Peaceful Process: Alta Montaña Peaceful Process of Reconciliation and Integration (Proceso Pacífico de Reconciliación e Integración de la Alta Montaña)

PRT: Revolutionary Workers Party (Partido Revolucionario de los Trabajadores)

Sembrandopaz: Sowing Seeds of Peace (Sembrando Semillas de Paz)

Victim's Law: Victim's and Restitution of Land Law 1448 (La Ley de Víctimas y Restitución de Tierras 1448)

Victim's Unit: Unit for the Attention and Integral Reparations of Victims (Unidad para la Atención y Reparación Integral a las Víctimas)

ZRC: Campesino Reserve (Zona Reserva de Campesina)

ZVTN: Transitory Rural Zones for Normalization (Zonas Veredales Transitorias de Normalización)

FIGURE 1. Archives of *Resistencia* with Jorge Pérez. Photo by author.

TO DEFEND LIFE
An Introduction

ON AUGUST 24, 2016, THE government of Colombia and the Fuerzas Armadas Revolucionarias de Colombia—Ejército del Pueblo (FARC-EP) announced that they had reached a final peace agreement after over fifty years of war. As major news networks broadcast then President Juan Manuel Santos's announcement from Havana, Cuba, I sat next to Jorge Pérez under the tin roof of his open-air living room in the Alta Montaña (High Mountain) of El Carmen de Bolívar, a municipality located along Colombia's northern coast. Jorge leaned back in a handmade chair, carefully propped up against one of the posts of his house, as he recounted the history of his community (*vereda*).[1] Stacks of papers sat in piles around Jorge's feet. He had placed small rocks on top of the papers to guard against the steady breeze that passed through the open living room. As he spoke, he sifted through the stacks, locating cherished and worn documents to tell his story.

I had traveled to Jorge's house at the invitation of Larisa Zehr, an accompaniment worker from the local peacebuilding organization, Sembrandopaz. Most recently, Larisa's work included accompanying the Alta Montaña's historical memory process. Facilitated in collaboration with the National Center for Historical Memory (CNMH), the community-based process responded to one of the reparation measures outlined in the signed accords between the campesino movement, the Proceso Pacífico de Reconciliación

e Integración de la Alta Montaña (Alta Montaña Peaceful Process of Reconciliation and Integration, shortened to Peaceful Process) and the state in
2013. Jorge formed part of the team of "narrators"—writers—and had begun
organizing his community's archives for the historical memory book. He had
asked Larisa to come and scan the saved meeting minutes, legal proceedings,
human rights violations, and records of the Junta Acción Comunal (Community Action Council, abbreviated JAC) into a cell phone application as part
of that process.

Larisa and I left the urban center of El Carmen in the afternoon. Seated
behind a trusted moto driver, we passed lines of jeeps full of the day's harvest at the busy intersection of Twenty-Eighth Street. I watched campesinos
unloading the jeeps and bartering with the intermediaries in charge of the
storage and export centers located along the highway as we headed up the
winding road to the Alta Montaña. The open grasslands characteristic of the
large cattle ranches that line the lower region of El Carmen passed from
view as we climbed into the Montaña's dry-tropical rainforest. The cool air
and shade from the old growth caracolí, mango, and ceiba trees provided
a respite from the hot temperatures and dusty streets of El Carmen. At the
highest point of the paved road, we turned off onto a steep and narrow dirt
path. The base of the Colombian Marine Infantry—replete with a helicopter
landing pad—came into view when we rounded the last hill before descending into the heart of the Alta Montaña. As the dirt road flattened, the peaks,
valleys, marshes, rivers, and reservoirs of Montes de María spread out before
us. I could glimpse the shimmering waters of the Caribbean Sea in the far
distance.

The beauty of the panoramic views belied the history and memories of
violence also held within the landscape. The armed conflict had taken a devastating toll on the fifty-two communities that compose the Alta Montaña.
Massacres, disappearances, arbitrary detentions, selective assassinations, and
massive, forced displacements form part of the litany of violence that campesinos experienced at the hands of multiple armed groups that operated in
the region. The isolated and thickly forested region served as a strategic base
for the FARC-EP, the Popular Liberation Army (EPL; Esperanza, Paz y Libertad), the National Liberation Army (ELN; Ejército de Liberación Nacional), the Revolutionary Workers Party (PRT; Partido Revolucionario de los

Trabajadores) as well as the United Self-Defense Forces of Colombia (AUC, or, paramilitaries), and the Colombian Marine Infantry. Campesinos found themselves "caught in between" competing armed groups over the course of decades.

"Ay-o!" Jorge greeted us as the motos descended the narrow path to his house. I dismounted, shaking Jorge's hand with a warm greeting. Hundreds of fallen old-growth trees lined the steep hillside below. He followed my gaze. "Here, before, these were mountains of avocado," he explained. "Here, there were avocado trees that reached thirty meters high, mountain after mountain of avocado," he gestured across the barren hillsides. "I could not see the neighbor's house. Now it is seen because all the avocado, *ajá*," his voice trailed off as we took in the ashen-white logs that blanketed the steep hillside.[2] "We are talking about 6,000 hectares of avocado," Jorge continued. "Since the time of my grandfather, these were farms of avocados. Imagine it!" He paused, giving us time to envision the thick, green forests. "This avocado farm was more than fifty years old. Look at what has been lost." Jorge shook his head. A donkey cried from the valley below, filling the space of silence, memory, and loss. "Here, before, one had everything one needed, one lived well. Here, there was a massive displacement. The death of the avocado has affected everything." Rather than separate the experience of forced displacement from the death of the avocado forest, Jorge connected the two experiences as inextricably linked, lifting out the human and environmental costs of war in his narrative. He turned away from the lookout and motioned for us to take a seat next to the stacks of paper that he had carefully arranged in the open-air living room.

Despite bombings, forced displacement, and the social upheaval wrought by war, Jorge had protected and preserved his community's history. The archives, carefully guarded and enclosed in makeshift cardboard folders, reflected the practices of campesino *resistencia* (resistance) found across Montes de María.[3] Jorge sifted through the papers, carefully maintained throughout the years, as he spoke. His grandparents started the first school, cradled in the valley below his house. "At that time, there were many children but no teachers willing to travel to the Montaña," he recalled, "so, my grandparents organized the children together to teach them. It makes one very proud to know this history, to know that their legacy lives on." He pulled out an aged piece of paper—the edges worn with small smudges across the front. The page contained the names and signatures of all the Community Action Council (JAC; Junta Acción Comunal) members since the organization's inception. He pointed to the name of his grandfather and, with his finger, traced the page until he found his own name. The signature marked an integral part of his life story, the moment when he first joined the JAC in the early 1990s. "This leadership," he said, looking up from the page, "is in my blood."

Violence offers only one part of the story that Jorge chooses to recount about his life and community. In his telling, the rich traditions of campesino organizing, *resistencia*, and agroforestry form the foundation of his narrative. Accounts that focus solely on war and suffering obscure the multigenerational struggle for peace that shapes how campesinos, like Jorge, narrate the history and territorial identity of Montes de María.[4] Popular depictions of Montes de María as one of the territories "most affected" by the armed conflict not only erase the long histories of campesino organizing that have fundamentally marked the region, but also conceal the localized dynamics and consequences of the armed conflict.

Jorge turned back to the paper in his hands as he continued the story. Next to his name appeared the name of the attorney from the urban center of El Carmen who legalized members of the JAC as part of the local governance structure. The same attorney, Jorge explained, later accused the JAC president of "collaboration" with the guerrillas, leading to his assassination. False accusations of campesino leaders became one of the primary forms of violence that local state authorities, like the attorney, used in collaboration with the paramilitaries to maintain power and territorial control. As the campesino movement in Montes de María grew in numbers and influence, the state increasingly engaged in violent repression to undermine the collective power, built through grassroots organizing, that threatened the country's elite political class. The criminalization of campesino organizations through the dual discourses of "security" and "insurgency" enabled the state to normalize violence against campesino social leaders.

"For many years, they said that this area was only full of guerrillas and *micos* (monkeys)," Jorge explained, outlining the ways in which the state denied recognition of civilians in the Alta Montaña. Dehumanizing representations of campesinos legitimized selective assassinations, helicopter bombings, and arbitrary detentions of social leaders throughout the course of the war. Such discourses also rendered more-than-human lives in the Alta Montaña disposable—collateral damage in the war against insurgency. The social and environmental devastation wrought by the war resulted in large-scale, forced displacements of campesino communities from the region.

A few families, however, remained "resistant," refusing to displace to urban cities. "I was part of the Asociación de Comunidades Olvidadas de los Montes de María [Association of Forgotten Communities of Montes de María, shortened to Forgotten Communities]"; Jorge leaned forward in his chair as he detailed the forms of community organizing that persisted throughout the war—yet, which remain largely absent in dominant accounts of the armed conflict. Working across the Alta Montaña, the Forgotten Communities formed to make civilian life in the rural high zone visible to outside authorities. At the height of violence, members of the Forgotten Communities led nonviolent marches to the urban center of El Carmen to demand their constitutional rights as citizens. They also developed communication and collective nonviolent protection strategies, creating shrewd, early warning systems to prevent the assassinations of friends and family members.

As the hot afternoon sun shifted into warm, evening light, Larisa scanned each page of Jorge's archives into the cell phone application. In addition, Jorge gave Larisa a five-page essay he had handwritten for the historical memory book, which focused on the role of social leaders in the Alta Montaña. He looked up, removing his bifocals. "I composed a *décima* [song] about what it means to be a *líder social* [social leader]." His voice rang out as he sang—from memory—his life story, wrapped in the poetic, ten-line stanza song. Jorge's *décima* did not focus on the violence he had endured. Instead, he sang of the "campesino struggle" to "defend life and the right to life."[5]

With evening descending, we said our goodbyes and began the journey back down to El Carmen. When we arrived at the start of the paved road that connects the Alta Montaña to the urban center, SUVs from various media news outlets lined the road. The glaring bright lights, video cameras, external generators, and crowds of newscasters that swarmed the community offered a jarring contrast to our slow afternoon of "swapping stories [*echando cuentos*]." Just hours before, Santos announced that the government and the FARC-EP had reached a peace deal. Reporters holding microphones stood, strategically, in front of the bullet-pocked and burned-out church that sits at the edge of the paved road to capture the reactions of "the victims" to the historic news. With no internet signal, no electricity, and no television, the announcement from Havana had not reached us at Jorge's house. Far removed, yet intimately connected, Jorge sang of the collective campesino struggle for peace at the same time televisions and radios blared Santos's declaration of peace from Havana, Cuba.

Jorge's intimate recollections of violence and peace, as lived and embodied, set against the distant and inaccessible backdrop of Santos's announcement from Havana, exposes the paradox of proximity that many social leaders in Montes de María faced as Colombia ushered in a "new era" of "postconflict." The camera spotlight, trained on spectacular displays of the "historic moment," cast a shadow over and drowned out the songs of the daily and decades-long campesino struggle for territorial peace that social leaders sustained throughout the war. Although many social leaders publicly advocated for the peace accords, the signed agreement posed new challenges for those who, like Jorge, had to find creative ways to make their work seen and heard amid the clamor of the *posconflicto* (postconflict) that dominated the airwaves.

This book makes visible what far too often is lost in mainstream depictions of war and peace. The stories and chapters to follow trace the collective, campesino struggle to build peace as the state's implementation process unfolded in Montes de María. With this purpose in mind, I critically examine the effects that spectacles of peace—often bound to sound bites and photo shoots—have on everyday practices of peace, lived and built in campesino communities. After noting the lack of anthropological engagement with peace as a conceptual category, anthropologist Liisa Malkki (2015) asks: "What would it mean to study peace ethnographically" (104)? This book responds to the concern that animates Malkki's question. I analyze the cultural practices, socioecological relations, temporal disjunctures, historical processes, and constellations of power that structure the uneven landscape of peacebuilding in Colombia.[6] In doing so, I advance a critical anthropology of peacebuilding as a site of struggle.

Throughout my research, campesino leaders repeatedly critiqued the state's approach to peace within distinct temporal registers to expose the varied forms of violence that permeate the postaccord context and to make their claims to peace seen and heard. By placing campesino critiques of "*los tiempos*—the times" as the central starting point for ethnographic inquiry into peace, this book offers a critical assessment of the temporalities that undergird the interlocking processes of political and environmental violence. Ethnographic analysis of the temporal continuities and contestations found in Montes de María affords theoretical insight into the technologies of power, dynamics of violence, and the practices of liberation that shape the postaccord landscape in Colombia. Grounded in the campesino call to build *paz sin prisa* (peace without hurry), I develop an ethnographic theory of slow peace. Although "slow peace" is not a literal translation of *paz sin prisa*, I use the terms interchangeably to place campesino theories of time in conversation with the wider literature on slow movements (Hickel 2019; Kallis et al. 2020; Parkins and Craig 2006; Petrini 2007; Tam 2008).[7] "Slow peace" more accurately reflects the multifaceted dimensions of *paz sin prisa* by foregrounding the relational, place-based, and affective practices that shape temporal experience.[8] Born from grounded theory, slow peace also extends Rob Nixon's (2011) influential concept of "slow violence" to the domain of peace and justice, highlighting the ways in which grassroots communities respond to—and creatively transform—the compounding effects of political and environmental violence. In the chapters that follow, I argue that the campesino call to build *paz sin prisa*—slow peace, gives primacy to everyday life (*cotidianidad*), where relationships are deepened, ancestral memories are held and reclaimed, and ecologies continuously regenerated.

ARRIVALS AND RETURNS

Located along the Caribbean coast between Sincelejo, Sucre, to the south and Cartagena, Bolívar, to the north, the fifteen municipalities that comprise Montes de María carry rich legacies of collective organizing and grassroots peacebuilding. While the region is known today as one of the territories most affected by the Colombian armed conflict, those who live there center the long history of intercultural coalition-building and resistance, born from Afro-Colombian, Indigenous, and Campesino struggles for liberation, in their narratives. I first arrived in Montes de María through an invitation from Ricardo Esquivia, the director of Sembrandopaz. Born to an Indigenous mother and Afrodescendant father on the Caribbean coast, Ricardo experienced the multiple forms of violence familiar to many in the region. He was also deeply formed by his mother's and grandfather's engagements in caregiving and healing work, respectively (Maring 2016). He began apprenticing with his grandfather, an Indigenous shaman, at the age of five. When Ricardo was eight years old, his father was diagnosed with Hansen's disease, more commonly known as leprosy. The state not only displaced and institutionalized his father in a quarantined sanatorium near the capital city of Bogotá, but also forcibly removed Ricardo and his brother Silfredo from their family, placing them in a state-run boarding school near the sanitorium—a twenty-hour bus ride from their rural, coastal home. Abuse, racism, classism, religious stigmatization, and hunger led Ricardo and his brother to eventually seek survival on the streets rather than face the daily onslaught of violation at school (Maring 2016). Two years later, Ricardo and his brother found shelter when the Colombian Mennonite Church opened a boarding school for Protestant children whose families had been diagnosed with leprosy. Drawn to the Anabaptist tradition of nonviolent action and social justice, Ricardo later became a key leader of the Mennonite church.

Ricardo's early childhood experiences shape his holistic vision of peace as part of a permanent process to build social justice. For Ricardo, peace requires close accompaniment of people as they struggle to transform multiple forms of violence in their everyday lives. Although his training as a shaman ended abruptly, his *proyecto de vida* (life project) as a healer did not. Indeed, his grandfather, who, "with his life, gave love," remains an important moral referent for Ricardo's approach to peacebuilding (Ricardo Esquivia quoted in Maring 2016, 196). While Ricardo's life history is distinct, his reverence for the *campo* (countryside), the centrality of environmental caretaking in his understanding of peace, and his intimate awareness of the multiple and interlocking forms of oppression that give rise to war all weave through—albeit in different ways—the narratives of social leaders dedicated to the work of peacebuilding in Montes de María. Their life stories—along with Ricardo's—animate this project.

I came to know Ricardo as a young child. At the time, I was living with my family in Costa Rica where my parents accompanied exiled, Nicaraguan Miskitu leaders seeking the right to territorial sovereignty amid the civil war between the Sandinistas and the US-backed Contras. US-sponsored death threats against my father and a failed kidnapping attempt on my life orchestrated by the CIA eventually forced my family to flee (see Lederach 1999). Ricardo, who had also come under increasing threats because of his work for peace and human rights in Colombia, formed part of the transnational solidarity network that accompanied my family during this time of uncertainty, providing important emotional support as they made the decision to return to the United States. Years later, when military-backed death threats forced Ricardo and his family to flee the country, they temporarily moved next door to us in Virginia. In exile, Ricardo continued his daily work for peace, expanding the transnational network that connected rural communities in Colombia to human rights organizations in the United States. Ricardo deepened my own understanding of peace—not as something that comes after war, but rather as part of a daily struggle to create a radically different world in the midst of violence.

My early childhood experiences led to an enduring interest in the dynamics of state violence, transnational solidarity, and peace—understood as part of a lifelong commitment to transform oppressive systems and cultivate a more just world. This book emerges from that commitment. Rather than feign neutrality, I want to be transparent about the relational ties that led me to this research and the multiple positions that I speak from as a young, white woman from the United States—a country deeply complicit in the violence endured by those with whom I work—and as someone whose life history has been intimately shaped by a transnational community of activists committed to the work of peace. I locate my research within the longstanding tradition of engaged anthropology (Hale 2008; Hale and Stephen 2013; Harrison 1991) and am particularly indebted to generations of feminist scholars who have advocated for an understanding of knowledge as situated (Haraway 1988), contingent and dynamic (Ackerly and True 2008; Ahmed 2017; Berry et al. 2017; Mahmood 2008; Sultana 2007), and profoundly relational (Boulding 1990; Enloe 2004; Krystalli 2019a; McLean and Zapata 2015; Nordstrom 1999). Rather than flatten the relational, social, and historical landscapes that I navigated as part of this research, I have sought to remain responsive to the individuals and collective struggles at the center of this book.[9]

In 2009, I initiated a conversation with Ricardo about the possibility of pursuing graduate study focused on grassroots peacebuilding in Colombia. After spending four years working in the field of international peacebuilding, I had become disillusioned with the colonialist structures that shaped the everyday practices of many international NGOs, which tended to obscure—rather than support—existing, grassroots peacebuilding efforts, even as they championed "local participation." I saw similar patterns reflected in the literature where studies of peace remained largely focused on high-level processes of negotiation. At the time, Sembrandopaz was at the forefront of accompanying campesino communities seeking to return to their land in the midst of war in ways that challenged linear models of "postconflict" peacebuilding, and I was interested in deepening my understanding of their practices and theories of peace. During that initial conversation, I naively asked Ricardo whether "return" was possible in the face of the severe social and political violence that continued to persist in Montes de María. "Angie," he paused, raising his eyes to meet mine, before asserting with a sharp tenderness, "anything is possible." The critiques of international peacebuilding that I offer throughout this book do not emerge from dismissal or cynicism, but rather from the grounded hope that Ricardo has instilled in me over the years. Like my colleagues across Montes de María, I remain fiercely committed to peacebuilding as a site of possibility. Drawing on the critical, social analyses that campesino leaders offer as well as their practices of peacebuilding, I aim to not only contribute to theories of peace but also to outline concrete possibilities for decolonial peace praxis.

In 2014, I began ethnographic and participatory research focused on grassroots peacebuilding in Montes de María with the support of Ricardo and Rosa Jiménez Ahumada, then director of the Observatory for Displacement, Conflict, and Peacebuilding at the University of Cartagena. The participatory framework for the research led me to join the Sembrandopaz team, which provided an inside view into the organization's daily work for peace through accompaniment. Distinct from other international accompaniment efforts aimed at providing nonviolent protection for grassroots communities across Colombia (Burnyeat 2018; Gill 2016; Koopman 2012; Mahony and Eguren 1997), most of the individuals who form part of Sembrandopaz are from the Caribbean coast and lived through multiple forms of violence as a result of the armed conflict. While foreigners, like myself, do work with Sembrandopaz, the organization locates accompaniment as part of their wider framework for peacebuilding, understood as a permanent commitment to walk alongside and amplify the work of grassroots communities engaged in creating spaces of dignified life amid violence.

Sembrandopaz introduced me to the Peaceful Process and the youth wing of the movement, the Jóvenes Provocadores de Paz (Youth Peace Provokers, abbreviated JOPPAZ). Over the course of six months in 2014 and 2015, I engaged in a series of dialogues with the coordinating committees of the Peaceful Process and JOPPAZ to co-construct a collaborative research design. In July 2016, I returned to carry out seventeen consecutive months of ethnographic research based on the design that we had developed together. The signing of the peace accords in September 2016 and the subsequent implementation of the accords in 2017, all of which occurred while I was living in El Carmen de Bolívar, also presented me with the distinct opportunity to examine the relationship between long-term, grassroots peacebuilding movements and the implementation of national peace accords. The accords' "territorial focus" offered one of the first systematic attempts to develop a participatory model aimed at integrating local peacebuilding actors into the national peace process.[10] As one of the pilot sites for implementation of the accords, Montes de María became a particularly rich location for research examining the everyday engagements between local and national actors within the contested landscape of peacebuilding. In the pages that follow, I analyze the contentious interactions between social leaders, International Nongovernmental (INGO) workers, state bureaucrats, donors, and private sector actors, offering insight into the conditions and practices that strengthen, constrain, and fragment grassroots peacebuilding. I ground my theoretical inquiry within a particular ethnographic context to move beyond static binaries of peace understood as either a utopian ideal or merely the absence of war. Instead, I outline the historical, political, socioecological, and temporal processes that have and continue to shape peacebuilding in Colombia. In doing so, I destabilize conceptualizations of peacebuilding as limited only to state-centric and top-down interventions. Instead, I offer an ethnographic theory of peace as a social practice—one that mobilizes political action, shapes subjectivities, and acts on the world.

This book emerges from a total of twenty-five months of research carried out between 2014 and 2021, the bulk of which took place from July 2016 until December 2017. Drawing on participant observation, twelve focus group sessions with 306 campesino youth, and 118 interviews with social leaders, human rights defenders, (I)NGO workers, state bureaucrats, private sector actors, and members of the FARC, I analyze peacebuilding as a site of struggle. I show how the technocratic delivery of "peace" by elite and external actors obscures grassroots peacebuilding processes, even though the text of the accords explicitly purports to do the opposite. Indeed, as I observed the implementation process unfold in Montes de María, I witnessed the continuation—not the transformation—of top-down approaches that *limit* rather than *expand* participation. *Feel the Grass Grow* offers a thick account of how campesino social leaders negotiate, refuse, and reconfigure global mechanisms of peacebuilding as they work to build peace "from and for the territory."

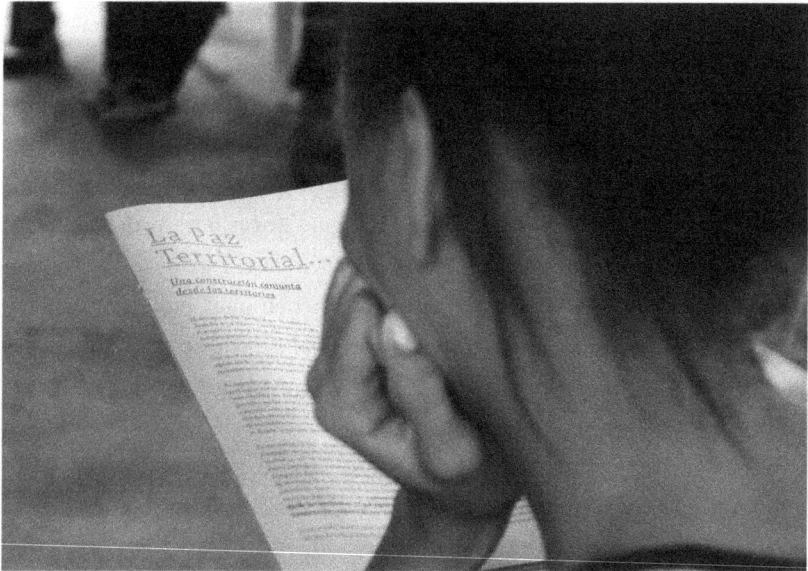

FIGURE 2. Studying the Peace Accords. A youth leader studies the Colombian peace accords in the Alta Montaña. The pamphlet reads: "Territorial Peace." Photo reprinted with permission from Omar Marcial Rodriguez Vides, audiovisual documenter for the Alta Montaña Peaceful Process of Reconciliation and Integration.

RESEARCHING TERRITORIAL PEACE

Over the course of my research, I made the journey from the urban center of El Carmen to the Alta Montaña hundreds of times. I gradually learned to know the place names, landmarks, histories, and families who live in the fifty-two communities of the rural high zone. My body learned to feel for rain before a downpour and move with the moto as we slid across muddy roads, traveled through rivers, and traversed the rocky hillsides of the Montaña. Planting season, rainy season, harvest season, and dry season not only changed the landscape but also the physical and relational journey. The thick mud and the rise of the rivers during rainy season meant that I often hiked when the motos could not pass. Walking immersed me in the rich soundscape of the campo—the rustling of the wind in the trees, the greetings called out between neighbors, the distinct cries of donkeys, the *vallenato* music that blared from billiards halls, and the low, eerie sounds of howler monkeys enveloped me on my daily trips through the Alta Montaña. I learned how to walk purposefully in order to preserve energy under the midday sun and remain alert to the snakes, wildlife, and flora that form an integral part of life in the campo. On lucky days, I caught glimpses of toucans and the endangered *mico titi* (cotton-top tamarin monkey) along the way.

Distinct from traditional ethnographic research, accompanying social leaders entailed constant movement across place. The "multi-locales" (Muir 2004) of territorial peacebuilding expand notions of place-based methodologies as dynamic and plural while still intimately tied to physical geographies and cultural processes of sensing place (Basso 1996).[11] Although I was based in El Carmen and spent most of my time accompanying social leaders in the Alta Montaña, ethnographic research with a social movement was not limited to a single location. Drawing on Shaw and Waldorf's (2010) understanding of "the local" as "the shifted center from which the rest of the world is viewed," I worked outward from rural community life in the Alta Montaña, accompanying members of the Peaceful Process, the Youth Peace Provokers (abbreviated JOPPAZ), and Sembrandopaz as they participated in the broad-based coalition known as the Espacio Regional de Construcción de Paz de los Montes de María (Montes de María Regional Space for Peacebuilding, shortened to Espacio Regional) (6). With representatives from Afrodescendant, Indigenous, Campesino, youth, feminist, faith-based, and LGBTQIA+ social processes in the region as well as allies from INGOs and state institutions, the Espacio Regional enabled me to observe the "sticky engagements" both between and *within* local, national, and international peacebuilding efforts, which I detail in chapters 5 and 6 (Tsing 2005, 6).

On some days, I attended early morning meetings in the Alta Montaña, returned to the urban center of El Carmen, and continued on to the bustling capital cities of Sincelejo or Cartagena. The "urban/rural divide," frequently invoked as an explanatory device for the root causes of the armed conflict, became part of my daily and embodied experience. The fact that popular media accounts, state projects, and INGO reports frequently collapsed the profound differences that I experienced within Montes de María into the generalized category of "rural Colombia" also directed my attention to the multiple—and competing—ways that people construct and deploy the terms "rural," "territory," and "local." As a result, I began noting *who* invoked the "urban/rural divide" and to *what ends* they did so, giving me purchase on the relations and technologies of power that structure the uneven landscape of peacebuilding in Montes de María. This, in turn, has allowed me to trouble assumptions about the "urban/rural gap," while still attending to the physical, political, and sociotemporal differences that exist within and between urban and rural geographies.

While a focus on grassroots peacebuilding is central to my analysis, many scholars have warned against the tendency to romanticize "the local" (Hughes, Öjendal, and Schierenbeck 2015; Mac Ginty and Richmond 2013). In response, Roger Mac Ginty (2015) argues for a "deterritorialized" understanding of the local as dynamically constituted through activity and relationships (841). I share Mac Ginty's concern that an essentialized and static account of "the local" undermines collective agency, reproducing colonialist relations through top-down interventions. However, in contexts of dispossession, place-based practices, socioecological relations, and physical geographies fundamentally shape how campesinos imagine and build "territorial peace." To this end, I find Daniel Ruiz Serna's (2017) discussion of the divergent ways that "territory" is conceived and defined particularly salient. Drawing on ethnographic research in Bajo Atrato, Colombia, Ruiz Serna writes against conceptual approaches to "territory" limited only to notions of property or framed merely as "discrete, limited places external from humans"

(95). Instead, he argues for an understanding of territory as a living body and form of "experience bound to specific places" that generate "feelings and meanings" (95). For Ruiz Serna, this conceptualization of territory also requires greater attention to the participation of more-than-human beings in processes of war and peace.

Following Ruiz Serna, I attend to the lives and histories of more-than-human species—rivers, fungi, avocado trees, mountains, monkeys, spirits, and ancestors—who have and continue to play a fundamental role in shaping the distinct socioecological niche of Colombia's dry tropical rainforest. To do so, I employ an understanding of "the local" as dynamic and relational in order to direct analytic attention to the "plurality of peace(s)" that exists in Montes de María, which includes more-than-human beings as integral actors in the process of world-building (Mac Ginty 2015, 11). As I moved across the physical and relational landscapes of Colombia, how "the local" was produced and what "territorial peace" meant shifted, providing a multiperspectival lens with which to analyze peacebuilding.

PEACE-SIGNING AND PEACEBUILDING

On September 26, 2016, the Colombian government and the FARC-EP signed a historic peace accord in the Caribbean city of Cartagena, marking a political end to over fifty years of internal armed conflict. Several weeks later, Colombian citizens narrowly rejected the accords through a referendum. The electoral map exposed the continued divisions between Colombia's periphery and the country's interior: In the territories where communities had lived through more than a half century of war, people voted overwhelmingly in favor of the accords. As social leaders in Montes de María sought to make sense of the referendum and its implications for their decades-long work for peace, they returned to a shared sentiment that emerged time and again throughout my research: "Peace is not signed, peace is built." Although the refrain may seem like a rejection of the accords, social leaders had placed their lives on the line to defend the peace accords. In the months leading up to the peace accord signing—and in the weeks prior to the plebiscite vote—grassroots leaders who publicly advocated for the accords came under death threats. Menacing pamphlets, anonymous phone calls, and rumors of planned assassinations circulated in an attempt to repress voter turnout, instill fear, and depress support for the peace accords. The distinction between peace-signing and peacebuilding, therefore, reflects the ways in which social leaders view the accords as a necessary, yet insufficient, part of their ongoing work to build peace.

The tension between "peace-signing" and "peacebuilding" lies at the heart of this book. Social leaders offer an understanding of peace as a permanent social process—one that began long before public declarations of war's end and one that will continue long after. The claim that peace is not signed across a negotiating table but rather built in everyday life recenters community agency in a national process dominated by elite interests. Peace, for social leaders, is not objectified as something you "have," "achieve," or "bring"—ushered forth through formal agreements made on paper. Instead, social leaders offer a more processual and dynamic conceptualization of peace as actively and continuously built in the *cotidianidad* (everyday).

In the days following the plebiscite vote, young people across the country took "peace to the street," organizing mass mobilizations throughout Colombia. The large-scale demonstrations, which lasted for over a month, successfully exerted pressure on the opposition, the state, and the FARC-EP. On November 24, 2016, the government and the FARC-EP signed a revised and final peace accord. Although the mass mobilizations for peace in the country's interior generated visibility for social leaders in Montes de María, death threats persisted after the signing of the accords. The sources of the threats remained unknown—or, at least unspoken and unnamed. Instead, vague references to "enemies of the peace" insinuated the involvement of armed actors who formed part of a loose network of illicit organizations known as "criminal bands" (BACRIM)—a generalized label ascribed to the array of armed organizations that emerged following paramilitary demobilization in 2005. Commonly referred to as a form of neoparamilitarism, the entanglements of the criminal, legal, and extralegal structures of power that fueled the war produced a climate of *incertidumbre* (uncertainty) in the postaccord context. *Incertidumbre* does not merely index ambiguity, but rather it reveals what Carolyn Nordstrom (1999) has called a "politics of not-knowing," which obfuscates the perpetrators of violence and reinforces a culture of impunity.[12] For social leaders in Montes de María, peace remained *peligrosa*—a dangerous and life-threatening endeavor—even after the signing of the accords. In contrast, on my trips to the cities of Bogotá and Medellín, people frequently remarked that peace had become *de moda*—trendy—with NGOs, universities, and foundations all vying for postconflict funding.

The majority of the research for this ethnography took place under the pro-peace administration of former president Juan Manuel Santos. While recognition of the increased incidents of violence enacted against social leaders under the subsequent presidency of Iván Duque is necessary for analysis, attention to the *continuities* of political violence found across Colombia's polarized political landscape is equally important. Indeed, the distinction between peace as "trendy" and peace as "dangerous" reveals the uneven distribution of bodily vulnerability in Colombia's "postconflict" landscape, exposing the effects that the wider, international political economy of peace has on postaccord contexts, where increased access to resources that abound for some are linked to the intensified exposure of harm for others.

Today, peace remains a dangerous endeavor for grassroots actors across Colombia, where nearly five hundred social leaders and 250 former FARC combatants have been assassinated since the signing of the accords (Indepaz 2021). While journalists and human rights organizations have made important strides to increase awareness of the violent deaths of social leaders, less coverage has focused on the substance of their lives. Throughout this book, I ask: What are social leaders in Montes de María risking their lives *for*? What social practices and sources of knowledge animate and sustain their collective struggle for peace? And how might an understanding of peacebuilding as a dangerous endeavor—one that necessarily upsets entrenched and unequal structures of power—inform anthropological theorization of peace?

This is not another book about the Colombian armed conflict. To focus the lens of inquiry on campesino peacebuilding is not only a theoretical endeavor but also an ethical stance. Accounts that limit analysis to social suffering carry grave consequences for how mass violence is remembered and the possibilities for peace imagined or circumscribed. Deficiency narratives that focus only on what the campo and campesinos lack fortify processes of dispossession (West 2019). I write against the "damage-centered" (Tuck 2009) research that proliferates the extant literature on Colombia. Instead, I situate contemporary campesino peacebuilding within a wider, multigenerational struggle for territorial liberation. Violence is never the whole story. Recent ethnographies have shown how creative "world-building" (Nordstrom 1995, 143), "love" (Bolten 2012a), and courageous acts of sacrifice and refusal (Theidon 2013) figure centrally into the ways in which people experience and narrate their lives in the midst and aftermath of war. As Roxani Krystalli and Philipp Schulz (2022) contend, "centering practices of love and care opens up different sites and spaces, and highlights a different set of actions, through which to understand the work of remaking a world in the wake of violence" (3). In Montes de María, the practices of solidarity, social memory, and *resistencia* live alongside the experiences of violation that social leaders have endured—and merit close, ethnographic attention as a result. Throughout the chapters that follow, I center campesino peacebuilding as a locus for understanding the holistic practices that social leaders engage to create conditions for dignified life in the midst and aftermath of violence.

For campesinos in Montes de María, daily living includes caretaking more-than-human relations. Yet, multispecies approaches remain largely absent from the anthropological literature on social recovery and transitional justice (Das 2007; Hinton 2010; Shaw et al. 2010). To this end, I build on the growing body of literature within multispecies anthropology to offer a close examination of how human and more-than-human relations are regenerated in the context of war and its aftermath (Cadena 2015; Escobar 2015; Fuentes 2010; Kirskey and Helmreich 2010; Lyons et al. 2019; Todd 2016; Tsing 2015). I engage with campesino ontological frameworks that understand the territory as living and animate to show how the death of the avocado forest in the Alta Montaña severed reciprocal relations of care between campesinos and the campo over the course of the war, disrupting social and legal orders that previously governed collective life. In response, campesino leaders have increasingly employed multispecies political actions to make their claims to reparative justice visible.

By expanding the temporal framework of peace research "beyond the human" (Kohn 2013), *Feel the Grass Grow* directs analytic attention to the possibilities and practices of multispecies resurgence. "Resurgence is acting beyond resistance," writes Mohawk scholar Taiaiake Alfred (2015), "It is what resistance always hopes to become: from a rooted position of strength, resistance defeats the temptation to stand down, to take what is offered by the state in exchange for being pacified" (151). Here, I take up Taiaiake Alfred's notion of resurgence to argue that campesino peacebuilding emerges from a distinct ecological imagination—one that mobilizes alternative understandings of temporality, relationality, and place. Drawing on intersectional feminist analysis (Cohn 2013; Cox 2015; Crenshaw 1991; Cross Riddle 2017; Hill Collins 2016; Lugones 2010; Méndez 2018; Paarlberg-Kvam 2019; Velásquez Estrada 2022), I examine campesino organizing strategies across the axes of generation, race, gender, class, sexuality, and territory. In particular, I show how social leaders make deep claims to land, place, and self in the face of ongoing processes of dispossession through embodied, intergenerational, and "land-based pedagogies" (De Leon 2020; McCoy, Tuck, and McKenzie 2016; Wildcat et al. 2014). Intergenerational movement-building emplaces and empowers campesino youth in ways that destabilize what Rob Nixon (2011) has called "slow violence." The daily labor of caretaking social and environmental landscapes marred by violence also subverts the linear and progressive temporalities that undergird the state's technocratic approach to neoliberal peacebuilding—opening possibilities for building a more emancipatory peace "from and for the territory."

SLOW PEACE

"Our times are not the same," became a common refrain that circulated among social leaders following the peace accord signing as a way to contest the continuation of top-down approaches to implementation. By invoking "the times," social leaders sought to expose the harmful effects that external interventions enacted against the territory in the name of peace. In particular, they criticized the state for carrying out the implementation process with "too much *prisa* [hurry]." As I will show throughout the following pages, the primary experience of the state's implementation process in Montes de María is one marked by perpetual delay. The paradox of *prisa*, therefore, raises significant questions for ethnographic inquiry. How are "the times" rendered meaningful in this context? What claims are social leaders making when they distinguish their times from the times of the state and the international community? And what possibilities for political action emerge when grassroots leaders explicitly name, expose, and refuse the "time of states" (Tilly 1994)?

Time shapes—and is shaped by—social and geographic relations, orients action, and has profound implications for how external interventions strengthen or harm grassroots movements (Mische 2009; Povinelli 2011; Tilly 1994; Watts 2013). In *Patients of the State*, Javier Auyero (2012) illustrates the ways in which "waiting time" naturalizes bureaucratic violence, fortifying state domination and social control. Mark Rifkin's (2017) *Beyond Settler Time* similarly outlines how dominant temporal formations render oppressive social orders inevitable, perpetuating the continuation of colonial violence. Building on this literature, I engage with campesino social theories of "the times" to analyze the temporal politics of postaccord reconstruction. I place Miriam Ticktin's (2011) critique of "emergency time" in conversation with Auyero's notion of "waiting time" to show how these discordant temporalities co-constitute *prisa* as the dominant temporal order for international peace interventions. When campesinos critique the implementation process for being carried out with "too much prisa," therefore, they are not suggesting that the state is fulfilling its mandate rapidly. Instead, *prisa* exposes the ways in which the liberal peace model reproduces colonial violence through technical, growth-driven, and temporally bounded projects that exacerbate inequality and perpetuate extractivism on a global scale (Diamond 2019; Hickel 2019; Paarlberg-Kvam 2021; Richmond 2011).

In *Vital Decomposition*, Kristina Lyons (2020) outlines how cyclical temporalities animate the "life politics" of grassroots soil practitioners at the forefront of regenerating poisoned landscapes in the coca growing regions of southern Colombia. Training our attention to the microbial lifeworlds that thrive amid decay, Lyons pushes past the linear times of technical development projects. I extend Lyons's findings to amplify the ways in which campesino social leaders in Montes de María theorize "the times" beyond the measurements of speed, limited to notions of acceleration and deceleration. For campesinos, time is subjectively experienced and relationally ordered through cooperative farming, environmental caretaking, ancestral presence, and community organizing. Indeed, when social leaders make claims to peace in the temporal register of *prisa*, they expose how technical, development interventions enact harm by eroding multispecies relations of care central to life in the campo. In doing so, they lay bare the dynamic relationship between environmental and political violence in ways that trouble the state's linear "postconflict" discourse.[13]

At the intersection of political and environmental anthropology, I develop an ethnographic theory of slow peace. Against the backdrop of a national process dominated by elite interests, the campesino call to build *paz sin prisa* recenters cultural practices of peacebuilding, grounded in the collective struggle for dignified life. Building peace *slowly* entails a permanent commitment to the daily and open-ended work of tending territorial relations of care in the wake of violence. Throughout the proceeding pages, I explore the multivalent practices of peace that shape "the times of social leaders" to advance an understanding of slowness as imbricated in "felt" experience and relationality (Million 2008). Slowing down does not exclude the sense of urgency that accompanies the collective struggle for peace in Montes de María but is, instead, central to the defense of life and territory. Slowness, understood as a way of relating and mode of attention, works against global processes that alienate, dispossess, and degrade human and more-than-human communities. In the aftermath of forced displacement, social leaders maintain that peace cannot begin from the desks of those who have benefited from the unjust power relations produced through colonial violence. Rather, to build slow peace requires the capacity to draw from the deep well of ancestral knowledge held within the territory. Slow peace offers a relational framework for peacebuilding as a multigenerational, multispecies, and permanent struggle to cultivate a world *otherwise*.

REMOVING THE UMBRELLA

"Writing is a responsibility. I have to think about each word, because each word is powerful," Dionisio Alarcón Fernández, a poet and campesino leader from the Alta Montaña, reflected as his hand drifted over the worn notebook on his lap. As the son of a mother who was widowed at a young age, Dionisio's formal studies were cut short because of the historic inequalities that exclude rural, campesino communities from access to public education. He did not, however, stop writing. Sitting next to me on a white, plastic chair, he read aloud the handwritten words as I transcribed the text into my computer.

The idea for the article emerged after Dionisio and I cofacilitated a workshop on the use of Investigación-Acción Participativa (Participatory Action Research, abbreviated PAR) as a tool to support community-based peacebuilding efforts. The 2017 Action Research Network of the Americas congress formed part of a wider celebration that marked the thirty-year anniversary of the first conference on PAR organized by Colombian sociologist Orlando

Fals Borda in Cartagena in 1977. With the support of Hernando González, Glenda Jaraba, and Larisa Zehr, we designed the workshop to focus on the common, extractive research practices that campesinos in the Alta Montaña had to increasingly navigate in Colombia's postaccord landscape. We also outlined alternative research methods that social leaders in the Alta Montaña had developed as part of their historical memory process. "We need the support of academia," Dionisio affirmed after reading his handwritten essay, "But academics don't often move beyond analysis. In order to feel that it is raining, you have to get wet, you have to remove your umbrella." This image, offered as a side reflection, later became the title of the article that Alarcón, González, and Jaraba (2018) published in the academic journal *Economía y Región*. In the article, they contend that conducting ethical research in regions affected by armed conflict requires long-term commitment to grassroots struggles for peace, visible recognition for the contributions that campesinos make to knowledge production, and the return of final publications to communities who participate in research. "We should not be treated as objects under the gaze of academia," they assert in the article, "but as actors in the elaboration of profound studies in our search for transformative peace" (336). The guidelines offered in their article inform my approach to research, shaping the lines of inquiry I pursue, the methods I use, and how I frame, write, and disseminate what I have learned.

Months after *Economía y Región* published the article, I asked Dionisio where the metaphor of the umbrella came from. "I found that image in the moment," he explained as we sipped sweet *tinto* (coffee) from small plastic cups. "Normally they have an editor that . . . takes away that voice. You see," he gestured out across the bombed-out church that stood at the edge of the hill overlooking Montes de María, "here, this is where we experienced the bombings and the armed confrontations. Here, I cradled my son to my chest because in that moment I was thinking if the bullet hits me in the back, at least my body will protect him, and he will survive." He took in the scene for a few minutes before concluding, "With the umbrella, it is also this—an understanding of what those decisions and moments mean. This is the knowledge that emerges from those of us that lived this . . . in our own words, our own ways of speaking."

Dionisio's visceral and embodied memories of fleeing direct combat with his small child held tightly against his chest remains alive in his body and the landscapes he calls home. These living memories—what people in the Alta Montaña call *memoria viva*—serve as a reminder of the limits of my knowledge (CNMH 2018a). As a foreigner and guest in the Alta Montaña, I learned that removing the umbrella not only requires long-term immersion in the campo but also close accompaniment from—and collaboration with—"those . . . that lived this." As Alarcón, González, and Jaraba (2018) admonish, research must move "beyond the academic bubble, to take root in our land, with our social processes of peacebuilding in order to become a tool of transformation" (337).

I position my methods and research within the wider genealogy of Investigación-Acción Participativa (PAR; Participatory Action Research) that forms an integral part of the history and collective struggle for peace in Montes de María (Fals Borda 1986; Hall and Tandon 2018; Negrete 2013; Rappaport 2021). In chapter 1, I trace the emergence of PAR as a methodology born from campesino organizing to outline the less visible contours of violence and peace in Montes de María, where knowledge has become a site of intense struggle that shapes both collective resistance and state violence. Throughout the armed conflict, the state systematically criminalized campesino intellectual thought as a strategy of territorial control. The localized expressions of violence that targeted campesino knowledge production implicate researchers as direct participants in, rather than neutral observers of, social and political struggles today. The state's criminalization of campesino knowledge production, used to legitimize the incarceration of social leaders in Montes de María falsely accused of "rebellion," contours the ethical dimensions of my research and shapes with *whom* and *how* I conduct research. Today, social leaders are engaged in reclaiming campesino knowledge production as a critical part of their peacebuilding work (Alarcón, González, and Jaraba 2018; CNMH 2018). This book emerges from my ongoing commitment to and collaboration with those efforts.

PAR offered me a set of methodologies responsive to the particular history in which I was working and my own positionality in that context. Preliminary research included a collaborative process that shaped the research design, questions, and inclusion criteria. In particular, both Sembrandopaz and the coordinating committee of the Peaceful Process emphasized the need for a plural account of grassroots peacebuilding with specific attention to the voices of youth and women. I not only received feedback and suggestions for the research design from campesino collaborators, but I have also translated and shared all my written work—including multiple drafts of this book—throughout the process as part of a wider form of peer review. The support and formation that I have received from my campesino colleagues in Montes de María—many of whom were at the forefront of creating and giving rise to PAR as a methodology in the 1970s—enabled me to also learn by doing (*aprender haciendo*). I have come to understand my own engagement in research as part of a wider and continuous process of collective reflection and action, central to the work of campesino movement-building. Participatory methods also generated new lines of inquiry, important critiques, and significant clarifications that have deepened and improved the conceptual and practical arguments found throughout this book.

While writing is often discussed as something that is done after leaving "the field," implicitly locating theory as external to the campo, research understood as *praxis* decenters the final product to prioritize ongoing, collective processes (Riaño-Alcalá 2006). Working within—rather than outside of—collectively defined processes of community organizing generated different kinds of theoretical insights through engagement with the "multiple contradictions" and plural standpoints that shape territorial peacebuilding (Hale 2008, 22). Furthermore, situating the research as part of my wider commitment to grassroots peacebuilding asked me to consistently center the sociopolitical *process* of movement-building over a single *project*, reflecting a central claim that social leaders make throughout this book. Although, at times, I had to navigate the dissonance and tension that emerged from the competing demands of multiple stakeholders who form an integral part of the research process, decentering the final project to work alongside social movement leaders not only deepened my understanding of campesino organizing but also my own political engagement in the work of grassroots peacebuilding. While these efforts will always remain partial and imbued with power, co-constructing research with social leaders in Montes de María has fundamentally changed how—and why—I write about violence and peace in Colombia.

Manuel Salamanca (2018) has pointed to the ways in which the linguistic shift between "peace research" in English and "*investigación* para *la paz*"—

research *for* peace in Spanish—shapes distinct orientations to knowledge production. The subtle difference gestures toward the contributions that Colombian scholars have made to politically engaged research methods (Abitbol 2010; Alarcón et al. 2018; Fals Borda 1986; Negrete 2013; Riaño-Alcalá 2006). The rich body of literature found in the Colombian tradition of "research *for* peace" works against the narrow frame of violence that often guides scholarly accounts of Colombia, offering insight into the practices of collective resistance, peacebuilding, and reconciliation that local communities have developed over a half century of war (Abitbol 2016; Barreto 2016; Bouvier 2009; Echavarría-Álvarez 2019; Esquivia 2009; García-Durán 2006; Hernández Delgado 2012; Jiménez 2004; Masullo 2015; Meertens 2015; Mouly et al. 2015; Ojeda, Quiroga, and Vallejo 2021; Paladini 2020; Riaño-Alcalá 2006; Rodríguez 2011; Rodriguez 2012; Sarmiento et al. 2018; Serrano-Amaya and Baird 2013; Valenzuela 1995; Valenzuela 2009; Vega and Bayuelo 2008; Zapata 2020). As Veena Das contends, close attention to the fragmented worlds found at the "limits of life" illuminate the "eventfulness" of the *cotidianidad*, where the seeds of peace are nurtured and grown (Das 2007, 218).

The knowledge that emerges from lived experience and campesino "ways of speaking" offer rich contributions to the theories and practices of peace. Yet, campesino concepts and social analyses are too often edited out, spoken over, and extracted—reduced to mere "data" in need of scholarly interpretation, rather than theories in their own right.[14] Rooted in oral tradition, storytelling—*echando cuentos* (swapping stories)—forms the theoretical scaffolding for campesino social theory. The collective process of storytelling offers a relational framework for collaborative reflection on the ethical and political dynamics of violence and peace. Throughout this book, I have sought to engage with campesino intellectual thought, foregrounding narratives, short stories, and poetry as generative sources of knowledge for theorizing peace.

Writing, understood as a "responsibility," also requires an ethical stance—a refusal to erase the contributions that people like Dionisio Alarcón, Hernando González, and Glenda Jaraba have made to analyses and practices of peacebuilding. As my understanding of the dynamics of violence in Montes de María deepened, social leaders' requests to be named and recognized for their contributions to theory also took on new meaning. Elsewhere I have written about how grassroots actors in Montes de María center *visibility* rather than *anonymity* in their understanding of collective protection (Lederach 2020). "I want my name to appear just as it is," youth leader Naún Álvarez González explained, "To take on a false name now is to repeat the history of the war, which is a form of revictimization. We do not want to return to those times. We do not want to disguise ourselves in the names of another. We want our words, experiences, and lives to be visible." Throughout this book, I have taken up Naún's assertion by using the names of individuals who requested I do so, thereby giving them direct credit for their contributions to ethnographic knowledge. For those who wished to remain anonymous, I have used pseudonyms and made changes to further obscure their identities. Rather than default unreflectively to the use of pseudonyms, Carole McGranahan (2021) argues for a more nuanced and relational approach to naming. "Knowledge grounded in the realities of people's lives," writes McGranahan, "requires this to be an ongoing and relational process, rather than a fixed institutional decision."[15] In the pages that follow, I have sought to foreground the theories and social practices of my campesino colleagues—as legitimate intellectual interlocutors—in conversation with academic scholars to deepen an understanding of peace as part of a permanent and collective struggle to create the conditions for dignified life in the wake of violence.

CHAPTER DESCRIPTIONS

In each chapter of the book, I peel back a different layer of meaning embedded within social leaders' critique of *prisa*—hurry, in order to bring the temporal politics of peacebuilding into focus. In doing so, I direct analytic attention to the historical (chapter 1), multispecies and intergenerational (chapter 2), political (chapters 3 and 4), sociotemporal (chapter 5), coalitional (chapter 6), and ethical (chapter 7) dimensions of campesino peacebuilding that shape an experience of time as embodied, affective, and emplacing. In chapter 1, I draw on the narratives, oral histories, memoirs, and collaborative scholarship produced through Investigación-Acción Participativa (PAR; Participatory Action Research) to reclaim Montes de María as a space of emancipatory peacebuilding. While popular and scholarly studies frequently locate the armed conflict as the starting place for understanding the context of Montes de María, this chapter traverses the historical landscapes of transgenerational organizing to uncover how campesino understandings of the territory as a space of liberation, collective resistance, and *interculturalidad* (interculturalism) inform the ways in which social leaders imagine and build peace today. I write against dominant depictions of Montes de María as a place of endemic violence to show how social leaders locate their contemporary peace movements as the continuation of the ancestral struggle for liberation led by Black, Indigenous, and destitute Spanish workers in the wake of enslavement and colonial violence. Here, the shift in "the times" that social leaders advocate for widens the temporal frame to recognize the multigenerational struggle for peace in Montes de María.

In the face of enslavement, genocidal violence, and debt bondage, coalitional organizing not only shaped the event of escape but also territorial relations. In particular, I outline how *interculturalidad* fashions a shared, territorial identity. As a sociopolitical framework, *interculturalidad* also deepens forms of coalition-building in a socioecological landscape fragmented by centuries of violence. For this reason, the *campesinado* in Montes de María is socially, historically, and materially constituted as a plural and political identity.[16] Indeed, many social leaders identify simultaneously as Afrodescendant, Indigenous, and Campesino and understand the category of "campesino" as inclusive, rather than mutually exclusive, of Indigenous and Afrodescendant struggles. Throughout this book, I employ "campesino" to reflect this plural understanding of the term. In tracing the emergence of campesino peacebuilding practices prior to the armed conflict, in this chapter I write against the rhetorical dispossessions that reify Montes de María as a place of violence. Instead, I argue that contemporary grassroots peace movements in Montes de María embody the continuation of the collective, campesino struggle for territorial liberation that began centuries ago.

Chapter 2 begins with the story of the death of the avocado in the Alta Montaña. Reading the armed conflict through the lens of the avocado forest, I examine the ways in which multispecies relations—and their violent severing—shape campesino theories and practices of peacebuilding as more-than-human. Multispecies temporalities destabilize the linear logic that undergirds the state's postconflict project, offering a more relational and place-based framework for decolonial peace praxis. Throughout the chapter, I show how the Peaceful Process and the Youth Peace Provokers movement engage in multispecies political actions to reaffirm the lives of avocados, cotton-top tamarin monkeys, soils, and rivers as lives that count in the face of environmental and political violence, giving rise to campesino resurgence.

In chapter 3, I direct analytic attention to the everyday interactions between grassroots social movements, state actors, and International Nongovernmental (INGO) workers to offer a thick account of the routine practices that structure the temporal regime of *prisa* (hurry). This chapter critically assesses the ways in which external interveners perform participatory peacebuilding through photos and signatures (*fotos y firmas*). The extraction of attendance sheets and photos, used to promote and publicize institutional presence and action, pervades international peace interventions at the expense of direct and meaningful political participation for local community members. I argue that the "theatrics of peace" is not limited to the realm of spectacular events—like peace accord signing—but contours the everyday encounters between social leaders, state bureaucrats, and the international community. Social leaders direct their critique of shallow performances of participation, enacted through "photos and signatures," to what they refer to as the *institucionalidad*. The term *institucionalidad* is used in reference to the state as well as international institutions. In this way, the term *institucionalidad* does not reflect a fixed notion of state institutions but instead gestures toward the processes, discourses, performances, and histories that produce the formal institutional structure of peace interventions as well as the feelings and perceptions that people attach to those institutions. Through engagement in contentious performances of peace, social leaders recast the gaze of the accords' "territorial focus" away from the campo and toward the systemic changes needed within the *institucionalidad*. Rather than locate campesinos as a passive audience, I attend to the ways in which social leaders appropriate the state's stage through a countertheatrics of peace.

Chapter 4 provides ethnographic analysis of the 2017 ñame (yam) crisis to outline how the temporalities of *prisa* operate as a technology of power, structuring the uneven landscape of peacebuilding in Colombia. I make direct linkages between the state's response to the death of the avocado and the subsequent ñame crisis to show how "emergency time" (Ticktin 2011) and "waiting time" (Auyero 2012) co-constitute the temporal regime of *prisa*. Punctuated, repetitive, and rushed meetings result in the perpetual deferral of basic public services at the expense of campesino lives and livelihoods. Throughout the chapter, I unpack how social leaders contest, subvert, and refuse the "times of the state" to foreground their claims to peace.

Chapter 5 traverses the everyday relational and geographical landscapes of campesino organizing to develop an ethnographic theory of slow peace. In distinguishing their times from the state and international community, campesino social leaders expose the ways in which the temporal regime of *prisa* erodes the relations of care and love central to life in the campo. Slowing down does not negate the urgency that animates the defense of territory in Montes de María but is, instead, a matter of life and death for social leaders engaged in the tenacious collective struggle to build justice and peace in the face of persistent political violence. I draw on campesino narratives, ethnographic analysis, and embodied, land-based methodologies to offer a social theory of slowness—one grounded not in clocks and calendars but in relations.

Chapter 6 directs attention to "the times of social leaders" with a focus on the Espacio Regional's approach to intercultural coalition-building. In sharp contrast to technocratic approaches to peace that rely on distant intermediaries and fleeting interactions, members of the Espacio Regional advocate for an understanding of peace as a political process that requires sustained proximity. While the theatrics of peace circumscribe participation to the extractive practices of *fotos y firmas* (photos and signatures), I show how the indeterminate temporalities that shape the work of the Espacio Regional usher forth a vision of political participation rooted in *voz y voto* (voice and votes). Participation understood as *voz y voto* centers sustained dialogue, political engagement, and democratic decision-making as vital for the work of peace. In a context of social fragmentation and repressive state violence, I argue that sustained dialogue through intercultural coalitional organizing constitutes an imaginative act of what Carolyn Nordstrom (1995) has called "world-building" (143).

Chapter 7 begins at a wake held for a social leader in Montes de María. As those gathered for the wake engage in an evening full of "swapping stories," they repeatedly highlight the blessings and abundant life found in the campo. In this chapter, I ask: What is seen—and made possible—when we widen the frame and focus the lens on life and love, rather than limit our field of vision to death and suffering in contexts of war? I take up Christina's Sharpe's (2016) conceptualization of the wake, which destabilizes the fixed temporalities of "the past as past" to recognize the "still unfolding aftermaths of Atlantic chattel slavery" in the present (2). The practices of slow peace examined throughout this chapter—including accompaniment, reforestation, river mapping, and living memory—constitute what Sharpe calls "wake work," which I argue derives from and deepens moral dispositions attuned to life amid violence (13).[17] I place Sharpe's conceptual frame of "the wake" in conversation with Ricardo Esquivia's notion of peacebuilders as *vigías* of hope (guardians of hope). Rooted in the Latin word for vigil, the figure of the *vigía* weaves together collective mourning, ancestral memory, protest, and wakefulness as creative acts of peace that usher forth campesino futurities. Slowness, as a practice of presence and mode of relating, cultivates dispositions alert to the emergent possibilities for liberatory peace found and nurtured in the territory.

FROM THE GRASSROOTS

On a clear, warm Caribbean day in 2016, I walked the trails of Villa Barbara with Ricardo Esquivia. Since 2010, Sembrandopaz has planted over three thousand trees on the outskirts of Sincelejo, reforesting a plot of land destroyed by the dual processes of cattle ranching and war. The Sembrandopaz farm serves as an experimental and educational space, bringing campesinos from Montes de María together for heirloom seed exchanges, workshops on traditional farming techniques aimed at regenerating damaged soils, and dialogues focused on creative approaches to sustainable reforestation in an increasingly arid landscape. The farm has also served as a sanctuary and refuge for those fleeing violence. With Ricardo as my guide, I spent the day learning to identify the different trees that give life to Villa Barbara, their uses, and the stories they hold. We talked about climate change, food sovereignty, and regenerative agriculture. We spent surprisingly little time talking about the strategies of coalition-building, community organizing, and peacebuilding— themes that usually enter our conversations. As the sun began to set, we sat on the porch of the small *cabaña* located at the edge of the farm, quietly taking in the scenic views of the Montemariana range. "You see," Ricardo said, breaking the silence to offer a final reflection, "the work of the *base* [grassroots] is to see, feel, and grow the tree held within the seed," he paused, bending down to let his fingers drift over the earth, "to be so close to the ground that you can feel the grass grow."

Ricardo's words form the title of this book. To "feel the grass grow" evokes the socioecological imagination that undergirds the holistic approach to peace that I have encountered across Montes de María. The deep connection that campesinos have with the land and their wider *entorno* (lifeworld) informs the ways in which social leaders envision peace as a permanent process of caretaking socioecological relations in the wake of violence. The daily and patient work of learning to see, tend, and feel "the grass growing" deepens one's presence and attention to the multiple relations that inhabit and give life to particular places. By cultivating moral dispositions attuned to the existence of the nearly imperceptible processes of life that persist amid violence, the practices of slow peace nurture and generate campesino futurities *desde la base*—from the grassroots. Peace, understood not as an ideal abstracted to a distant future but rather as part of the collective struggle to defend and generate conditions for dignified living, is made possible and present in the daily work of social leaders across Montes de María who, with their lives, give love.

Part I
MEMORIAS VIVAS—
LIVING MEMORIES

Recordando al futuro—Remembering towards the future
  —*Ricardo Esquivia Ballestas*

FIGURE 3. The Youth Peace Provokers March for Peace in El Carmen de Bolívar. A nonviolent march in support of the peace accords following the October 2016 referendum. Photo by author.

CHAPTER ONE

FROM AND FOR
THE TERRITORY

The Campesino Struggle for Peace

"IN ORDER TO KNOW WHERE we are going, we need to locate ourselves. And in order to locate ourselves, we need to know where we have come from." Ricardo moved to the edge of the couch in the upstairs meeting room of the Sembrandopaz office as he spoke. We sat in a circle for Sembrandopaz's annual evaluation. After a tumultuous month, the government and the FARC-EP had recently signed a revised peace accord. The atmosphere was light and celebratory as we gathered one last time before the holiday break. "We need to look at the context and learn to read 'the signs of the times,'" Ricardo continued, quoting a favorite biblical passage, "what we do today in the present is our future, but we cannot forget that the present is also nourished with what has already happened. It is good to reflect on this." A large poster with the words "Sowing Seeds of Peace: We Make Life Projects Possible" and an image of a campesino harvesting produce hung on the wall behind Ricardo as he spoke:

> We have had a situation of social inequality for the last two hundred years. What they call the state of Colombia emerged from the violence that the Europeans brought to our land. The Spanish Empire took their privileges

Subregiones

- Alta Montaña
- Montaña
- Pie de Monte Occidental
- Troncal Río Magdalena
- Límites departamentales

Cartagena

BOLÍVAR

Mar Caribe

Barú

El Guamo

María la Baja

San Juan Nepomuceno

San Onofre

San Jacinto

MAGDALENA

El Carmen de Bolívar

Zambrano

Golfo de Morrosquillo

Chalán

Colosó   Ovejas   Córdoba

Toluviejo   Los Palmitos   Río Magdalena

Río Viejo   Palmito   Morroa

Sincelejo

SUCRE

Río Chicagua

Río Sinú

CÓRDOBA

Río Cauca

Centro Nacional
de Memoria Histórica

*Procesado por:
Centro Nacional de
Memoria Histórica (CNMH)
Georreferenciación:
Julio E. Cortés
Jun-2022*

Río San Jorge

MAP 1. A map of Montes de María, Colombia. Source: Centro Nacional de Memoria Histórica. Georreferenciación: Julio E. Cortés. *Un Bosque de Memoria Viva, Desde La Alta Montaña de El Carmen de Bolívar.* Informe Del Centro Nacional de Memoria Histórica y Del Proceso Pacífico de Reconciliación e Integración de La Alta Montaña de El Carmen de Bolívar. Bogotá: Centro Nacional de Memoria Histórica, 2018, 21.

and put it in a constitution, and they called this a new country. There was not space for Indigenous people, for people who were not Catholic, for the enslaved Africans, and this has been maintained throughout history. We can look at the gallery of presidents, all men, all connected by their names. This is not because women aren't smart or Black people are not smart or Indigenous people couldn't have these roles, but because the system maintains this, the structures maintain this. And, here, this has been maintained with violence. . . . The problem with colonization is that it not only forces itself onto culture, but also imprints itself on language. In my case, I am African, but I don't even know where I come from and everything I do is through the language of the conquistador. We have been taught a universal history only of Europe and this affects us. How can we achieve independence from this? An organization like ours, who works in peacebuilding, must be attentive to these dynamics. Montes de María is a region that has been devastated by violence for many years, but it has an interesting history. This region was not parceled out when the Spanish arrived. The Spanish wanted the plains and this was a mountainous region. So, when the enslaved fled, they came to this region. And not just the enslaved, but also Indigenous people, and poor Spanish workers. The Black communities created over seventeen *Palenques* [Free Black Communities] and there were more than twenty Indigenous *Resguardos* [Indigenous reserves or territories]. And all of these diverse groups of people lived together and created *rochelas* [communal living spaces], where they sought refuge from enslavement and incarceration here, in the high zone, what today we call Montes de María.[1]

Ricardo paused, allowing for a moment of silent reflection before connecting the past to the present context. "Today, the war has not ended. The FARC is one of the armed groups—the largest group, but only *one*. It's not that we shouldn't be excited, but we need to have a realistic excitement. The war is not over. We need to have this history and context clear."

In sharp contrast to prevailing accounts of Montes de María that begin with the arrival of armed organizations fifty years ago, Ricardo situates the recent peace accords within the ancestral history of the territory to outline the repeated cycles of violence, political settlements, and forms of grassroots resistance that have marked the region for centuries. For Ricardo, territo-

rial peacebuilding did not begin with the language of the accord or declarations of war's *end*, but instead *preceded* the armed conflict. By analyzing
"the times" within the deeper history of Montes de María, Ricardo locates
the peace agreement as the continuation of a multigenerational struggle for
liberatory peace in Colombia, not as a beginning.

In this chapter, I draw on oral life histories, historical memory materials, and early participatory action research studies to historicize territorial
peace in the context of Montes de María. I apply a multigenerational lens to
bring the constellations of power, recurrent patterns of violence, and external
interventions that gave rise to the armed conflict in Montes de María into
focus. By tracing the long history of violence and resistance in Montes de
María, from colonial to contemporary, this chapter takes up Ricardo Esquivia's analysis to scrutinize the linear temporalities that undergird prevailing
postconflict discourses. Montes de María is home to one of the largest campesino movements in Colombian history, the birthplace of participatory action
research, the pilot for US-Colombian counterterrorism strategies, and one
of the European Union's first "peace laboratories"; grassroots organizing as
well as external interventions have fundamentally marked territorial relations
in Montes de María (Barreto 2016; Castaneda 2012; CNMH 2014; Gaviria
Betancur 2011; Negrete 2013; Peréz 2010; Zamosc 1986).

In this chapter I traverse the historical landscapes of transgenerational
organizing that have shaped the territory—and which continue to animate
grassroots peacebuilding today. In doing so, I write against dominant depictions of Montes de María as a place of endemic violence to show how
social leaders narrate and embrace the territory as a space of liberation—one
rooted in *marronage*. Drawing on Neil Roberts (2015, 10), Deborah Thomas
(2019) defines marronage as "a state of being in which 'agents struggle psy-
chologically, socially, metaphysically, and politically to exit slavery, maintain
freedom, and assert a lived social space while existing in a liminal position'"
(214). Local archival research and life histories with social leaders in Montes
de María further Thomas's argument "that it is in conditions of marronage
that repair is possible" (214). The linguistic move that Thomas makes from
reparations to repair reflects how social leaders understand their daily and
multigenerational struggle for peace as "deeply historical and relational"
(213). I argue that social leaders' daily work for territorial peace embodies the

temporal shift present in Thomas's conceptualization of repair. Whereas the state begins analyses of the region with the official start date of the armed conflict—used to delineate reparations measures in Colombia—social leaders advocate for a deeper understanding of the territory that considers the centuries-long grassroots struggle to create conditions for dignified life in the wake of enslavement and colonization. For social leaders, to build a more emancipatory peace "from and for the territory" requires a shift in "the times (*los tiempos*)"—the temporal frame of peacebuilding.

"Our presence in the territory is ancestral," write members of the grassroots coalition known as the Mesa de Interlocución y Concertación (2014 [MIC]; Roundtable for Dialogue and Coordination). In the essay, which outlines the rights of Black, Indigenous, and Campesino communities to "dignified permanence" in the territory, they contend that this ancestral history has also "permitted the construction of historical relationships of coexistence as well as the use of the soil and natural resources" (14). Montes de María, they write in the conclusion, "has been and continues to be a diverse and intercultural territory" (14). Intercultural coalition-building did not only result in *mestizaje* in Montes de María but also allowed the continuation of cultural and linguistic traditions across difference. *Interculturalidad* not only shapes a shared, territorial identity across difference but also operates as a sociopolitical framework that grassroots movements in Montes de María engage as central for the work of coalition-building, which they position over and against the state's approach to "neoliberal multiculturalism" (Hale 2006).[2] Tracing the concept of *interculturalidad* to Indigenous struggles in Ecuador, Walter Mignolo (2005) contends that interculturalism makes a particular claim to "epistemic rights" as central to the work of decolonization (118). For Arturo Escobar (1995), the campesino struggle is, therefore, not only about land, but rather a "contest over views of history and ways of life" (19). In this chapter, I take up MIC's assertion that *interculturalidad* forms a vital part of Montes de María's territorial identity to direct attention toward the multigenerational processes of coalition-building that continue to animate the grassroots struggle for peace today. Although land disputes have also occurred among the *campesinado*, less attention has been given to the centrality of *interculturalidad* found in campesino narratives of the history and identity of Montes de María. In placing social leaders' accounts as the central starting point for analysis, this chapter also casts a critical lens on the less-visible role external interventions have played in sowing internal division.

While outside scholars and journalists frequently depict Montes de María as a cauldron of Colombia's violence—unleashed, unfettered, and naturalized in the campo (countryside), Montemarianxs[3] tell a different story; their narratives weave through and beyond the violence to portray a territory of collective struggle for liberation, rooted in intercultural solidarity. The saliency of *interculturalidad* in the construction of the collective Montemarianx identity reflects the decolonial peace praxis that plural, social movements engage today—one that arises from and contributes to the fashioning of "worlds and knowledges *otherwise*" (Escobar 2008, 17).

KNOWLEDGE, POWER, AND THE CAMPESINO STRUGGLE FOR TERRITORIAL LIBERATION

Nestled between the Magdalena River and the Caribbean Sea, Montes de María is home to the distinctly fertile lands and waterways of the dry-rainforest ecosystem. The ancestral territory of the Mocaná, Malibú, and Zenú Indigenous peoples, Spanish colonizers renamed the region the Mountains of María in the 1500s (Porras 2014). With the capital city of Cartagena serving as one of the hemisphere's largest ports for the transatlantic slave trade, colonial violence and enslavement fundamentally shaped the political economy of the northern Caribbean coast. Led by Pedro de Heredia, Spanish colonizers engaged in systematic "reduction" campaigns and genocidal violence, forcibly displacing Indigenous peoples from the port city to the rural mountainous region (Zamosc 1986). This, in turn, expanded the exploitation of labor from enslaved Africans on the one hand and indentured servitude among poor Spanish *colonos* (settlers) on the other. Over time, the hacienda system formed, producing sharp class divisions between the *campesinado* (peasantry) and the hacendado (landowners) (Porras 2014).

The isolated mountainous terrain provided refuge not only to the Zenú but also to enslaved peoples from Africa who organized collective liberation movements, declaring Montes de María an "autonomous zone of Black power" (Porras 2014, 337). The collective struggle for liberation in the face of enslavement, genocidal violence, and debt bondage sharpened forms of coalitional organizing that shaped not only the event of escape but also the construction of social and communal life in Montes de María, fashioning a collective territorial identity rooted in *interculturalidad*. The dense forests, fertile soil, and robust marshlands provided protection and food sovereignty for Indigenous, Black, and poor Spanish laborers as they worked to cultivate a space of freedom together. Based on a cooperative model of exchange and solidarity, Indigenous practices of *minga* (communal work) emerged as the primary economic system in the region, laying the foundation for what many refer to today as the "campesino economy" (Pérez 2010, 17). The *campesinado* in Montes de María is, therefore, socially and historically constituted as a plural and political identity—one positioned over and against the hacendado. Historian Eduardo Porras (2014) contends that the convergence of histories, peoples, and forms of collective organizing created a distinct "intercultural ethos" in the region where a "long process of *convivencia* (coexistence)" continues to inform the campesino struggle for peace (340).

With the abolition of slavery in 1851, colonial administrators shifted their focus toward the industrialization of tobacco, expanding political and economic reach into Montes de María (Porras 2014, 345). As the demand for tobacco soared, the region attracted attention from foreign investors who seized large extensions of land for cattle ranching, igniting renewed coalition-building efforts among the *campesinado*—this time with a focus on land (PNUD 2010, 12).[4] With an organized tobacco union as well as *ligas campesinas* (campesino leagues), grassroots leaders led protests, strikes, and land recuperations to prevent the expansion of agroindustries beginning in the early 1900s (Fals Borda 1986; Porras 2014).[5] The rise of the leftist populist movement led by Jorge Eliecer Gaitán, which focused on organized labor, economic equality, and land distribution, resonated with the burgeoning campesino movement in Montes de María (Zamosc 1986). With support from the national Colombian Confederation of Workers (CTC) union, the campesino movement also began connecting their regional struggle to national politics (Daniels Puello and Múnera 2011). Intensified tensions between the Liberal and Conservative Parties carried strong rippling effects across the rural territories as the state began incarcerating leaders tied to the CTC who they accused of being "liberal guerrillas" (Pérez 2010, 10). The volatile political situation resulted in the forced displacement of campesinos throughout the thirties (Porras 2014). On April 9, 1948, the assassination of Gaitán ignited a civil war between Liberal and Conservative factions in Colombia, leading to what many refer to as the period of "*La Violencia* [The Violence]."[6]

In 1958, a bipartisan coalition known as the National Front formed in response to growing authoritarianism, successfully electing Alberto Lleras Camargo to the presidency. Under Lleras Camargo, the National Front implemented a series of reformist policies focused on coexistence, reconstruction, historical memory, and agrarian reform (Karl 2017). Although the National Front's approach to peace maintained the top-down and centralist political structures that had sown collective discontent in rural communities, this period also expanded possibilities for campesino organizing (Pérez 2010, 11). In particular, the 1961 Agrarian Social Reform Law established Community Action Councils (Junta Acción Comunal, JAC), giving campesino associations a way to directly articulate their demands to the state (Karl 2017, 127). Despite the fact that the state failed to include campesino representation in the design and implementation of agrarian reform, the wider political climate gave rise to the largest nationwide campesino movement in Colombian history, the Asociación Nacional de Usuarios Campesinos (ANUC) (Zamosc 1986). Jesús "Chucho" Pérez (2010), one of the primary organizers of the ANUC, highlights the importance of agrarian reform in his memoir while also underscoring that previous movements, including the tobacco union and the campesino leagues, also laid the foundation for the rise of the ANUC in Montes de María. "Without these organizational experiences," Pérez writes, "the ANUC would not have had the strength that it had in this region" (18).

Between 1967 and 1970, the ANUC began organizing Community, Municipal, and Departmental associations throughout the country (Zamosc 1986). On July 7, 1970, the ANUC held the First National Campesino Congress. Campesino representatives from departmental associations across Colombia ratified the ANUC's constitution. *Tierra p'al que la trabaja* (land for those who work it) became the movement's official slogan (Pérez 2010, 12; Zamosc 1986). In a radical departure from the centralist practices of the elite political class, the ANUC offered a compelling model for participatory politics from the ground up. "In the history of social movements and agrarian struggle in Colombia," León Zamosc (1986) writes in his pivotal study of the campesino movement in Colombia, "the ANUC is the only organization that was able . . . to articulate autonomously the demands of the peasants on a national scale" (2).

As their national visibility grew, ANUC leaders began facilitating popular education trainings for campesinos across the country. By 1970, five thousand ANUC members from three hundred municipal associations had received training on their legal and constitutional rights, community organizing, and public policy (Zamosc 1986, 56). Drawing on the long-standing history of campesino resistance, ANUC organizers began refining their strategies based on lessons learned from previous generations to coordinate large-scale land recuperations. In 1971, the ANUC recuperated more than eight hundred lots across Colombia in a single day (CNMH 2014, 10). The unprecedented scale and coordination of the collective recuperations threatened elite economic and political power. With the presidential election of Misael Pastrana Borrero from the Conservative Party, state agencies that had previously worked alongside the ANUC began to employ top-down policies in an attempt to control and contain the movement, fracturing the relationship between the campesino movement and the government (Zamosc 1986, 69).

In 1972, the ANUC led five thousand campesinos from Montes de María to Sincelejo, the capital city of Sucre, to demand a redistributive and participatory approach to agrarian reform, outlined in a document known as the Campesino Mandate (Zamosc 1986, 70). Although scholars have characterized the Campesino Mandate as part of a significant and more revolutionary shift within the movement, social leaders argue that the Mandate marked the culmination of generations of campesino organizing aimed at advocating for their basic constitutional rights (personal interviews July 8, 2017, and October 7, 2017; Negrete 2013; Pérez 2010).[7]

The march—and the Mandate—served as a tipping point for the already strained relationships between the state and the ANUC. Elite landowners denounced the march as a communist takeover and began hiring private "self-defense" forces in the months that followed, laying the foundation for paramilitarism in the region (CNMH 2014; Fajardo 2014). With heightened accusations leveled against the ANUC on the part of landowning elites, Pastrana Borrero announced that the administration would no longer negotiate with the ANUC and severed all ties with the organization. The state's antagonistic relationship toward the ANUC led to the Chicoral Agreement, which restricted agrarian reform and expanded agroindustries in the region (Pérez 2010; Zamosc 1986). Tensions between the ANUC and the state also exacerbated internal divisions *within* the campesino movement. During the ANUC's 1972 national association conference in Tolú, representatives voted to uphold the demands outlined within the Campesino Mandate. However, the decision was not unanimous. The Pastrana administration capitalized on internal divisions to negotiate with those who had opposed the Campesino Mandate, leading to a split between the government-recognized "Armenia Line" and the independent "Sincelejo Line" (Zamosc 1986, 101).

Following the split, campesino organizers began collaborating with local scholars to deepen their engagement in *praxis*—collective reflection and political action. The participatory process led to the emergence of the co-constructed research methodology known as *Investigación-Acción Participativa* (PAR; Participatory Action Research) (Fals Borda 1986). Led by sociologist Orlando Fals Borda, PAR challenged the positivist undercurrents prevalent in the social sciences, driven largely by US and European academic centers.[8] Instead, early proponents of PAR explicitly engaged in research as a participatory and politically engaged process (Rappaport 2021). In particular, they argued for new forms of knowledge production that centered subjectivity and lived experience through "*sentipensante* (feeling-thinking)" methods, explicitly placing research at the service of movement-building (Fals Borda 1986, 25B; Negrete 2013, 55).

Through critical, historical retrieval, storytelling, and *décimas* (songs), PAR celebrated and reclaimed campesino intellectual traditions as valid sources of knowledge (Robles Lomeli and Rappaport 2018). Víctor Negrete, a key protagonist in the creation of PAR, writes that local researchers created community spaces where people reflected on campesino "history and life" in order to "defend, connect, and improve . . . the positive elements" of campesino culture as the foundation for social change (Negrete 2013, 30). The PAR teams also worked with local artists to produce accessible materials about the history of campesino organizing, including graphic novels, leaflets, and radio programs (Rappaport 2021). With a focus on campesino "figures of exceptional significance," these materials reclaimed the history of campesino organizing and resistance, otherwise absent from extant accounts of the region (Negrete 2013, 17).

One of the first illustrated booklets focused on the life of Felicita Campos. An Afro Caribbean leader from San Onofre, Campos played a central role in the organization of the campesino leagues that formed in the 1920s. Throughout the 1920s and 1930s, she also organized successful land recuperations and made multiple trips to the capital city of Bogotá to demand campesino rights to land. Imprisoned on at least thirty different occasions, her ceaseless commitment to campesino organizing embodies the multigenerational struggle for liberation in Montes de María (Fals Borda 1986, 156B). As Negrete later reflected, "it was our intention to know, in depth, these past struggles . . . efforts which remained mostly unknown by the popular sectors and distorted or condemned by the dominant groups" (Negrete 2013, 12).

Drawing on the work of Paulo Freire (1970), PAR researchers situated their methods within the wider pedagogy of *aprender haciendo*—learning by doing. As a form of praxis, the pedagogy of "learning by doing" situates research as an ongoing and collective process of action and reflection aimed at creating spaces for grassroots activists to analyze and act on political experience. By locating research as a vital part of movement-building, PAR researchers did not limit their understanding of knowledge production to project-based endeavors with a finite end, but instead embraced research as a permanent, participatory, and explicitly political process (Negrete 2013; Rappaport 2021). Facilitating focus group interviews, public forums for collective deliberation, and a national newsletter, the PAR teams developed methods that aimed to strengthen the organizing capacity and visibility of the national campesino movement. The PAR studies also helped campesino leaders articulate their demands within the framework of legal and constitutional rights, historically denied to the *campesinado* (Pérez 2010, 20). In this way, campesino knowledge production became a powerful tool for political organizing. "This work," Negrete (2013) concludes, "was the genesis . . . of what today is called participatory research . . . widely known and applied in many parts of the world" (82).

During the Second National Congress of the ANUC-Sincelejo line, members once again ratified the Campesino Mandate, solidifying their "political position of independence before the State" (Pérez 2010, 43). While unified in support of the Campesino Mandate, the assembly exposed tensions across gendered lines. Women, who had been at the forefront of the land recuperation campaigns, remained marginalized in the state's land policies, which only recognized the nuclear family for land deeds. In response, campesina women organized the first Regional Women's Conference in Ovejas, Montes de María, where the ANUC formally included women as independent members of the household in their official platform (CNMH 2014).[9] Decades of organizing spearheaded by campesina women culminated in the creation of the Women's Secretariat in 1977, laying the groundwork for the 1984 National Policy for Campesina Women (Grupo de Memoria Histórica 2011).

Despite the split between the Sincelejo and Armenia lines, Chucho Pérez (2010) asserts that the independent gathering of ten thousand campesinos from departments across the country during the Second National Congress reflected the realization—and not the disintegration—of the campesino struggle. "It was the moment that the *campesinado* truly understood their situation," Pérez writes in the introduction of his memoir. "Our sincere struggle [*franca lucha*] during the entire decade of the 1970s was not only for land, but also to liberate ourselves from the orders of a State that had excluded us since the beginning (20)." The government, however, reacted to the Second National Congress with severe repression.

"We were abused by the state," explained Catalina Pérez Pérez, an ANUC leader who participated in the early PAR studies and helped organize the Women's Secretariat. "I was first imprisoned in 1974. A policeman imprisoned me, hit me, took me to jail, and they marked me, as if I was the biggest delinquent in the world, with numbers here," she recalled, outlining an invisible box across her forehead. "If we were found reading books, then we were stigmatized as *guerrilleras*," she explained. "They would take away our notebooks, our books, our histories." Catalina's voice softened as she paused to reflect on the state's criminalization of campesino knowledge and history. "We started to bury them out of fear and when we dug them out, many of the books had decomposed."

Campesino knowledge became a key site of state violence and territorial control. As Catalina details, the state carried out targeted campaigns against teachers, PAR researchers, community educators, ANUC members, and grassroots leaders who knew how to "speak well"—those who engaged in public social analysis. Drawing on racist, colonialist, and patriarchal tropes of campesinos—and rural women in particular—as backward, premodern, and incapable of articulate social analysis, the state legitimized violence against social leaders who they claimed had been co-opted by the guerrillas. State repression generated a widespread "fear of speaking" among community leaders who bore the brunt of state-sponsored violence. Grassroots organizers and educators hid educational materials, and "lowered" their public profiles in response.

Amid the increasingly tense relationship between the ANUC and the state, various guerrilla organizations also began establishing bases in the region, including the Fuerzas Armadas Revolucionarias de Colombia—Ejército del Pueblo (FARC-EP), Ejército Popular de Liberación (EPL), Ejército de Liberación Nacional (ELN), Partido Revolucionario de los Trabajadores (PRT) and the Corriente de Renovación Socialista (CRS). Many of the guerrilla organizations initially sought to build trust through educational campaigns focused on campesino rights, agrarian legislation, and community organizing rather than armed revolution. The initial relationship between guerrilla movements and campesino communities in Montes de María, therefore, was not primarily marked by hostility but rather tenuous coexistence as civilians navigated living side by side armed organizations. Although these relationships undoubtedly influenced segments of the campesino movement and their varying strategies for political participation, the ANUC-Sincelejo line remained staunchly independent (Negrete 2013; Pérez 2010). As guerrilla organizations intensified their armed recruitment campaigns, however, their relationship with campesino communities deteriorated. Over the course of the war, guerrilla factions carried out assassinations and kidnappings, established illegal checkpoints to monitor communities' movements, planted land mines, appropriated community meeting spaces, and forcibly disappeared civilians (CNMH 2014).

Despite the widespread victimization of campesino communities at the hands of the guerrillas, the state used the presence of guerrilla organizations in the region to justify the violent repression of campesino leaders, characterizing the ANUC as a "subversive" organization. Through the dual discourse of security and criminality, the state eroded the distinction between armed revolutionary organizations and nonviolent social mobilization.[10] With the election of right-wing candidate Julio César Turbay Ayala in 1978 and the implementation of the administration's "Security Statute," an emboldened class of landowning elites ramped up their collaboration with the "self-defense organizations" that had formed in the early 1970s (Pérez 2010, 161). Campesino leaders were systematically assassinated with impunity (CNMH 2014, 28). "The coercive treatment of the land invasions, the persecution of the peasant leaders, the use of military justice under the state of siege, and the continuous harassment of ANUC," concludes Zamosc (1986), "became, after 1972, the official policy toward the peasant movement" (104).

The state's strategic conflation of campesino organizing with armed revolution through the discourse of "national security" has remained a potent tool that continues to normalize violence against social leaders today. Furthermore, the state's criminalization of campesino intellectual traditions, beginning in the 1970s, became a recurrent pattern of violence used throughout the armed conflict—one that persists in the postaccord landscape. "The leaders from the sixties and seventies are still on file, and if they speak out again, they are killed immediately," Jesús Pérez reflected in his 2010 memoir.[11] "For this reason, I told a *compañero* recently in Cartagena, 'The campesino leadership has more fear today, because they do not let us speak openly' " (174).

THE ROUTE OF TERROR

The early 1990s marked a turning point for the war in Montes de María. First, guerrilla organizations increased their focus on territorial control and military strategy. Second, armed organizations began to increasingly fund their military operations through narcotrafficking. With access to major highways, the Magdalena River, and the Caribbean Sea, Montes de María became a strategic corridor for the military, paramilitaries, and guerrilla organizations alike, situating the region as a key axis of the armed conflict (Porras 2014, 361). Third, the rise of "militias," hired to carry out targeted assassinations on behalf of the various armed organizations vying for territorial control, created a climate of chaos (PNUD 2010). Finally, the consolidation of the paramilitary organization, the Autodefensas Campesinas de Córdoba y Urabá (ACCU) into the Autodefensas Unidas de Colombia (AUC) led to mass violence and large-scale forced displacements (CNMH 2014, 28).

The intensification of organized violence in the 1990s, however, too often overshadows the significant peacebuilding processes that also emerged during this time. In 1990, the government signed agreements with the M-19, PRT, and the EPL, which placed political participation at the center of the national conversation (García Durán, Grabe Loewenherz, and Patiño Hormaza 2008, 22).[12] The demobilization of the PRT, which took place in Montes de María, also played a pivotal role in the creation of the 1991 Constitution, ushering in a period of hope for a national peace process rooted in social justice. With the new constitution, the 1993 "Law 70" guaranteeing ethnic communities the right to collective land ownership and "*consulta previa* (prior consent)," passed.[13] These gains emerged from—and opened a space for—a more engaged citizenry focused on human rights and peacebuilding. As Ricardo Esquivia notes (2009), over ten million people participated in various marches for peace across Colombia throughout the 1990s (296). With new opportunities for political participation, the campesino movement also organized successful electoral campaigns in Montes de María, catapulting social leaders into political positions as mayors and municipal council representatives. Their rise to power, however, was once again met with violent backlash.

In 1997, the first paramilitary-led massacre in Montes de María besieged the rural community of Pichilín (CNMH 2014, 30). Formed through an ANUC land recuperation action in the 1970s, Pichilín became the first site of over one hundred massacres[14] that took place in the region between the 1990s and 2000s, violently paving what the National Center for Historic Memory has called the "route of terror" (De los Ríos et al. 2012, 11).[15] Although guerrilla organizations also carried out violence against civilians, the paramilitaries were responsible for the majority of civilian deaths in the region (CNMH 2014). Campesinos accounted for 90 percent of the victims, many of whom occupied leadership roles as teachers, health-care workers, and human rights defenders (PNUD 2010). The hypermasculinity that shaped paramilitary violence further reified male-dominated structures of governance in rural communities, disproportionately affecting girls, women, and lesbian, gay, bisexual, and transgendered individuals (CNMH 2015; CNMH 2011; Serrano Amaya 2018). Rooted in white supremacist ideologies that privileged white individuals, the paramilitaries targeted and occupied historically Black communities, with Black women, girls, and LGBTQIA+ individuals bearing the brunt of the direct and structural violence that emerged from everyday social control (Rocha 2010; CNMH 2011, 165).

Furthermore, the establishment of the AUC's Bloque Héroes de los Montes de María (Heroes Block of Montes de María) unleashed a wave of violence against local representatives, including community leaders, mayors, municipal council members, and members of the Unión Patriótica political party, contributing to what is known as the "*parapolítica* scandal" (CNMH 2018b; Tate 2015).[16] Politicians with direct ties to the paramilitaries rose to power at the local, regional, and national levels, producing a culture of impunity and providing paramilitary commanders with direct access to public contracts and land.[17] Notary and Land Registry officials in Montes de María worked in collaboration with the paramilitaries to change land deeds, "donating" lands acquired by force to specific families in order to cover the paper trail that linked paramilitary violence to dispossession (García Reyes and Vargas Reina 2014).

As the National Center for Historic Memory has outlined, the state's shift away from land redistribution policies and toward rural development further depoliticized the agrarian question, obscuring the connections between forced displacement and the massive purchase of land by elite business owners (CNMH 2014). Under the Agrarian Reform Law 160 of 1994, campesinos could only access land through a combination of subsidies and development projects (PNUD 2010). In order to buy the genetically modified seeds that the state, in alliance with multinational corporations, required for participation, campesinos began taking out loans. State officials raised interest rates and evicted families who defaulted on their loans (CNMH 2014; García Reyes and Vargas Reina 2014). With the threat of eviction, campesinos began selling their land at extremely low prices (PNUD 2010, 8). The state's nefarious and exploitative use of debt facilitated what David Harvey (2005) has called "accumulation by dispossession" (63). Political instability and economic strain further perpetuated the massive sale of land, coinciding with the arrival of the palm oil industry to the region (García Reyes and Vargas Reina 2014; Ojeda, Quiroga, and Vallejo 2021).

"I had the picture clear. I knew that there were interests in the land," Rafael, a social leader, reflected,

When we displaced to Cartagena, we were living in complete misery and there were people who said, "this is never going to improve so why don't you sell me this land." Some people sold 20 hectares for 500.000 pesos [$158.00USD]. And so, I said to them, "okay, if this is not going to improve then why are you interested in buying this?" But I have to tell you, many people were taken advantage of and sold their land. Later, I watched as the palm oil industry expanded, generating more displacements. It is a form of modern slavery for our campesinos. Those who work in the palm oil plantations are paid a miserable salary and, additionally, they now have to buy yams, yucca, and rice because they no longer have farmland.

As Rafael makes clear, the powerful nexus between paramilitarism, state development contracts, and multinational corporations that led to the acquisition of land in the hands of a few elite business owners continues to shape socioecological, political, and economic relations today. Indeed, Rafael's account reflects what Diana Ojeda and colleagues (2020) have called "geographies of everyday dispossession" where the reconfiguration of space through monoculture plantations results in a lack of access to water, farmlands, and mobility for local communities (30).[18] For this reason, Porras (2014) argues for a distinction between "land conflicts" and "territorial conflicts"—terms that are frequently collapsed in scholarly and policy-making circles. For Porras (2014), analyses that focus solely on land reduce an understanding of the dynamics of the armed conflict to sheer economic terms without adequate attention to the sociopolitical relations that also shape the ways in which the state's neoliberal development model "favors elite landowners and businesses . . . to the detriment of the rights, interests, and expectations of the rural population" (354). Instead, he contends that an understanding of the struggle for *territory* allows for more fine-grained analysis of the sociopolitical constellations of power that undergird the "control of strategic zones" across Colombia in relation to the dominant economic model that guides state action (345).

In 2000, the implementation of the US foreign policy Plan Colombia under former President Bill Clinton provided funding for Colombia's military operations, doubling the size of the Colombian Armed Forces (Isacson, December 2012).[19] Despite the dramatic increase in military and police presence in the peripheral territories, state absence became the preferred trope among US foreign policy makers, used to justify increased military support and training. As Winifred Tate (2015) details, US policy makers also focused their analyses on the FARC, attributing paramilitary violence to a generalized "category of chaos" (107), which they legitimized as a "localized reaction of the middle class to guerrilla violence" (96). As a result, the paramilitaries became "the foundation of counterinsurgency efforts, operating outside the law but unofficially sanctioned by the state" (84).

The election of Álvaro Uribe to the presidency in 2002 and the immediate implementation of his administration's "Democratic Security" policy intensified state violence in Montes de María. Uribe capitalized on the post-9/11 discourse of counterterrorism to deny the existence of the internal armed conflict in Colombia, further eroding the distinction "between civilians and combatants" in the rural territories (Mason 2003, 401). Following his inauguration, Uribe declared Montes de María a "state of commotion," legitimizing extrajudicial force (Presidencia de la República 2003). Referring to it as a "Zone for Rehabilitation and Consolidation," the military and police set up roadblocks and checkpoints, enforced curfews, and blocked the entry of external visitors into the high zone of Montes de María (PNUD 2010, 32; Rojas 2015).

The state also targeted campesino knowledge production, once again incarcerating those who carried books and writing materials, occupied professional posts as teachers and community health-care workers—charging campesinos who knew how to "speak well" with "rebellion." From 2002 to 2004, the state arbitrarily detained more than six thousand campesinos in Montes de María alone (CSPP 2020). Heavy military surveillance and restrictions on the movement of people and goods severely limited campesinos' access to markets, collapsing the strained campesino economy. Daily military interrogations were hostile and violent, with women reporting cases of sexual harassment and assault at checkpoints and roadblocks (Personal interview, April 3, 2017; Focus group interview, September 24, 2017). Despite the fact that the Colombian Constitutional Court declared the Zones for Rehabilitation and Consolidation unconstitutional, the use of military checkpoints, interrogations, and arbitrary detentions continued in Montes de María until 2006 (García Reyes and Vargas Reina 2014; Mason 2003). Massacres, selective assassinations, torture, "false positives," rumors of paramilitary incursions, arbitrary detentions, disappearances, and violent confrontations between armed groups led to massive, forced displacements of campesinos from Montes de María.[20] Between 1995 and 2012 "110,000 people, over half the population" were forcibly displaced from just four of the region's sixteen municipalities (Isacson, January 2012).

PEACE IN TIMES OF WAR

Although the armed conflict severely weakened campesino organizations, social leaders refute prevailing narratives that suggest the war led to the complete dissolution of the campesino movement (CNMH 2018a; Pérez 2010). "People who remained, who resisted [displacement], began organizing," recalled Alejandro, a social leader from the Alta Montaña:

> We formed one organization between many communities. We called the organization the Association of the Forgotten Communities of Montes de María. When the paramilitaries entered in '99, they caused massive displacement. Organizing helped us because whatever small thing occurred in one community, we all showed up there. I have never been able to forget this accompaniment that we had with each other, this solidarity. The day that the guerrilla arrived at my dad's house to *ajá* [kill him], more than 120 campesinos showed up and surrounded his house.[21]

As Alejandro details, the armed conflict led to renewed and concerted community organizing efforts that became vital for survival in the face of guerrilla, military, and state-sanctioned paramilitary violence. Social leaders created innovative communication strategies to notify neighboring communities about impending invasions by armed groups and staged nonviolent protection actions like the human barricade used to save Alejandro's father. "We realized that unity," reflected William Jaraba Pérez, a teacher and community leader in the Alta Montaña, "that social organization, was the only way to resist and survive."

The commitment to continue meeting clandestinely also deepened a shared understanding of the localized dynamics that fueled the armed conflict as campesino leaders began identifying key actors and patterns of violence in order to hone their strategies of nonviolent resistance. Throughout the armed conflict, social leaders engaged in both "hidden" and highly visible forms of organized nonviolent resistance to ensure the survival of campesino life (Scott 1990). At the height of the violence in 2003 and again in 2006, campesinos from the Alta Montaña led marches to the urban center of El Carmen to present local authorities with petitions demanding that the state recognize the civilian population in the rural high zone. They also requested an end to military interrogations, increased access to transportation and roads, and a response to a fungus that had begun to kill the avocado forest across the high region of Montes de María (CNMH 2018a). The state responded once more with force, leading to a surge in arbitrary detentions in the Alta Montaña. The protests, however, also generated visibility, catching the attention of key human rights organizations.

The first human rights delegation visited the Alta Montaña in 2006, marking a significant turning point for campesino leaders who had endured decades of state violence (CNMH 2018a). Over five hundred campesinos traveled to participate in the humanitarian visit, where they documented violations that their communities had suffered at the hands of the state, paramilitary, and guerrilla organizations. The visit, which took place in a community stigmatized as a guerrilla stronghold, drew significant backlash from the state. Local military commanders cited the mass gathering of campesinos as evidence of increased guerrilla presence, justifying the arrests of the leaders who organized the delegation. Jorge Luis Montes Hernandez, a charismatic and young community health-care worker recently elected to El Carmen's municipal council, became the state's primary target. Soon after the humanitarian visit and prior to Jorge's inauguration to the municipal council, the state arbitrarily detained and imprisoned Jorge on charges of "rebellion." A lack of evidence for the charges led to his release, but his legal case—like those of campesinos arrested during this time—remained "open," leaving him vulnerable to future imprisonment and excluding him from electoral politics.

Around this time, members from the community of Macayepo began to organize the collective return of their community to the Alta Montaña. The birthplace of one of the region's most notorious paramilitary commanders, Macayepo was stigmatized by the FARC-EP as a paramilitary stronghold, carrying out high levels of violence against civilians in the community. Land mines, forced disappearances, death threats, assassinations, and the guerrilla occupation of farmlands eventually forced the community to displace. Severe hunger and unemployment in the city, however, created an equally untenable situation. Several leaders approached local authorities to demand state-accompanied return to their land. The fact that the community had fled primarily FARC-led violence opened different avenues for forging relationships with local military commanders who sought to increase their presence in the region. The first group of families returned with military accompaniment in 2004. Young soldiers based in the community led de-mining efforts, allowing campesinos to safely access their farmlands once more. Many soldiers lost their lives in the process.[22] Their commitment to de-mining the area at great personal risk established strong bonds of trust between campesinos and soldiers based in Macayepo (personal interviews, September 26, 2017, and October 6, 2017; Sarmiento et al. 2018).

While this time marked a period of hope and joy for those returning to their land, the state-accompanied return raised profound suspicions for people located in neighboring communities where heightened military presence coincided with an uptick in arbitrary detentions, armed confrontations, and targeted assassinations of community leaders (CNMH 2018a). The militarization of community life deepened lines of enmity across the Alta Montaña, intimately felt and internalized by those stigmatized as either "guerrilla" or "paramilitary" due to the proximity of their communities to the bases of armed actors.[23] "The violence created hostility between the communities in the Alta Montaña," Miledys Vásquez Navarro, a social leader from the Alta Montaña explained:

> There was an invisible line that existed between the communities, based on the proximity of the different armed groups that operated in the region. One group operated in one sector and other groups operated in different sectors, and they had different ideologies and they were enemies and this also affected us, the campesinos. There was an atmosphere of terror in the region where we didn't just fear the armed groups, we also feared each other, other campesinos. We lost trust [confianza], there was no one we could believe. And the public forces, who were supposed to defend us, well, the armed conflict turned them into our oppressors who, like the criminal organizations,

sometimes controlled our daily movements through blockades and threats. And all of these dynamics created what we call "invisible walls" across the region.

As guerrilla organizations and state security forces exerted control over the daily movements of individuals through roadblocks and death threats, limiting the possibility of organization and trade between the communities, rumors of collaboration with armed groups responsible for violent acts fortified what many in the Alta Montaña refer to as "invisible walls" throughout the region. Like Michael Taussig' s (1987) description of a "culture of terror," Miledys underscores how the "intermingling of silence and myth" generated widespread fear, unraveling the social fabric that had previously united the region (8).

There is no single, unified story of the armed conflict, forced displacement, and return in the Alta Montaña. Some people were displaced for extended periods of time, others were displaced sporadically and periodically—returning when direct confrontations between armed groups struggling for territorial control decreased—and still others remained "resistant." While many families voluntarily returned *gota a gota* (drop by drop) and without state assistance, several communities returned with military accompaniment. For some, the humanitarian visit marked a turning point that opened possibilities for life beyond daily survival, while for others, rumors about a mass gathering of FARC insurgents ignited fear. Finding ways to work across deeply entrenched lines of enmity posed a significant, yet not impossible, challenge for social leaders in the Alta Montaña. The shared demand for dignified return and commitment to campesino life with attention to the ecological well-being of the territory created possibilities for collective organizing in the Alta Montaña.

Across Montes de María, grassroots organizations led numerous nonviolent marches, declared autonomous "zones of peace," organized unaccompanied returns to their land, documented and denounced human rights violations, created early warning systems, innovated arts-based approaches to community healing,[24] and initiated reintegration processes with combatants who had defected from various armed groups (Sarmiento et al. 2018). At the height of forced displacements in 2000 and following a bombing by the

FARC-EP, the Colectivo de Comunicación de los Montes de María Línea 21 (Montes de María Communications Collective: Line 21) hosted a movie night in the public square of El Carmen de Bolívar (Rodríguez 2011, 103). Despite the Colectivo's doubts that anyone would venture outside at night in the aftermath of the bombing, over three hundred people showed up. In the years that followed, the Colectivo began hosting itinerant movie nights across the territory. A popular education cooperative founded by Soraya Bayuelo in 1994, the Colectivo boldly reclaimed public spaces, disrupting the campaigns of terror that both the paramilitaries and the guerrillas used to exert territorial control.

LGBTQIA+ leaders in El Carmen similarly organized safe houses across the region, providing refuge for queer individuals fleeing severe, homophobic violence perpetuated largely by the paramilitaries, Colombian Armed Forces, and police (personal interview, August 30, 2017). Their early organizing efforts gave rise to multiple queer movements in the region, including the Corporación Todos Somos Iguales (We Are All Equal) and Caribe Afirmativo (Affirmative Caribbean). One of the most influential LGBTQIA+ movements in the country, Caribe Afirmativo later played a central role in advocating for the inclusion of measures attentive to the distinct needs of the LGBTQIA+ community in the 2016 peace agreement, the first comprehensive peace accord in the world to do so (Serrano Amaya 2018).

The proliferation of grassroots peacebuilding movements that formed in times of war distinguished Montes de María as a territory with a deep history of peacebuilding and conflict transformation (Bouvier 2009; Sarmiento et al. 2018). The challenge that social leaders faced, however, was how to unite the multitude of peacebuilding efforts that existed across the region yet remained fragmented. After more than twenty years of exile in Bogotá,[25] Ricardo returned to Montes de María and founded Sembrandopaz in 2005. In addition to providing direct and sustained accompaniment to campesino communities who sought to return to their land, the organization renewed forms of coalitional organizing in the region with the explicit aim of networking across the multiple—yet disconnected—peacebuilding processes that had emerged during the war. In collaboration with social leaders across the region, Sembrandopaz began building what they called an "Infrastructure for Peace in Montes de María" (Esquivia 2009, 302).[26] After years of collective organizing, the broad-based coalition known as the Espacio Regional de Construcción de Paz de los Montes de María (Montes de María Regional Space for Peace-building, shortened as Espacio Regional) formed in 2014, with representatives from over three hundred distinct social processes committed to the work of territorial peace.

Although repressive violence and the dynamics of the armed conflict weakened and fractured the campesino movement, the war did not eliminate the principles of *interculturalidad* and solidarity that had shaped the territorial identity and history of Montes de María for centuries. The peacebuilding processes that emerged in the 1990s drew explicitly from the structure and lessons of the campesino movement. "La Asociación Nacional de Usuarios Campesinos [ANUC] did not disappear," Jésus "Chucho" Pérez (2010), who later became a member of the Espacio Regional, asserts in his memoir, "Even though we have other organizational names, we are the same people" (15).

A "LABORATORY" OF PEACE: TRANSITIONAL JUSTICE AND INTERNATIONAL INTERVENTIONS

In 2003, the Uribe administration signed a peace accord with the AUC that initiated the demobilization of the paramilitaries between 2003 and 2005 (Rojas 2015, 167).[27] For social leaders, the clear ties between the state and the paramilitaries raised concerns about the legitimacy and intent of the demobilization process (Nussio 2011, 88). By 2005 all violent acts attributed to paramilitaries ceased to exist in official state records. Instead, the state began ascribing such violence to the generalized category of "criminal bands," or BACRIM (*bandas criminales*). The demobilization process, including nefarious arrangements such as the overnight extradition of paramilitary commanders to the United States, resulted in the emergence of "neoparamilitarism" (PNUD 2010; Tate 2015)." As Porras (2014) contends, the complex new reality that materialized following the demobilization was best summed up by paramilitary commanders themselves. "Here," Diego Vecino, a paramilitary commander in Montes de María declared, "the AUC has demobilized, but not paramilitarism" (quoted in Porras 2014, 371).

Alongside demobilization, the Uribe administration initiated the National Plan for Territorial Consolidation. Widely seen as "phase two" of Plan Colombia, Consolidation received financial and military support from the United States. In 2007, the Armed Forces killed the commander of the FARC's 37 Front during combat in the Alta Montaña. With the dissolution of the 37 Front, the state proclaimed the arrival of the "postconflict" to Montes de María (De los Ríos et al. 2012). Despite such declarations, documented cases of arbitrary detentions, surveillance, and false positives continued until 2008 (CNMH 2018a).[28]

The state's shifting approach to agrarian reform from land redistribution and toward development came into full fruition under Consolidation. The Ministry of Defense formed the Center for the Coordination of Integrated Action (CCAI) with support from the US Southern Command as well as USAID (De los Ríos et al. 2012). The partnership between USAID and the US Southern Command resulted in what Diana Rojas (2015) has called the "securitization of development," which played a central role in the state's strategy to regain territorial control (218). Montes de María became a pilot site for CCAI, receiving high levels of funding from USAID for development projects. Framed as a technical problem, the depoliticization of the historic land struggle carried steep consequences for campesinos committed to the defense of life and territory. Under CCAI, then Minister of Agriculture Carlos Roberto Murgas Guerrero, created "strategic, productive alliances" for "rural development" that directed state subsidies to the palm oil industry—a trend that continued through 2010 (PNUD 2010, 8; Rutas del Conflicto 2017).

The expansion of palm oil plantations facilitated massive land sales that led to renewed cycles of "economic displacements" of campesino communities from their land (PNUD 2010, 35). Between 2008 and 2010, more than seventy external businesses, primarily from the country's interior, purchased over 60,000 hectares of land in Montes de María (PNUD 2010).[29] During this time, 17,768 new cases of forced displacement occurred in just six of the region's municipalities, the majority of which took place along the palm oil corridor (De los Ríos et al. 2012, 29). Today, Carlos Murgas owns the largest palm oil industry in the region, exemplifying the ways in which international development worked in tandem with the state-paramilitary-agroindustry complex to normalize dispossession in Montes de María (Ballvé 2013; Ojeda et al. 2015).[30] As Tate (2015) writes, "the transformation of the agrarian sector through legislative and financial incentives (including USAID-sponsored programs in some areas) to privilege agribusiness monocrops such as palm oil has contributed to the conservation of paramilitary structures of land ownership" (229).

The passage of the Justice and Peace Law 975 following the AUC demobilization in 2005 also jump-started international mechanisms of "transitional justice" in the midst of war, leading to a wave of international funding and interventions led by International Nongovernmental Organizations (INGOs), including the United Nations (UN) and the International Organization of Migration (García Godos and Lid 2010; Meertens 2015; Porras 2014). The European Union (EU) also announced support for a five-year initiative focused on participatory peace and development programs. Positioned as an alternative to the United States' Consolidation program, the EU named Montes de María one of the first "Peace Laboratories" in the country (Barreto 2016). While aimed at funding "bottom-up" peacebuilding projects, the budgetary and administrative protocols perpetuated externally driven mandates in ways that undermined and fragmented the fragile grassroots coalitions that had begun to revitalize across the region.

In response to the fractured landscape of peacebuilding, the Citizen's Commission for Reconciliation in the Caribbean (shortened to Citizen's Commission) formed, bringing civil society representatives from social movements, trade unions, human rights organizations, religious institutions, and universities together. The Citizen's Commission sought to develop a shared, regional vision for reconciliation and transitional justice, evaluate the implementation of the Justice and Peace Law, and increase possibilities for citizen participation in national peace processes (Esquivia 2009, 310). Drawing on past experiences, the coalition once again directed their efforts toward popular education, creating a space for collective deliberation focused on comparative and translocal experiences of transitional justice. The coalition also advocated for renewed negotiations between the government, the FARC-EP, and the ELN, placing emphasis on the role of civil society in the construction of comprehensive peace accords. The work of grassroots coalitions like the Citizen's Commission became pivotal for the inclusion of key sectors of civil society during the negotiations that led to the 2016 peace accords.

In 2010, Juan Manuel Santos, the former Minister of Defense under Uribe, was elected president. In a sharp departure from Uribe, Santos passed the Victim's and Restitution of Land Law 1448 (Victim's Law) in 2011, which recognized victims of the armed conflict for the first time. The Victim's Law replaced the mechanisms of the Justice and Peace Law, establishing the Unit for the Attention and Integral Reparations of Victims (Victim's Unit), the Land Restitution Unit, and the National Center for Historical Memory (CNMH) as the agencies tasked with implementing war reparations. However, the legal distinction between land dispossession (*despojo*)—limited to cases of direct, physical violence—and abandonment (*abandono*) which included those who fled their homes during the war—obscured the mundane and bureaucratic practices that the paramilitaries used in collaboration with state officials to dispossess campesinos throughout the war. As Porras (2014) notes, the distinction resulted in the uneven application of restitution where the state's "typology of *abandonment* prevails over that of *dispossession*" (375). The assassination of at least four land restitution advocates in Montes de María between 2010 and 2011 and an upsurge in cases of sexual violence along the palm oil corridor further weakened trust between grassroots communities and the state (Isacson, January 30, 2012).[31]

The lack of material implementation and the persistent threat of forced displacement led community leaders from the municipalities of Mampuján and Las Brisas to organize a weeklong, nonviolent march from Montes de María to the capital city of Cartagena to demand collective reparations in December 2011 (Ruiz Hernández 2013). Extensive planning for the march, which included support from Sembrandopaz and local human rights organizations, led to a highly organized and visible action that received national and international attention. In the face of a weak implementation process, the march reflected the power of social mobilization and campesino organizing in the pursuit of territorial peace, offering a significant referent for other communities across the region.

THE 2016 PEACE ACCORDS AND TERRITORIAL PEACEBUILDING

In 2012, Santos surprised many with the announcement that his administration had renewed negotiations with the FARC-EP in Havana, Cuba—a process the administration confidentially began in 2011. "At the center of the Government's vision for peace is concern for territory and a concern for rights," Sergio Jaramillo, the High Commissioner for Peace, who led the government's negotiation efforts with the FARC-EP, declared at the beginning of a public lecture given at Harvard University (2013). The speech, which marked Jaramillo's first public presentation of "territorial peace," became the cornerstone of the Santos administration's framework for the accords. "Territorial peace" resonated with social leaders in Montes de María who saw the framework as the fruition of their decades-long work for peace. "The proposal of territorial peace is a proposal that has been emerging for a long time," Ricardo later explained:

> If we look at the example of the ANUC, the whole trajectory of Orlando Fals Borda and participatory action research, this is what we have been working on for a long time. Colombia is a country where the state tries to be a nation but has never been a nation. Why? Because it is a state that occurs only from Bogotá and is controlled by an elite class. So, if you want there to be a lasting and stable peace then you have to transform this. That is where the concept of territorial peace emerges from.

In the spring of 2016, as talks faltered between the government and the FARC-EP over transitional justice mechanisms, over three hundred social leaders from across Montes de María organized a march in the public square of El Carmen. Carrying a banner that declared, "We Sign the Peace," members of the Espacio Regional publicly asserted their unwavering commitment to the accords. While the symbolic political action served as a form of support for the national peace process, social leaders also made clear that their work for peacebuilding would continue regardless of the outcome of the negotiations in Havana. "We were there to support the peace process, but we also wanted to make clear that these accords are not Santos' or the FARC's," a member of the Espacio Regional later reflected, "these are *our* accords."

On September 26, 2016, then President Juan Manuel Santos and FARC commander Rodrigo Londoño signed a historic peace agreement in Cartagena, Colombia. Two weeks later, Colombian citizens narrowly rejected the peace accords in a plebiscite referendum. While the outcome of the plebiscite exacerbated the climate of "uncertainty" that pervaded Montes de María, the mass mobilizations that erupted across the country generated a sense of hope for social leaders who faced a renewed wave of death threats as a result of their public advocacy for peace. The sustained activism that took "peace to the streets" succeeded in exerting pressure on the opposition led by former President Uribe, resulting in renewed negotiations. On November 24, 2016, the government and the FARC-EP signed the Final Accord to End the Conflict and Build a Lasting and Stable Peace (Alto Comisionado 2016). This time, the signing took place behind closed doors in the Colombian capital, Bogotá.

"We must look beyond the plebiscite, because this vote has many political roots," Ricardo reflected at the end of Sembrandopaz's annual retreat soon after the revised accord was signed:

> More than fifty years ago, we witnessed what we call *La Violencia* between the Conservatives and the Liberals that left 300,000 dead. The National Front emerged, but this was a contract between elite politicians and the war did not end. Populist leaders were killed, and the FARC emerged from this. The ELN, PRT, EPL, M-19—all of these groups have been here, but the [political] system is entrenched, and they couldn't break it. With agrarian reform, campesinos in this region began organizing with the ANUC to recuperate land. It is very interesting to listen to the history of Pichilín and if we interpret the "signs of the times" based on what they say, we realize that this was an ANUC sector, a sector that was organized, that formed a farm within three days. But once again the large landowners decided to take this land and we witnessed massacres. This history helps us understand the situation in Montes de María. When the elite class saw campesino groups organizing within a wider political climate focused on human rights and solidarity, what did they do? On the one side, Congress started to shred the Constitution and, on the other, the paramilitaries emerged. There are steps that have been made to end the war, but the war is not over. We must remember that the peace accords are only the beginning, and it fills us with hope and we must support it. This is a key moment for our work. In 1996, we began what we called the Platform for an Infrastructure of Peace in Montes de María that initiated an era of peacebuilding that continues today. Sembrandopaz is not an NGO, we are an organization that works to be a community, and we have a vision. We are facing strong challenges; the political situation puts the peace accords in danger, the elections are coming, and the next presidency could dissolve the accords. It is within this context that we are living, it is within this environment that we are working, and so we must engage with this, ask questions, and clarify the times.

The grassroots struggle to build peace is not new in Montes de María but deeply embedded in the territory's history and identity. While prevailing discourses and reports frequently begin and end descriptions of Montes de María with the armed conflict, reading the territory through a deeper, temporal lens reveals different contours of violence and peace that have shaped the region. By clarifying "the times," social leaders illuminate the ways in which collective care, solidarity, and peace live alongside histories of violence. In positioning their work for territorial peace as part of the multigenerational struggle for liberation, their accounts echo the Campesino Mandate published decades ago. Indeed, as Jésus "Chucho" Pérez (2010) later reflected, drawing on the words of the Campesino Mandate, the only way to transform social inequalities and build territorial peace is through "the permanent and organized struggle of the *campesinado*, the working classes, and popular sectors committed to structural change and liberation of our nation from all forms of domination and colonialism" (41). Campesino peacebuilding does not rest solely on national negotiations—although the accords have clear implications for their work. Instead, the struggle that began generations ago endures today as social leaders advocate for and work toward a more holistic approach to peacebuilding—one that requires recognition of the ways in which the historical processes that have shaped Montes de María are deeply rooted in relations with the land and territory. To understand how campesinos imagine and build liberatory peace, therefore, demands close awareness of the socioecological lifeways and multispecies relations that animate and sustain campesino organizing and life—the subject to which I now turn.

CHAPTER TWO

THE EARTH
SUFFERED, TOO

*The Death of the Avocado Forest
and Multispecies Resurgence*

WITNESSING THE AVOCADO DIE

In 1995, as armed groups increasingly arrived in the Alta Montaña, Giovani, an avocado farmer, started to notice a strange discoloration on the leaves of his trees. The avocado trees, which typically boasted broad, dark green leaves, had taken on an alarming yellowish hue. Giovani dedicated additional time to care for the avocado forest, which not only served as his main income-generating crop but also provided expansive shade cover for subsistence farming. He carefully cut back the weeds around the base of the trees, making sure to expand access to water and soil nutrients. He monitored, documented, and analyzed shifting changes in the foliage on a daily basis. Throughout the next year, Giovani compared the size and color of leaves from different avocado trees, examining the trunks for signs of new or increased worm and fungi life. He also took careful measurements of the avocado fruits throughout their life course. As the discoloration of leaves began to spread throughout the farm and the harvest resulted in smaller, yellow-tinged avocados, Giovani decided he needed to act, fast.

From 1996 to 1997, Giovani sent three different samples from the trees along with letters to the Colombian Corporation for Agricultural Research (CORPOICA) requesting the state's urgent attention to prevent further damage ("El cultivo" 2017). He received no response. By this time, increased levels of violence in the region had forcibly displaced many of Giovani's friends and family members. The already scarce presence of state institutions that provided agricultural support disappeared entirely in the wake of violent clashes and rumors of guerrilla takeovers. The volatile situation eventually forced Giovanni to displace as well, leaving the avocado forest to fend for itself.

Campesinos recall watching the slow progression of the fungus as the yellow foliage began to spread across the hillsides of the Alta Montaña. The intensification of violence and forced displacements prevented campesinos from adequately tending to their forests. For those who resisted displacement, the constant need to flee to the hillsides amid open combat upended traditional ways of caring for the land. Furthermore, the severe constraints placed on campesinos as a result of military checkpoints made travel to the agricultural agencies nearly impossible.

In 2004, after years of failed communication attempts, Giovani received a letter from the Colombian Agricultural Institute (ICA) with the test results from the samples he sent nearly a decade before, confirming the presence of *Phytophthora cinnamomi*. A soilborne fungus that infects the root system of trees, preventing the absorption of water and nutrients, *Phytophthora cinnamomi* contaminates surrounding soil life in ways that often damages wider ecosystems, necessitating containment to prevent the spread (Department of the Environment and Heritage 2004). However, ICA did not respond, act, or address the crisis for another five years, at which point the *Phytophthora cinnamomi* had killed over 70 percent of the avocado forests ("El cultivo" 2017).

Finally, in 2009, ICA alongside the UN-led Inter-Agency Standing Committee arrived in the Alta Montaña to verify and analyze the fungus. *Twelve years after* Giovani requested the state's urgent attention, the commission declared the infected avocado forest *an emergency* that required an "immediate" response ("El cultivo" 2017, 20). ICA (2009) issued a report initiating a plan to remove 6,000 dead avocado trees. Implementation, however, did not occur until two years later—fourteen years after Giovani appealed to the state for support. By this time, the vast majority of the avocado forest in the Alta Montaña had died.

Campesinos in the Alta Montaña center the death of the avocado tree—and with it, the unraveling of a fragile ecosystem—in their narratives of the armed conflict. In this chapter, I ask: What does dignified return mean and how is it enacted in the context of a destroyed environment? How do communities regenerate socioecological relationships in the midst of ongoing political and environmental violence? And how does the inclusion of more-than-human species as living and vital actors in territories that have endured the consequences of war reorient approaches to peacebuilding? I contend that the distinct ecological imagination that animates campesino peacebuilding mobilizes an alternative understanding of time, relationality, and place in ways that challenge the dominant, project-based, and technocratic frameworks that undergird international interventions. By giving primacy to caretaking ecologies marred by the compounding effects of political and environmental violence, campesinos offer a more integral approach to peacebuilding—one that brings the violent effects of neoliberal peace and development projects into sharp relief.

Through analysis of the everyday assemblages forged between people, animals, avocado forests, spirits, and fungi, this chapter brings the reciprocal relations of care between humans and more-than-humans in the Alta Montaña into focus (Kirksey and Helmreich 2010). "A relational approach," write Kristina Lyons, Lina B. Pinto-García, and Daniel Ruiz Serna (2019), "considers, on the one hand, the intimate socio-ecological relationships between human and non-human beings and, on the other, the joint participation of all these entities in phenomena such as violence and peacebuilding" (16). In doing so, multispecies anthropology challenges prevailing, Western environmental discourses that exoticize nature as devoid of human life and directs attention to the often-overlooked environmental practices that campesinos engage as they care for their *entorno*—lifeworld (Cadena 2010; Descola 2013; Fuentes 2010; Imanishi [1941] 2002; Kohn 2013; Ruiz Serna 2015).

Following campesino social theories, this chapter offers a reading of war and peace through the lens of the avocado. While devastating, the shared loss of the avocado reignited campesino organizing in the Alta Montaña, giving rise to the Peaceful Process of Reconciliation and Integration (Peaceful Process). I outline the multispecies political actions that the movement has taken to make the death of the avocado legible as a victim of the war and direct attention to the regenerative peacebuilding practices that campesinos engage within an ecology of care forged between humans and more-than-humans in the Alta Montaña. The temporal framework of relationality that guides campesino peacebuilding contrasts sharply with technocratic approaches to peace implementation. With a focus on measurable and isolated indicators, technical peacebuilding frameworks erase the relational webs that shape how campesinos understand and experience violence as more-than-human. Consequently, local practices of peace are also obscured, with dire costs for those most affected by the war. As Duván Caro Tapia (2021), a youth leader in Montes de María, eloquently writes, "Due to the violence perpetuated against our people, the relationships between community and ecosystems, between plants and humans, were lost, as well as the knowledge surrounding them, leading to the abandonment of environmental practices that had maintained the environment since ancient times." (85)

By decentering the human and reorienting theoretical inquiry toward relationality, multispecies ethnography offers a more capacious conceptualization of peace—one that recognizes the full lifeworlds of people as they seek to reweave—and create anew—the socioecological fabric of their communities.

A SECOND VIOLENCE

"We have had a very big loss in the Alta Montaña with respect to the environment and that has been the death of the avocado," Miledys Vásquez Navarro, a leader from the Alta Montaña, explained. We sat at the edge of the veranda, looking out across a hillside covered in fallen avocado trees. "The avocado formed the mountains and served as the shade for the head of the rivers. And so, what happened? Well, the avocado died and the rivers are now dry." She paused, searching for the right words to explain the magnitude of the loss. "The avocado was like a second violence, which left us displaced and in the situation in which we live today."

For nearly two decades, Montes de María was the leading producer of avocados in Colombia, harvesting 71,962 tons annually at the peak of production (Yabrudy Vega 2012, 7–10). The avocado economy formed a dense web of social relations between communities, providing employment opportunities for farmers, harvesters, cooks, transporters, shop owners, and buyers. In a context of acute social inequality and historic disenfranchisement, the avocado created a sense of autonomy for campesinos, providing access to basic services like transportation, education, and health care. "Before, the campesino did not need the government," Jairo explained to me as we climbed over the fallen, old growth avocado trunks scattered across his farm. "The avocado provided enough so that the campesino could also plant their ñame, yucca, and plantains. For the campesino to feed their family, to put a child in school, the avocado provided for that. But today, there is no avocado." We stopped at the top of the hill overlooking a barren field. "Now, campesinos must go to the banks to take out loans just to plant their crops. And there are very high interests, 10 percent per month, and agriculture does not pay monthly [but by harvest season]. For many this has gone badly, and they have had to displace to the city to find work."

Situated as a second violence, the death of the avocado reveals how campesinos experience displacement as an ongoing process—with implications for how peace and dignified return are understood and enacted. The death of the avocado fundamentally altered social and economic relations in the Alta Montaña. Unable to generate enough income for subsistence farming, campesinos now rely on state programs, loans, and development projects run by the state and private foundations who, in turn, dictate the terms and conditions of agriculture in the region. The loss of shade for subsistence farming, the endangerment of native animal and plant species, and the dramatic depletion of waterways demand careful reconsideration of the multiple lives lost as a result of the war. "The loss of the avocado," reflected Dionisio Alarcón,

> is the opposite of being rooted. The avocado summoned us, the avocado brought us together, united us. When the avocado died, we were uprooted. All of the droughts that we have had, we didn't feel as much before because we lived in the shadow of the avocado, which also formed part of the mountain. And this allowed for ravines, and streams, and watering holes to maintain water. And so, the fauna has also fled. Before, the climate was always cool, which made the land fertile, and the crops produced more, and the animals fed on the trees. When the avocado dies, we must cut the dead trees, and the felling of the trees creates environmental impacts like erosion,

because the roots no longer have the strength of the forest and so the land
erodes. Today, we are suffering the consequence of that great scourge, which
brought us the loss of our native forest.

As Dionisio makes clear, the compounding violence of armed conflict, historic disenfranchisement, and environmental degradation severed mutually
constitutive relationships between campesinos and the campo, contributing
to people's sense of being uprooted (*desarraigado*). Rob Nixon (2011) expands
Johan Galtung's (1969, 12) theory of structural violence to center "questions of
time, movement, and change" into his conceptualization of "slow violence."
The overwhelming attention to dramatic single events of environmental destruction, Nixon contends, elides the gradual and multigenerational processes
of slow violence that disproportionately affect disenfranchised communities
across the globe. The practices of mutual care forged between campesinos
and the campo gesture toward what is lost when ecologies are torn asunder
by armed conflict. Multispecies accounts of the armed conflict, like those
offered by Dionisio and Miledys, reorient our understanding of displacement
to consider how political violence also uproots the land "slowly over time"
(Nixon 2011, 12).

"I was displaced and maltreated, but I have never left the campo. I have
always remained here," recounted Angelina González Jiménez, a teacher and
community leader who remained resistant throughout the armed conflict despite repeated, near-death experiences at the hands of various armed groups.[1]
A passionate, older woman with a quick wit and contagious energy, Angelina's role as a community leader threatened armed actors vying for territorial control. After confrontations with a *comandante* of one group, Angelina
immediately became suspected of collaboration by another. As a result, her
name rotated across the hit lists of the eight different armed organizations
that had set up bases in and around her community.

"One of the worst displacements is for those who remain," Angelina responded when I asked her what she meant by displacement if she had never
left the campo. "In those moments, when everyone fled, I stayed alone in my
house, and I composed a lot," she continued, turning to a poem she had written. "This one is called *el sentir del campesino*" (The feeling of the campesino).[2]
Closing her eyes, she recited the poem from memory,

I am a campesina and single mother
I am proudly single, with much honor
I am displaced, a title that I did not look for because I did not study it
Criminal organizations dragged me out and took everything
As a single mother, many times I cried because my children had nothing
  to eat
But God was there and lifted me up over and again
As a campesina, I have heard many combats
I saw massacres of many places
I saw many campesinos run, terrified, taking everything, including their
  memories
I saw them massacre my spouse, my friends, my compañeros
I saw them castrate the education of many children
I saw the burning of many homes
Loneliness suffocates me, the uproar torments me
I walk and walk the streets and I see only loneliness and destruction,
I have been alone, very lonely.
Where is my flowering campo?
Where are my birds that sing?
Where are my mountains? Where are the spaces of green?
I look for it and I do not see it, it lies only in my heart because it is my
  only illusion.

Angelina's poem speaks to the experience of becoming uprooted as the earth displaces from underneath one's feet. "Where is my flowering campo?" She asks, unable to locate herself in the place she calls home. "I look for it and I do not see it."

Angelina was the first person to alert me to the central significance of more-than-human relations in the constitution of not only campesino economies but of life itself. Seated under the palm-thatched roof of her home, she turned to a favorite saying to convey the profound devastation wrought by forced displacement. "The campesino was born for the campo and the campo for the campesino," she asserted. "The campesino is like a fish. The fish out of water chokes and the campesino out of the campo dies.[3] The campo without the campesino is also a desert that lacks fertile land, like a garden without flowers." She paused, looking out over the valley below. "You see," she concluded, turning back toward me, "the campesino gives life to the campo and the campo gives life to the campesino." Angelina extends Nixon's theory of slow violence to illuminate the interlocking vectors of political and environmental violence. For those who, like Angelina, remained resistant during the armed conflict, slow violence produced an experience of "displacement without moving" (Nixon 2011, 19). Without the care of campesinos, the campo also withered as the flora and fauna fled.

In their official report on the struggle for land, the National Center for Historical Memory (CNMH) asserts that displacement is not an isolated, one-time event but rather an ongoing process of rupture. Cycles of physical violence and displacement threaten people's sense of belonging, citizenship, and survival (CNMH 2014). Although I agree that displacement is an ongoing cycle, I contend that the process of becoming displaced (*desplazado*) is not one solely of repeated ruptures but also one that includes everyday violence that weaves itself into the backdrop of "ordinary" life (Das 2007, 7). For campesinos who cultivate the land and are, in turn, nurtured by the land, ordinary life includes daily farming practices founded on relationships of reciprocity forged between humans and more-than-humans. As Miledys, Dionisio, Jairo, and Angelina attest, the violent severing of these relationships results in an extended sense of being lost (*perdido*) and uprooted (*desarraigado*) even as people remain in place.

The experience of displacement as an ongoing process troubles the temporal register of the state's "postconflict" discourse. For those caught in the midst of slow violence, peace is understood as a permanent social process where "resistance, resiliency and flourishing" are made simultaneously available—rather than sequentially ordered—through relationships of mutual care (Lederach and Lederach 2010, 54). Campesino peacebuilding, therefore, reflects an understanding of self and world creation as, in the words of Arturo Escobar (2015), "always in movement, made up of materials in motion, flux, and becoming" (18). The entanglements of human and more-than-human relations in the Alta Montaña not only shaped the experience of violence but also reignited community organizing efforts across the region (6).[4] "We have learned that the conflict divided us," Miledys explained, "but today, we have ended this division. It is this union that gives us strength. . . . I think that it was this shared misery, this *olvido* [neglect] by the state that permitted us to create a space to begin trusting one another." The shared loss of the avocado mobilized campesino leaders across the "invisible barriers" that divided the region, giving rise to the Peaceful Process of Reconciliation and Integration of the Alta Montaña.[5]

REACTIVATING THE MOUNTAIN

In 2010, as *Phytophthora cinnamomi* ravaged the avocado forest, several leaders began to reach out across the divided communities of the Alta Montaña. After the state failed to respond to the petitions presented during the 2003 and 2006 marches to El Carmen, they decided that any future action would need to include *all* the sectors of the Alta Montaña to make the magnitude of the crisis visible to the national authorities. As a trusted teacher and member of the Seventh Day Adventist church, William Jaraba Pérez drew on his wider relational networks to connect community leaders across the "invisible barriers" of the Alta Montaña. Eventually, six leaders agreed to meet to discuss the avocado. Profound distrust as well as anger marked the first dialogue. Despite the tension, however, the shared concern for the death of the avocado moved the conversation—at least momentarily— beyond past grievances. Drawing inspiration from the nonviolent march led by the neighboring community of Mampuján, Ciro Canoles Pérez proposed a similar action with the aim of petitioning the state for reparations for the avocado. The idea sparked the imaginations of those present, cutting through the tense environment.

Following the meeting, Ciro reached out to Larisa, a member of Sembrandopaz who had accompanied the Mampuján march and who lived in a nearby community. Together, they arranged a meeting between several community leaders and Sembrandopaz. A trusted organization across Montes de María, Sembrandopaz's presence eased the tensions that inflected the initial dialogue. With the assurance of Sembrandopaz's support, the leaders agreed to organize a public assembly for all of the communities in the Alta Montaña. Nearly one hundred people attended the meeting. Those gathered unanimously approved the decision to organize a nonviolent march from the Alta Montaña to the capital city of Cartagena to demand integral, collective reparations for the death of the avocado under the 2011 Victim's Law of 1448.

The dialogue marked the beginning of a long journey toward rebuilding trust in the Alta Montaña.

Over the next six months, the leaders began to organize the march. They traveled in pairs—with representatives from different sides of the divided region—to each of the fifty communities in the Alta Montaña. At each meeting, they provided a space for people to air grievances and share their individual experiences of the armed conflict. The opportunity to speak openly and honestly about the lived experiences of the war—and their perceptions of others' complicity in the violence—created a space for what Deborah Thomas (2019) has called "deep recognition," establishing the *confianza* (trust) needed for collective organizing in the Alta Montaña (219).[6] "People spoke sincerely during those meetings," Jocabeth Canoles Canoles, a coordinator of the youth wing of the movement, later reflected. "We realized that we were all stigmatized, that what we had thought before was not really what had happened, that we were all victims of the war."

As social leaders walked physically through the geography of the Alta Montaña, they also documented the extent of the death of the avocado across the region. During each community meeting, they discussed the health of the avocado and the presence of the fungus, documenting when the fungus had first arrived, how many trees had died, and the economic, social, and environmental toll that the death of the avocado had taken on the community. They listened to people outline multiple reasons for the avocado's death: Some had seen helicopters drop dust across the mountain ranges and suspected that the military had intentionally targeted the forest in order to eradicate the guerrilla's protective hiding grounds, others suggested that the movement of armed groups across the region had unintentionally brought the fungus to the Alta Montaña, others focused on historic state abandonment and the state's failure to respond to the fungus, while others suggested that forced displacement had prevented campesinos from caring for the trees, leading to the spread of the fungus. Despite different theories about the arrival and spread of *Phytophthora cinnamomi*, they all agreed that the death of the avocado was a direct consequence of the war (CNMH 2018a).

After six months of organizing, the Peaceful Process of Reconciliation and Integration of the Alta Montaña was born with two primary and related objectives: First, to reunite communities that had been divided as a result of the armed conflict; and second, to demand collective reparations for the avocado as a victim of war under the 2011 Victim's Law of 1448.[7] The leaders also declared *¡La Montaña se mueve por la reparación integral!* (The Mountain moves for integral reparations!) the slogan of the march, reflecting the multiple and entangled agencies that animate campesino theories of peace as an active, multispecies process. In communities where there is no electricity, little cell-phone reception, and limited internet connection, collective organizing requires continual movement across the region's mountainous terrain. In *The Mushroom at the End of the World*, Anna Tsing (2015) asks: "What if our indeterminate life form was not the shape of our bodies but rather the shape of our motions over time?" (47). *¡La Montaña se mueve!* offers one response to Tsing's inquiry. As social leaders moved across the frayed landscapes of the Alta Montaña, their sense of place and belonging (*sentido de pertenencia*) deepened. The embodied movement through the physical, social, and ecological geographies of the Alta Montaña created a process of "transformation through encounter" (Tsing 2015, 47). Roots were not established through stasis, but rather through constant motion.

As the leaders prepared petitions for the march, they also confronted the challenging dilemma of how to make the avocado legible within the state's definition of victimhood. In response to the "representational bias" present in the state's approach to reparations, the leaders of the Peaceful Process decided to make the cotton-top tamarin monkey—the *mico titi*—the symbol of the movement (Nixon 2011, 13). Endemic to the region, the *mico titi* had become endangered over the course of the armed conflict as a result of the loss of its primary habitat: the avocado forest. Close to extinction and forcibly displaced as their homes became uninhabitable, the *mico titi* exposed past and continued threats to life in the Alta Montaña. In particular, the *mico titi* served as an important reminder of the state's extermination campaigns that rendered the lives of campesinos, *micos*, and avocados invisible—and therefore disposable.

"At one point, the state said that there were only guerrilla and *micos* (monkeys) here. In other words, they were saying that there was no civilian population," Jorge Pérez recounted.

When we started to organize, we wanted to show that there were civilians here. We said if this is a region of guerrilla, then we are the *micos* and we identified with the *mico titi*, which is native to this zone and which is also threatened with extinction. We wanted to show that the 6,000 hectares of avocado also formed the habitat of the cotton-top tamarin monkey and that, here, we also care for them and maintain them in the territory even though they are threatened with extinction, because we identify with those two things. If we were labeled as *micos* before, why not identify with those monkeys? And by doing this, we are also able to show that the *mico titi* is endangered.

The presence of the *mico titi* in the work of the movement affirms the lives of monkeys and campesinos as lives that count. Invoked in meetings and assemblies, etched on T-shirts and hats, and displayed on motorcycles and houses, the *mico titi* makes powerfully present the absence of the human and more-than-human lives destroyed by war. As the symbol of the movement, the *mico titi* allowed social leaders to situate their claims to "integral reparations" firmly within campesino social and legal orders that include obligations to care for more-than-human beings. "You see, what we are trying to do here is to reactivate the Mountain again and in order to make this visible we have the *mico titi*, which is threatened with extinction," Jorge concluded, "And with this, we are also able to make visible the threats against the movement, to show how they wanted to extinguish us as well."

The *mico titi* unearths the ways in which campesinos experience political and environmental violence as interlocking—integrally bound up with the multiple lives that constitute the lifeworld of the campo. Drawing on local-level entanglements between human and more-than-human communities in the Alta Montaña, the Peaceful Process not only sought to make the state's complicity in campaigns of mass extinction visible but also worked to "reactivate the Mountain" by regenerating multispecies relations of care in the aftermath of war. "To be entangled," Kristina Lyons (2014) writes, "is not simply to be intertwined, as in the joining of separate and preexisting entities, but to lack an independent, self-contained existence outside the relation itself" (224). Indeed, the *mico titi* did not merely serve as a strategic political tactic or abstract symbol, but rather formed a vital part of the movement's work for community reconciliation.

In April 2013, after months of planning, the Peaceful Process led over 1,500 campesinos in a nonviolent march toward Cartagena. Two days into their march, the national government requested that they meet to negotiate in San Jacinto—a municipality located between El Carmen and Cartagena. During negotiations with local, regional, and national institutions, the leaders of the Peaceful Process repeatedly prioritized their demand for state subsidies for the avocado, citing previous precedent for coffee, cacao, and palm oil farmers ("El cultivo" 2017, 30). However, former Vice minister of Agriculture Andrés García,[8] refused to entertain the possibility of a monetary subsidy for the avocado, citing "insufficient" legal tools.[9] As a compromise, the Peaceful Process agreed to a series of productive projects focused on ñame (yams) and yucca. These projects included access to bank loans that state representatives argued would provide campesinos with the financial resources needed for agricultural production. The state also agreed to carry out a study on the death of the avocado, provide trainings focused on prevention and control of the fungus, and implement a "renovation project" with avocado seedlings known to be resistant to the *Phytophthora cinnamomi* ("Acta Mesa de Agricultura" 2013). On April 7, 2013, the Peaceful Process signed ninety-one accords with the state, making the Alta Montaña one of the largest collective reparations processes in the country (CNMH 2018a).

PROVOKING PEACE: INTERGENERATIONAL ORGANIZING IN THE ALTA MONTAÑA

As the first symbolic act of reconciliation, the Peaceful Process organized a regionwide soccer tournament, reviving a favorite cultural tradition that brought communities across the Alta Montaña together. Over six hundred youth participated in the tournament, revealing a surprisingly large number of young people who had returned to the region. The tournament challenged the underlying assumption that rural areas lacked youth—a dominant perception that INGO workers, bureaucrats, and community elders alike shared. "After we signed the 91 accords," Jose Niño, one of the young organizers of the Peaceful March recalled, "we held the first reconciliation tournament in the Alta Montaña, and it was there that Ricardo asked us the question: How many youth are here? What do they dedicate themselves to? And that is when we began to analyze things."

With accompaniment from Larisa and support from the Peaceful Process, several youth began traveling across the Alta Montaña to hold open
forums about the lived experiences, concerns, and desires specific to young
people. After months of organizing, youth from communities across the Alta
Montaña held their first general assembly where they democratically elected
representatives to form the Youth Peace Provokers movement (Jóvenes Provocadores de Paz de la Alta Montaña, abbreviated JOPPAZ). The youth also
ratified their constitution, declaring higher education, peacebuilding, and
environmental care the three pillars of their movement.

Participation in JOPPAZ is not confined to narrow definitions of youth
based on age (below eighteen), gender (coded male), or social markers such
as parenthood or property ownership. Instead, youth identity construction
emerges from participation in community organizing, commitment to the
territory, and social formation as the *relevo generacional*—generational successors—of the movement. While much of the current literature on youth
often limits analysis to discrete generational cohorts, the saliency of the *relevo
generacional* in the narratives of young people from the Alta Montaña reflects
a relational understanding of youth (Lederach 2019). JOPPAZ challenges representations of youth in contexts of violence as either in need of protection
or prone to violence, orienting analytic attention toward the multiple positions and intergenerational landscapes that young people navigate (Berents
and McEvoy-Levy 2015; Bolten 2019). The meaningful participation of youth
in a nationally recognized and intergenerational movement enabled young
people to revitalize their life projects (*proyectos de vida*)—a central part of
the transition from "youth" to "adult" that the war disrupted. "It is through
the work of peacebuilding, through this movement," Naún Álvarez González
explained as we traveled to meet with one of the youth committees, "that I
began to dream again." We swayed back and forth in the Jeep that transported us across the Montaña. "You see," Naún continued, raising his voice
over the sound of the engine,

> When the social fabric is broken, it's not easy to restore it, which is why it
> is important to reclaim our culture as people and as campesinos. And this
> is beautiful, where there are *relevos generacionales* [generational successors],
> where adult leaders form youth leaders, that is what will always keep this pro-

cess going. We are the children of this movement. That is, we are born from the Peaceful Process and we are working together so that the adult process and that of the young people is what sustains the movement, so that this is a movement that will never end.

While seemingly future-oriented, becoming the *relevo generacional* requires intergenerational processes of social and political formation. For youth born into the war, cycles of forced displacement and social upheaval became a permanent, rather than aberrant, aspect of daily life. Intergenerational processes of social memory are, therefore, central to youth emplacement and belonging in the aftermath of war. The word *provocar* means both "to *desire*" and "to *agitate*," reflecting the interplay between affect and mobilization that shapes young peoples' understanding of peace as an active, social process where desired futures come into being through the daily work of intergenerational movement-building. "We, the youth, are not only the future," Jocabeth Canoles explained when I asked why the youth had chosen the name *provocadores*, "We are the future, but we are also the present."[10]

Centrally concerned with finding a way to "maintain youth in the territory" in the face of the socioecological and economic insecurity, JOPPAZ's decision to include gender parity in the leadership structure of the movement brought the generational and gendered consequences of the avocado's death into sharp relief.[11] The avocado not only provided jobs, secondary educational opportunities, and health care for communities "abandoned" by the state, but also offered the economic means for young people to pursue higher education. "This place has always been characterized by the avocado," Miguel, a JOPPAZ coordinator, reflected,

> So, when the avocado died, well, everything was left uncovered—the watering holes dried up, the animals displaced. I heard that before there were *mochuelos* [owls] here. I don't know the *mochuelo*, the canary no longer exists, and the deer have fled. The death of the avocado displaced these animals, the flora and fauna. When the avocado died, everything changed. My community has always been known for having youth that study in universities. My grandfather sent many children to study in universities because there were resources, and there you see a clear example—the parents are professionals, but their children cannot study because of the death of the avocado.

The socioecological losses that the death of the avocado produced were especially acute for young women who played key roles during the avocado harvest—and gained economic autonomy within their families and communities as a result. "Before, you could climb to the top of these hills and you wouldn't be able to see across, you wouldn't see all those dead trees," Darlis Hernández explained as she guided me to the top of the overlook located above her home. "Before, this was a lot different," she continued, gesturing toward the barren hillsides that stretched out before us,

> Before, all of this was green and you desired to see this, you desired to walk
> through the forest. Before, the river had lots of water, which gave us a sense
> of serenity to know the stream was flowing. Now, you see the deterioration
> of the environment. For young people, and for young women especially, the
> avocado offered one of the ways to move forward because the economic pro-
> duction was high, and they could earn money. But now, the avocado is dead.

Miguel and Darlis understand community flourishing and economic opportunity as inextricably linked to ecological well-being. Displaced to urban centers in search of work, youth not only struggled to find a sense of place but also encountered heightened forms of stigmatization and social marginalization. "When I arrived to the city," Gloria explained during a circle dialogue facilitated by JOPPAZ, "I was treated as if I were a guerrilla. This is the gap, the stigmatization of the campo. Many [in the city] do not know what war is, what truly happened here, and because of that they stigmatize us, they treat us badly, they believe that we are inferior." Tears welled in her eyes. She looked down and took several deep breaths before proceeding,

> Here I am, with these tears, because it still touches me, because I am still
> living in the city, and they say, "there goes the campesina, the villager [*pueb-
> lerina*]" or they call me things like *corroncha* [backward].[12] What we live
> here [in the campo] and there [in the city]—because I have lived in both
> places—are two different kinds of violence. They are not the same, they are
> two distinct violences.

Rather than situate the city as a place of opportunity, Gloria speaks to the "distinct" violences enacted against campesino bodies across urban and rural landscapes. "But now," Gloria declared, energy inflecting her voice as she recalled her experience with JOPPAZ, "Well, now, I just laugh, it does not make me feel less, because I am what I am and I love what I am. *I'm a campesina* and that's how I love myself, wherever I am."

Intergenerational movement-building generates a sense of pride for youth as they work to reclaim their campesino identities in the face of dispossession and stigmatization. In particular, community organizing expands young peoples' understanding of the histories and politics that have and continue to shape territorial relations in the campo, allowing youth to cast a critical lens on their experiences of violence in both rural and urban contexts. As the guarantors of campesino life and social organization, youth position themselves as sociopolitical actors within their communities in ways that deepen their sense of belonging and desire for the campo. "I am no longer embarrassed to go to any of the communities, because they recognize me," Jose Niño explained. "The integration of the youth and the adults, well, the movement is very important for the region, and it is important that it does not end." He paused, gathering his thoughts, before offering a more personal reflection on the significance of the movement,

> When I was a young man, I had no vision of anything. But, when I entered the movement, my mind opened, and I started to notice possibilities for many things. What I learned, I learned there [in the movement], to value myself, and that is something that has touched my heart. Wherever I go, I say: "I am a campesino." I cannot deny it because I was born and raised in the campo. Today, when I arrive and say that I am a Youth Peace Provoker, it is as if I am carrying an ID card, it identifies me.

As Jose's narrative attests, in a context where the state has only recently acknowledged the existence of civilian victims—and only then because of grassroots nonviolent mobilization—the social construction of youth identities as the *relevo generacional* (generational successors) generates collective agency in ways that work against the violent processes of social disenfranchisement and marginalization.

The stigmatization that many of the youth leaders outline is not merely located in the realm of interpersonal experiences but also structures political violence, which fuels the continued criminalization of campesino organizations. In the months following the Peaceful March of 2013, the leaders of the

Peaceful Process as well as Sembrandopaz received anonymous death threats. The state also threatened to deport Larisa and another international accompaniment worker, but the unsubstantiated charges were eventually dropped. Less than a month after JOPPAZ established their constitution, the state unexpectedly arrested and unjustly imprisoned Jorge Luis Montes, one of the principal leaders of the Peaceful Process. On the day of his arrest, Jorge willingly traveled to the public prosecutor's office to report the death threats that he and other leaders in the Alta Montaña had received following the march. When he arrived, the state unexpectedly detained and incarcerated Jorge in a maximum-security prison located over eight hours from the Alta Montaña, where he remained for the next three years awaiting trial. The state drew on Jorge's open case file from the early 2000s to justify his incarceration, evading accusations that his imprisonment was a form of social repression following the Peaceful March of 2013. The state accused Jorge of participation in the high ranks of the FARC-EP, holding him responsible for orchestrating violence against the very communities he had dedicated his life to defending. International human rights organizations, local organizations, and state officials from the Ombudspersons office and the Victim's Unit denounced the unsubstantiated charges against Jorge. Campesinos across the Alta Montaña also decried the false accusations, expressing distrust in the state's willingness to uphold the campesino right to peaceful protest and dignified return.

The fear that Jorge's arrest generated was unevenly distributed across generational and gendered lines, posing a significant challenge to JOPPAZ's budding movement. "When they captured Jorge, the youth were in a meeting," Miguel recalled, "and I remember the parents became worried saying 'don't go to the meeting, because they are capturing leaders, they are threatening them [with death]' and in this moment I remember thinking, well, it's over." For young women, fear of state repression exacerbated the barriers that often limited their participation in community processes. The fear was particularly acute in communities where the state had disproportionately imprisoned campesina women who occupied leadership positions during the war. Rather than disintegrate the movement, however, Jorge's detention further mobilized leaders who saw the arrest as a direct assault on their right to dignified return, guaranteed by the Victims Law. Jorge also remained adamant that the movement continue organizing for reparations. With a grant from the Washington Office on Latin America (WOLA), several youth traveled to visit Jorge in prison, which sustained their relational ties to Jorge and deepened their commitment to campesino peacebuilding. "We started thinking," Miguel later reflected, "If they scare us with whatever threat they throw at us, we will remain in the same conditions. Maybe it was this that made us *seguir pa'lante* (continue on). We said, 'if they capture one, well then, let ten of us emerge screaming, "We are also here!"'"

Intergenerational relationships with Jorge and movement elders helped youth, like Miguel, situate the threats leveled against the movement within a wider history of state violence. "In reality, our identity as campesinos, as Afrodescendants, has been very silenced," Naún explained,

> For us, when one leader, when one campesina woman, or one youth is engaged in advocacy, they look for a way to silence our voices. And this, too, has made us realize that we must be organized, we must be united, we must regenerate these bonds of friendship, because today, they will not silence one leader, but rather a whole *pueblo* [people], a whole territory, a whole region. For this reason, we are organizing today.

THE EARTH SUFFERED, TOO

On a hot afternoon in September 2016, Jocabeth, Naún, and I sat huddled together over the audio recorder as we discussed the implications of the peace accords for the work of JOPPAZ. The negotiating team had recently announced that a final agreement had been reached and preparations were underway for the historic peace signing in Cartagena. "There used to exist beautiful fauna and flora in the Alta Montaña," Jocabeth explained, reflecting on the work of territorial peace,

> But due to the solitude, due to the displacement, due to the bullets, due to the presence of armed groups, many birds died, many displaced. Without someone planting crops, the birds had nowhere to eat and they died. The earth suffered, too. The violence inflicted on our communities requires that we fight to build peace from here. The territory is where we live, where we

feel good and, therefore, we must accommodate the territory so that we can live in peace. The war has also been violent to the environment, and we must reconcile with her.

"It's true," Naún interjected,

> The land felt so battered that this affected the avocado trees to the extent that today there are more than seven thousand hectares of avocado that are dead. This is also abandonment because the land felt alone without her people. One must live in a way that the earth feels that connection, they go hand in hand, so that while we are working the earth, we are also, at the same time, protecting her.

"Maybe it is strange," Jocabeth continued, "But there are things that make you think that the earth realizes things are happening. That was something I experienced during the violence. The day of a massacre or right before a direct combat, one would hear the hens go quiet, the trees also became silent, a deep shadow would descend and a slight breeze would pass through. You could feel it in the atmosphere."

"A coldness," Naún added.

"A coldness," Jocabeth repeated, "or what we call an *'ambiente pesado'* [heavy atmosphere]."[13] Jocabeth paused as she sought to explain the experience. "There are myths and legends in the Alta Montaña," she continued, "For example, the *llorona* [weeping woman] came when the violence was heavy. I lived this and I don't know if it is a myth, but it is something real because I lived it. I heard the *llorona* when the violence was very intense. When there was death, the *llorona* would appear. I heard her crying. And it was something that one feels, that something strange was happening." Jocabeth's voice softened to just above a whisper. "When the massacre happened, I heard the *llorona* and when we held the vigil afterward, we heard the *llorona*, we heard her wailing alongside us."

Naún nodded, "What Joca says is true," he affirmed, "when she began to speak of this, one also remembers these moments. This is the reality, this is what happens." We sat in silence for a few minutes and then Naún added,

> I say that today, the people that have the most connection with the land are campesinos. When one lives, works, and feels the land, I believe that the land

also feels this connection. And so, in the moment when something is about to happen to the campesino, the earth also cries out. Today, as young people, we can struggle to maintain what is important for us, which is this love of the earth. For us, peace is to be in our territory.

For Naún and Jocabeth, the land is sentient—feeling, speaking, and communing with campesinos as they labor, love, and grieve in the campo. The affective sensations that accompany violence—the passage of cold winds, the silence of hens, and the descent of shadows—reflect multispecies experiences of war. The *llorona* is not just a myth, but an embodied and ontological reality, "something one feels."[14] Birds, avocados, shadows, and spirits all collaborate in the creation of the *entorno*—the deep ecology that shapes campesino frameworks of relationality.[15] The land cries out—not figuratively, but literally—experiencing the violence alongside campesinos.

Jocabeth and Naún's insistence on the mutually constitutive relationship between land and life resonates with Vanessa Watts's (2013) articulation of "Indigenous Place-Thought," which is "based upon the premise that land is alive and thinking and that humans and non-humans derive agency through the extensions of these thoughts" (21). Campesino narratives of war require close attention to the *sentipensante* (feeling-thinking) experiences that emerge from a deep connection to place, where mutual relations of care with the land are forged and sustained. "Our ability to speak to the land is not just an echo of a mythic tale or part of a moral code," affirms Watts (2013), "but a reality" (32). The land, within this framework, is a central actor in the work of territorial peacebuilding.

"Our territory identifies who we are," Naún concluded at the end of our conversation. "Our identity distinguishes our culture, the context in which we live. Our territory and our identity is something that speaks for us, because it represents our culture, our actions.[16] The context in which you live, the territory, that is what you reflect." Naún's central identity as a campesino is inextricably bound together and only made possible through a particular set of relations and material practices. Territorial peacebuilding, therefore, cannot be circumscribed to the confines of a single event—like peace signing—but must be continuously nurtured in the everyday—the *cotidianidad*. Tending multispecies relations of mutual care is a permanent, dynamic, and place-based process. The relational framework found in campesino peacebuilding operates with distinct temporalities that recognize ancestral presence and future imaginaries as inextricably intertwined. Indigenous women leaders in southern Colombia advocate for a similar understanding of time. "Time returns every once in a while, to remind us that history is guided by a *churo* or spiral," they write. "Therefore, the struggle for land is not something new for indigenous peoples; they have always sought to leave something to remind us that the land is ours" (CNMH 2021, 20).

THE ECOLOGICAL CACICAZGO: CAMPESINO RESURGENCE AND THE *RELEVO GENERACIONAL*

"Where, before, armed groups made their bases, today, we the Youth Peace Provokers have reclaimed this space as one of beauty and environmental recreation that promotes integration and peace. This is transformation. Where before people in camouflage with weapons generated fear, today there are sounds of joyful youth," Jocabeth's voice boomed through the loudspeakers across the open field, reaching over three hundred youth who had gathered for JOPPAZ's signature community integration event, the Ecological Cacicazgo. "This Cacicazgo Ecológico is not just a fun event, but an act of recuperation—we are reclaiming the spaces that before were used to harm the community." A line of young people, dressed in elaborate outfits made from recycled materials, stood on the makeshift stage behind Jocabeth. "Our history tells us that there used to be auctions to sell our ancestors. The Spaniards would sit there and say: 'give me this one.' This is very ugly to remember." Jocabeth continued, "As Youth Peace Provokers, we promote gender equity and so we said, 'No, we will not have a *reinado* (pageant).' Instead, we will have a *cacicazgo*. The figure of the *cacique* is our ancestral leader. But you never hear reference to the *cacica* (gendered female) and in *reinados* you never have a masculine touch. But we said, 'we will have both the *cacique* and the *cacica*.'"

Jocabeth's opening convocation subverts the colonialist origins of *reinados de belleza* (beauty pageants) to reclaim traditional Indigenous governance structures as the foundation of the Youth Peace Provokers movement.[17] As Jocabeth explains, *Cacicazgo* refers to the Indigenous cacique. Jocabeth, however, challenges the dominant masculine marker to lift up Indigenous women leaders, the *cacicas*, as well. In doing so, she simultaneously undermines the

hyperfemininity of *reinados*—pageant shows—and hypermasculine representations of the male cacique. The critical, feminist retrieval of the *cacicazgo*
positioned over and against *reinado* reinscribes women into ancestral governance structures, reflecting what Stuart Hall (1997) has called an "imaginary
political re-identification" from which "a counter-politics" emerges (52). For
Hall, reclaiming histories that are otherwise erased from the public imagination gives rise to "the language of that which is home in the genuine sense,"
allowing those living in the wake of enslavement and dispossession to establish roots (52).

The annual Ecological Cacicazgo is a multiday event facilitated by the
Youth Peace Provokers (JOPPAZ) that includes workshops for youth focused on human rights, peacebuilding, environmental care, and political
participation—concluding with an eco-fashion show. Public performances of
the Ecological Cacicazgo in rural communities previously occupied by armed
actors, allows young people who participate in JOPPAZ to reclaim stigmatized histories and territories as places of peace. In the Alta Montaña, youth
are at the forefront of what Justin de Leon has called "resurgent political
praxis," dedicating themselves to regenerating multispecies and multigenerational relations of care and solidarity (de Leon 2019).[18] The struggle to recover
a sense of belonging (*sentido de pertenencia*) in the aftermath of displacement
lies at the heart of JOPPAZ's daily work to build territorial peace—one that
requires intergenerational solidarity. While much of the peace studies literature focuses on transformation, Jocabeth's opening convocation reflects the
dialectic relationship between social transformation and social reproduction
as equally important for claims to land and futures in a context of dispossession (Alfred 2005; Corntassel 2012; Daigle 2018; Hatala et al. 2019). Through
the daily work of caretaking social and ecological landscapes in the aftermath
of war, youth also reclaim campesino identities as beautiful and worthy of
dignified life.

VIOLENCE IN THE TIMES OF "POSTCONFLICT"

While the Peaceful Process succeeded in having the avocado officially recognized as a harm of war in the state's diagnostic report, the implementation process continues to privilege technocratic measures that create a
fragmented—rather than integral—approach to reparations (Unidad de Víc-

timas 2014). Consequently, the state's framework fails to address political and environmental violence as mutually reinforcing processes. "The government is reluctant to provide monetary reparations to the victims of the conflict," Ciro Canoles explained. "And now, to provide reparations for a plant," his voice trailed off as he shook his head. "They don't see it from an environmental point of view, but what was lost in the Alta Montaña is an environmental harm that is gigantic and to recuperate itself will require many years." Rather than view the avocado as a replaceable crop, Ciro underscores how the death of the avocado forest disrupted the fragile ecosystem of the dry tropical rainforest—one that will require decades to regenerate. "Here, the campesino is not used to cultivating crops," he continued, challenging dominant perceptions of the *campesinado* as solely engaged in exploiting the land, "here, the campesino is used to cultivating forests." Ciro gestured toward one of the remaining forested hillsides behind his house, "The avocado is an old growth tree that thrives without technical assistance. It is a tree that becomes dense vegetation, and it is there that you see the monkey, the squirrel. You see all the animals that live there, and this is beautiful. How beautiful!" he exclaimed. "You see," Ciro continued, "this is a forest. More than a crop, this is a forest."

State projects that privilege crop-based agroindustrial farming shatter the hidden relations and actors who breathe life into the campo. By questioning the truncated temporalities that guide the state's approach to reparations, Ciro also interrogates widely accepted notions of expertise, positioning campesino environmental knowledge—born from generations of working the land—as critical for understanding local ecosystems. The burden campesinos face to make themselves legible as experts is tremendous in a context where long histories of racism and discrimination continue to guide external peace interventions (Lyons 2016; Ruiz Serna 2015). As Ciro notes, the state refused to provide direct subsidies to campesinos, sending technocrats from the capital cities to implement agricultural projects instead. Such projects, built uncritically on the nature/culture binary, obscure the ways in which humanitarian efforts work in tandem with neoliberal logics to legitimize violent dispossession across the world (Cronon 1996; Guha 1989; Igoe 2010; West 2019). Drawing on the discourses of "sustainable development," agribusinesses in Montes de María continue to legitimize their claims to the land by positioning campesinos as lacking technical expertise, unable to operate with long-term perspectives, and, therefore, destructive.

For campesinos in the Alta Montaña, the threat of violence has not ended with the signing of the peace accord. The arrival of megaindustries like palm oil has radically transformed the region's socioecological landscapes, negatively affecting human and more-than-human relations (Coronado and Dietz 2013; Junieles 2017; Ojeda et al. 2015; Rey 2013; Rutas 2017). "Today we are being displaced by the massive purchase of land that is, once again, displacing us from our territory," a young social leader reflected soon after the government and the FARC-EP signed the accords.

> This is one of the most fundamental challenges for youth and for the future generations. Big companies, like palm oil and teak trees, companies that have a lot of power from the outside, see that campesino lands are very fertile. Today, these companies want to empower themselves through profit, through development. But they do not see the importance of the land for the campesino. And so, these private companies are implementing projects, things that will make them profitable and for that reason they want to remove us from our land. But with land and education, we can maintain our territory so that from generation to generation we can live in our territory. But this requires that projects are not created on the desks of someone from outside of the territory, but instead that the people from the grassroots are the ones who create and implement the projects.

Campesino environmental knowledge exposes the damage that monocultures perpetuate against local ecosystems, drawing attention to the socioecological relations that constitute life in the campo. As this young organizer underscores, peace interventions "created on the desks of someone from outside of the territory" undermine campesino legal orders fashioned through multispecies relations of care in ways that violate the state's guarantee of permanent and dignified return. "The avocado economy was one of the most important that we had in Montes de María," Geovaldis González Jiménez, a social leader, who has been at the forefront of social efforts aimed at preventing the expansion of palm oil, explained,

What is happening here alters the whole *campesinado*. Monocultures alter
our entire ecosystem. Palm oil plantations generate agrochemicals that seep
into the land and reservoirs. What we see is a monopoly between the environmental authorities, state institutions, and palm oil companies who are in
favor of anything that generates profit. The environmental and social implications do not matter, the only thing that matters is production. We have
denounced interventions that are negatively impacting our environment, but
the authorities have done nothing. What it has generated are threats against
leaders who challenge the palm oil monoculture. We are not against palm
oil. What we are against is the damage it has done to our bodies of water.
What we are against is the damage it has done to our environment. Palm oil
has displaced us again.

With the loss of the avocado, the struggle to prevent the expansion of palm oil
has intensified, revealing ongoing processes of dispossession perpetuated by
the state-agribusiness-development nexus in the name of peace. As Geovaldis
makes clear, neoliberal peacebuilding interventions that expand monoculture
agroindustries enact, rather than transform, violence against the territory. "If
the past of slow violence is never past," writes Nixon (2011), "so too the post
is never fully post" (8).

In contrast to the state's framework of postconflict peacebuilding, campesino leaders engage in a more relational, processual, and dynamic approach
to peace as they work to transform the interlocking vectors of political and
environmental violence. As a result, campesino peacebuilding operates with
alternative temporalities, not easily legible to institutions that privilege
project-based and growth-driven frameworks (Lyons 2014). As Watts (2013)
contends, repairing right relations in a context of dispossession "is not a question of 'going backwards,' for this implies a static place to return to . . . it is
not a question of accessing something, which has already come and gone, but
simply to listen. To act" (32). Multispecies resurgence does not come from
outside projects, but instead arises, in the words of Anna Tsing (2015), from
"the force of the life of the forest, its ability to spread its seeds and roots and
runners to reclaim places" (178).

In the Alta Montaña, peacebuilding is not objectified as part of a linear
project with a finite end but rather understood as a permanent social pro-

cess. "Watching the palm oil expand made us change our strategy," Rafael explained, reflecting on how social leaders have responded to emergent forms of political and environmental violence: "We began to educate the communities. I feel proud of the work we have done. We have been able to stop the expansion of the palm oil company, because people see things more clearly. This is the reality we must bring to communities, we must continue this work."

As families in the Alta Montaña struggle to survive in a changed and changing environment, they are continuously nurturing multispecies relations and lives threatened with erasure. Today, JOPPAZ and the Peaceful Process facilitate campaigns focused on logging, sand extraction, and the protection of precious waterways, safeguarding their territory against the expansion of monoculture industries through community-based environmental efforts. "As a leader, I say let's not destroy this environment because it's what permits us to stay, it is what permits the continuation of the campesino economy," Geovaldis concluded.

> As a leader, I keep watch over these resources so that this beautiful campesino economy that we have will be preserved and will survive over time because, for us, the campo is our life. Do you understand? And if the campo is our life, it is unjust to murder or exploit something that gives us life, and which helps us give life to many others. There is not more to say than my life is the campo, my life is the campo, and I will die for the campo, for leadership, because it is in my blood.

LOVE AND DESIRE IN TIMES OF SLOW VIOLENCE

I opened this chapter with the story of Giovani who began noticing subtle changes in the avocado forest beginning in the mid-1990s. Decades later, as we slowly traversed the footpaths around his home, Giovani reflected on the state projects that have come in response to the avocado's death. He bent low to the ground, sifting soil between his fingers as he spoke, "The problem is that institutions and businesses come with projects already set. They bring trees or they put forward a project as an alternative without asking those who are farming to provide input. What they need to do is ask: 'What is it you want? What would you like to plant?'" He stood, brushing the dirt from his hands. "We were *aguacateros* [avocado farmers]," he continued, lingering on the word to place emphasis on the subjectivity of the avocado farmer, "We *loved* avocado, we loved planting avocado, and so what is needed now is for them to ask us: 'What is it you want to do? What do you want to plant?' Because when the people express their *desires*, when it comes from the *desire* of the people, that's where you find the love for farming." For campesinos in the Alta Montaña, love and desire—rather than technocratic prescriptions—are the central modalities for regenerating socioecological relations in the face of slow violence. Technical projects that focus solely on growth and profit ignore the environmental wisdom and multispecies relations of mutual care that shape campesino life in the Alta Montaña.

"As soon as one starts talking about peace, one must start with the environment," Domingo Rafael Deavila Buelvas, a campesino leader, declared when I asked about the relationship between environment and peace. "The violence left its own contamination, but despite all that, nature itself is returning once more to the region. If we care for the environment, we are caring for ourselves, and if we care for ourselves, we will live in peace," he paused, before concluding, "and so, I think this is the point." Campesinos in the Alta Montaña advance a processual and multispecies conceptualization of peace as an emergent, multispecies, and permanent process, fashioned through everyday relations of mutual care that generate life in the campo. The daily practices of intergenerational movement building, environmental caretaking, and agroforestry work against the temporal forces of slow violence, enabling campesinos to establish roots in a context of displacement. Territorial peacebuilding is, therefore, inextricably tied to the multispecies struggle for dignified permanency in the territory. As Robin Wall Kimmerer (2013) reminds us, "the word ecology is derived from the Greek *oikos*, the word for home" (85). Careful analysis of the everyday assemblages forged between campesinos, avocado forests, cotton-top tamarin monkeys, waterways, and spirits bring into sharp relief the multivalent practices that social leaders in the Alta Montaña employ as they work to regenerate their lifeworld. An "anthropology beyond the human" recognizes how the daily routines of harvesting yucca and caring for avocado trees are deeply intertwined with social and political organizing (Kohn 2013).

"I composed a poem." Dionisio opened his notebook, exposing the tattered edges of the leather binding, worn from years of use as he carefully searched the pages until he found the handwritten poem,

> *When it rains, the dry grass will stop crackling under my bare feet,*
> *I will not remember the embrace of the hot sun on my skin,*
> *If it does not rain, the earth will claim from my pores the moisture that*
>   *irrigates its cracks,*
> *My hands will caress the dryness of the crease, praying for the seed to*
>   *germinate*
> *If it does not rain, the campesino will die in the shade of a tree waiting*
>   *for rain.*[19]

He paused and looked up from the weathered pages of the notebook before offering a final reflection: "This poem interprets the anxiety and all of the uncertainty that drought generates. The earth gives one food, life. So, this poem interprets the roots that one has with the land. The land is the *love* of the campesino. The true campesino loves (*ama*) the earth, loves it as their own life because everything, their way of life, their way of being, is composed of the earth."

Part II
PRISA—HURRY

Tiempo es justicia—Time is justice
— *Ricardo Esquivia Ballestas*

FIGURE 4. Mesa de Seguimiento (Monitoring Committee Meeting), Ñame Crisis 2017. Photo reprinted with permission from Elmer Arrieta Herrera, youth documenter for the Alta Montaña Peaceful Process of Reconciliation and Integration.

PHOTOS AND SIGNATURES

Contested Performances of Peace

A SEA OF WHITE UMBRELLAS decorated with doves boasting the tricolored Colombian flag danced under the rays of the late afternoon Caribbean sun. Against the backdrop of the colonial city of Cartagena and the Caribbean Sea, foreign dignitaries, high-ranking state leaders, and celebrities dressed in white—the symbolic color of peace—proceeded toward the stage to witness the signing of the historic peace accords between the government and the FARC-EP, marking a political end to over fifty years of war. Mellow electronic music, rather than music traditional to the coast, played across the loudspeakers, creating an atmosphere more akin to an elite club found in the urban capital cities. Local and national authorities had blocked the main highways and streets leading into the old city with security checks. Only those with VIP passes could enter to witness the historic event. Once inside, the staging for peace signing was further segmented: a gated and secured area with plush white chairs and the shade of tall palm trees was reserved for guests with special passes. Officers ushered those of us without special passes to a series of bleachers that had been set up behind the VIP seating. There, many social leaders from Montes de María who had experienced the intimate consequences of the armed conflict gathered, reuniting with old friends.

I had accompanied members from the Montes de María Regional Space for Peacebuilding coalition to the peace signing. The hierarchically divided arena was not lost on many of the leaders, who made note of the typically elite-class politics that framed the historic moment for peace in Colombia, which they had worked tirelessly for over the last several decades. And yet, they remained joyful with anticipation. As the ceremonial procession began, cheers erupted for the politicians and celebrities who had become public advocates of the peace accords. The cheers became even louder for the emblematic victims who promenaded forward as special guests to witness the peace signing. After being asked to take their seats, the Colombian national anthem blared across the sea of white. The event had begun.

When President Juan Manuel Santos took to the podium, he began his speech with the words of the national anthem, "Oh unfading glory! Oh, immortal joy! In furrows of pain, good now germinates. In furrows of pain, peace now germinates" (Santos 2016). Throughout the speech, Santos continued to invoke the lyrics of the national anthem, inscribing the peace signing as the central starting point for a "new" and unified postconflict nation—one that sought to bring those previously criminalized and victimized into the state's care. "Today, I want, in this context of openness to peace, to make a sincere tribute, from the bottom of our hearts to all the heroes of the Armed Forces of our country," Santos declared,

> who fought with honor to defend the tranquility and security of Colombians. Thanks to soldiers and police of Colombia, because their sacrifice, their courage, led us to this great day! I also want to pay tribute to the millions of innocent victims; to human rights defenders; to Indigenous, Afro-Colombian and Campesino communities; to so many women and mothers who, in the midst of tears, paid for peace. No more young people sacrificed, no more young dead, no more mutilated young by an absurd war!

In proclaiming a unified nation, Santos wove the experiences of those who had endured the consequences of the "absurd war" together with the sacrifices of the Armed Forces into a single and cohesive narrative, effectively erasing the different forms of violence that state actors had carried out against the civilian population. In his concluding remarks, Santos returned to the national anthem,

This is a *new country* that we see today. A Colombia in peace, a Colombia with more equity, a better educated Colombia that allows us to progress and be happy. Dear friends of peace in Colombia, I started by recalling the phrases of our national anthem and I will also end with the anthem, which today moves us more than ever. Colombians: "The horrible night has ceased!" The horrible night of violence that has covered us with its shadow for more than half a century has ceased. . . . Today, I invite you all—young people and adults, in the countryside and in the cities, the skeptics and the enthusiasts, to all! Let us open our arms, our eyes, our minds, and welcome the *new day*. Let us open our hearts to the *new dawn*; to the bright sun, full of possibilities that looks out on the Colombian sky. The dawn of peace! The dawn of life! (Santos 2016, emphasis mine)

The crowd erupted in applause. President Santos lifted the pen from the table in front of him and signed his name to the agreement, reaching out to shake the hand of the FARC commander, Rodrigo Londoño Echeverri, in a final gesture of peace. Cheers spread as people stood to celebrate the "dawn of peace."

Celebrities, journalists, government representatives, and foreign dignitaries filed out of the plaza as the ceremony came to a close. With salsa music now blaring across the loudspeakers, we danced our way down from the bleachers and into the empty streets of the old city of Cartagena. *"Amiga!"* Catalina Pérez Pérez declared, taking my hands in hers as she spun us around, "We have worked so long for this day! They said it would never happen, but *nosotras*, the social leaders who lived the violence, we have always known that peace is possible."

How does the state's declaration of a new, unified and postconflict nation reconfigure—or reinforce—uneven relations of power within the postaccord landscape? And what implications do such declarations have for grassroots peacebuilding efforts led by social leaders like Catalina? In "A Performative Approach to Ritual," Stanley J. Tambiah (1981) draws on J. L. Austin (1962) to outline how rituals are not merely reflective, but constitutive of social worlds (136). Speeches, ceremonies, and rituals are sites where the nation is imagined and where state power is enacted (Adams 2010; Geertz 1980; Postero 2017; Stasch 2011). The narratives of war and peace that inflect state performances of the *posconflicto* (postconflict), therefore, reveal practices and discourses that are constitutive of the state. In *Guerrilla Marketing*, Alexander Fattal (2018) argues that the Colombian state sought "postconflict status" long before the signing of the peace accords with the FARC-EP. Through rich, ethnographic insight into the state's marketing and branding campaigns, Fattal shows how the "postconflict state is built upon images that stimulate imaginaries" of a unified nation state—one free of violence (1).[1]

Spectacles of peace—like the signing of the peace accord and the commemoration of civilian massacres—took place across the country both leading up to and following the peace accords. These spectacles became key sites for national and regional authorities to consolidate power, gain political legitimacy, and demonstrate state control in the rural countryside. In *Red Tape*, Akhil Gupta (2012) distinguishes between "spectacular displays of state power" and the "everyday practices" of the state. Nancy Postero's (2017) ethnography, *The Indigenous State*, similarly locates state performances as a site of power produced through "clearly framed events set off from normative everyday reality" (74). In this chapter, I show how performances of peace in Colombia are not only limited to the realm of spectacular events but have also become one of the primary ways rural communities experience and interact with the state in the postaccord context. I extend ethnographic theories of bureaucratic violence (Gupta 2012; Jaramillo 2012) and state performances (Fattal 2018; Postero 2017) to show how the ritualization of "postconflict" performances structure external peacebuilding interventions in Montes de María. In doing so, I push past the binary of "the spectacular" and "the everyday" to draw out the continuities between national performances and everyday intervention practices as both emanating from what I call the "theatrics of peace."

Over the course of my research, campesino leaders repeatedly criticized the state's shallow approach to participatory peacebuilding as limited to the extraction of *fotos y firmas*—photos and signatures. *Fotos* (photos), *firmas* (signatures and attendance sheets), *mesas*[2] (negotiating tables), *discursos* (speeches), and *chalecos* (vests) form a repertoire of performances that shape the theatrics of peace. In this chapter, I contend that performances of peace have become constitutive of state action—the vehicle through which the state makes claims to *cumplimiento* (compliance) in postaccord Colombia (Tilly

2008). I take up Tilly's notion of "contentious performances," to argue that the theatrics of peace is not unique to Colombia but rather offers insight into the everyday practices that shape international peacebuilding interventions in comparative postaccord contexts across the world.[3] For Tilly (2008), repertoires exist when particular performances are "recurrent," consistently patterned, and recognized by all of the participants involved in contentious interactions (27). Throughout this chapter, I show how state actors draw on an internationally legible script, focus the spotlight on particular subjects, and make a presence (*hacer presencia*) through a recognizable set of performances.[4]

Since these performances are celebratory, rather than repressive, the theatrics of peace offers a key site to analyze how productive power relations are forged in Colombia's postaccord context (Adams and Rustemova 2009; Foucault 2003, 242). Drawing on Miriam Ticktin (2011), I outline how the theatrics of peace creates "new forms of subjectivity and inequality" through the clear delineation of roles between victims and experts (127). The category of victimhood simultaneously casts those who fall outside the state's framework as deviant, criminalizing more politically engaged approaches to peacebuilding. Furthermore, the victim/expert binary masks the ways campesinos in Montes de María experience multifaceted and often contradictory state practices and functions that simultaneously oppress, arbitrate, detain, provide, accompany, and defend grassroots movements. Indeed, when social leaders employ the term *institucionalidad*, they are not offering a fixed notion of state institutions but are instead referring to the processes, discourses, performances, and histories that not only make the state but that also produce the feelings and perceptions that people attach to the state.

Performances are always dialogical and multivocal, revealing multiple, competing, and dynamic visions of peace (Cox 2015). As a site of contestation, performances offer ethnographic insight into how social leaders rework and refuse the prevailing and universal discourses of peace on the ground. In this chapter and the next, I show how grassroots leaders flip the state's script to reclaim the peace accords as the fruit of their multigenerational struggle for liberatory peace, built "from and for the territory."

WHAT WE NEED IS MUD

On October 2, 2016, Colombian citizens narrowly rejected the peace accords through a popular referendum. Led by former president Álvaro Uribe, political organizers of the "no" vote built their campaign around targeted fearmongering and disinformation, invoking the discourse of criminality in ways that increased threats against social leaders at the forefront of advocating for peace. In the aftermath of the plebiscite vote and with the support of mass mobilizations that erupted across the country, the Santos administration also engaged in a broad, public campaign aimed at generating legitimacy for a revised peace agreement. Despite increased threats against social leaders, however, the Santos administration placed "the victims" at the center of its publicity campaign while simultaneously excluding grassroots actors from the renewed negotiations that took place among elite politicians in the capital city.

In the week leading up to the signing of the final, revised peace accords between the FARC and the government, I attended a state-led ceremony for land restitution in the Alta Montaña. The ceremony focused on the state's delivery of formalized land titles to sixty families in the Alta Montaña. As my moto climbed the dirt hill that led into the community, a temporary military checkpoint came into view. Armed military personnel sifted through my personal items, checked my identification, and eventually permitted me to continue my descent into the community. A large, white tent with a banner came into view, declaring the state's presence: "The Land Restitution Unit in the Alta Montaña." The usually tranquil soccer field was abuzz with people. Music blared from the sound system that state officials had temporarily set up for the ceremony as a stream of state bureaucrats emerged from white SUVs. The bustling scene, set against the backdrop of the daily movement of campesinos descending from their farms with the day's harvest, accentuated the spectacle as out of place.

A podium displaying the Land Restitution Unit logo stood at the edge of a large stage that had been constructed for the ceremony. State officials, dressed in different colored *chalecos* (vests) that marked their institutional affiliations, passed around an attendance sheet to the campesino families who sat below the stage. The tan clipboard holding the attendance sheet eventually reached me. I filled out the familiar table, which included columns for name, identification number, phone number, organizational affiliation, and a request to check the box next to the appropriate identity marker: Afrodescendant, Campesino, Indigenous, Victim. I signed my name in the final column labeled *firma* (signature) and passed the clipboard to the family next to me. As others seated around me went through the routinized motions of signing the attendance sheet, the emcee called the individuals scheduled to receive land titles to the front of the tent in order to rehearse the ceremony. Each recipient practiced walking up to the stage to receive the land titles before taking a seat in the bleachers located directly behind the podium. Halfway through the rehearsal, the emcee abruptly requested that everyone take their seat. The general director of the Land Restitution Unit had arrived. The peace campaign hymn blared across the speakers as the director walked ceremoniously down the aisle of the great, white tent, making his way to the stage. The emcee welcomed all of the entities that had come to make a presence (*hacer presencia*) in the territory, before asking everyone to stand for the national anthem.

"Peace," the emcee announced when the national anthem concluded, "is what is going to be done today in the hands of the state entity that will play a fundamental role in the implementation of these peace agreements." The emcee then called each of the state representatives forward to give their *discursos* (speeches). The brigade commander of the Colombian Marine Infantry stood, taking his place behind the podium. "Since the times of violence, we have always been here with you," the comandante began. "When this area was consolidated, we provided humanitarian accompaniment at all times. The fruit of this labor is what we see here, the delivery of land to you, the campesinos." Throughout his speech, the comandante underscored the military sacrifices made to protect civilians, locating military presence in the region as part of the state's legacy of peace and security—that which had "brought the *posconflicto* [postconflict]." With no mention of the violence that most of the families who sat in the chairs below had suffered at the hands of the Colombian Armed Forces, the comandante seamlessly transitioned the militarization of daily life—replete with checkpoints, surveillance, roadblocks, and bases—from times of war to times of peace as a fundamental part of how the state "makes a presence in the territory."

With the government speeches concluded, the emcee initiated the ceremony, calling each of the recipients to the stage. As they had rehearsed, the campesinos ushered forward, one by one, to receive their titles. After the last person walked across the stage, the emcee requested that the campesinos hold their folders out in front of them to display the land titles for one, final photo. A wave of multicolored *chalecos* (vests) rushed to the stage. State bureaucrats snapped photos with their cell phones, populating twitter feeds with images of campesinos holding their land titles. "With this," the emcee announced,

> We are making evident that Colombia is changing. We are writing a new history, that we are different people, a different country, that it is justice and peace we are bringing to the campo, that it is our institutions that will make our nation free of blood, hate, and the horror of violence. Let's applaud! Let's applaud! This is a historic moment for Colombia, for the nation, for the people of Montes de María, one of the regions most affected by the violence.

When the applause subsided, the emcee called Ciro Canoles, the representative of the Peaceful Process of the Alta Montaña, to the podium.

"We want to thank the national government for this land restitution program, a program that came with the Victim's Law for those of us who were dispossessed," he began. "I am thankful that finally, after ten years of working as a leader, this project has emerged." Ciro chose his words carefully, situating expressions of gratitude within the tireless and decades-long campesino struggle for land rights. "But, Doctor," he paused, turning his head to make eye contact with the director, "I want to say something. This group that is here," he gestured toward the sixty representatives seated in the bleachers behind him, "is much smaller than that group there," he turned toward the hundreds of families seated below the stage. "This other group," Ciro continued, "they are also campesinos. Today, they call them victims, but I have always said, I am not a victim. I am a campesino. To make us victims rids us of our name, campesinos, which is what we call ourselves." Ciro turned once again to look directly at the director:

> Today, we are empowered in our regions, and we have risen up. . . . At one point, the national government had forgotten us, but today they are saying, "here we are." Our territory also wants peace. Peace is life. Peace is the ability to produce food. I have been analyzing the accords that the government and the guerrilla created in Havana, and I have said to myself, here, what they are negotiating are our rights, there is nothing more than this. The government,

for a long time, denied us our rights and with the Victim's Law and the restitution of land and rural development we see that this can advance.

Ciro paused, allowing time for the echo of the microphone to dissipate before proceeding,

> But I want to say to you today, 70 percent of the families in the Alta Montaña of El Carmen de Bolívar still do not have their land titles. We also have a message that we want you to take to the national government, to President Santos: Are the [postconflict] agencies that they are creating travel agencies [*agencias de viaje*], or will they be rural agencies [*agencias rurales*]? Because travel agencies fly in and then leave, but the agency that we are waiting for is one that is in the hands of the people.

Affirmative murmurs of "*así es*" (that's right) punctuated Ciro's words as he reached the apex of his speech. "Today, we are crying out for the government to continue working hand in hand with us. When there is money, but there is no food, well, no one can eat money—and food is what *we campesinos* produce." Scattered applause rippled across the tent. "It is beautiful to have this title," Ciro ceremoniously held out his land title once more, pausing for emphasis. "But," he continued, "it would be even more beautiful to see that all of my *compañeros* also receive this title." A wave of applause erupted for an extended period of time.

"Doctor," Ciro said, directing his concluding remarks to the general director after the applause subsided, "For us, we do not like the city. We do not like pavement, we don't really like any of this," he waved his hand toward the white tent and the SUVs parked outside,

> For us, we prefer *mud* to pavement. In order to sow yucca, what we need is mud. We need mud for the ñame [yams] to grow, which is why we like this better. So, take this message to President Santos. Tell him that there, where you were, these people want peace, but a peace that includes equality [*igualdad*]. As a representative of the Peaceful Process of the Alta Montaña, we demand that the national government legalize our land. We ask that in the new negotiations they do not change this part of the Havana peace accords. We thank you for your presence here and we wish God to bless you so that this work continues.

In making claims to peace as cultivated from the fertile ground of the campo, Ciro rejects prevailing "postconflict" discourses that frame peace-building as originating from the state. Instead, he flips the state's script to retrieve the land titles as part of the historic campesino struggle. To do so, he inverts the state's construction of the territory as empty and backward, reclaiming the vibrant, lifeworld of *mud* as the groundswell for transformative peace—that which feeds the nation. "Peace," he explains "is life. Peace is the ability to produce food. And food," he repeatedly asserts, "is what we campesinos produce." Peace, in other words, cannot come from the desks of state institutions located outside of the territory but is cultivated by campesinos within the fertile lands of the campo. Ciro does not completely reject a relationship with state institutions but rather shifts the ground on which that relationship takes place. The state cannot merely "make a presence" through helicopter approaches to peace (*agencias de viaje*), with bureaucrats flying in and out of the territories. Instead, territorial peace requires the construction of permanent state agencies (*agencias rurales*) that are "in the hands of the people." Ciro recasts the gaze of the accords' "territorial focus" away from the campo as the site of transformation and toward the systemic changes needed within the *institucionalidad*—calling into question the structure, mandate, and actions of state bureaucracies.

Furthermore, by situating the territory as the source of life—and campesinos as the experts who tend and grow life—Ciro subverts the deficiency narratives that dispossess campesinos of their knowledge, agency, history, and identities. "I am not a victim," he boldly proclaims, "I am a campesino." Ciro's refusal of the category of "victimhood" challenges the ways in which the state positions campesinos as helpless beneficiaries of state care, rather than social and political actors engaged in the difficult work of peacebuilding. "*We* are empowered," "*we* have risen up," and "*we* created the accords," he reiterates in a rhythmic oratory, reclaiming the accords as the fruit of the multigenerational campesino struggle for peace, land, and life. Through his speech, Ciro reminds those gathered that land restitution is not a gift from a benevolent state, but a *right*, guaranteed by law in the aftermath of dispossession.

When the ceremony ended, state bureaucrats stacked chairs, removed banners, and began taking down the tent as they prepared to return to the capital city. Amid the bustle of the cleanup, I caught a glimpse of Javier leaning against a shade tree, his mule still tied to one of the branches. He waved and I made my way across the open field in order to greet him. The leader of a remote and densely forested community in the Alta Montaña, he would need to leave soon to make the long journey across the rugged, mountainous terrain before nightfall. Javier was a well-respected social leader who had dedicated his life to advocating on behalf of his community. He didn't speak often, but when he did, people listened carefully. He began organizing for collective land rights long before armed actors entered the region—and he continued to do so throughout the war. He endured arbitrary detention, torture, and near-death confrontations with multiple armed groups yet remained resolutely committed to the collective defense of life and territory. "How exciting," I naively proclaimed as I approached Javier, shaking his outstretched hand. "How do you feel?" I pointed to the title that he held underneath his arm, wrapped in a soft, faux leather folder. He opened the folder and looked down at the title. "We have struggled for this land for a long time," he reflected, taking the last drag of his cigarette before stepping on the butt with his rubber boot. "But this," he said waving toward the tent, "Well, here, this is just a lot of photos and signatures [*fotos y firmas*]."

The widespread critique of *fotos y firmas* (photos and signatures), which circulated among campesino leaders across Montes de María imbued the phrase with social meaning, making me attuned to the multifaceted material practices and political effects that accompany the state's claims to *cumplimiento*, the fulfillment of its mandate. The discursive circulation of "photos and signatures" not only casts a critical lens on how the state circumscribes and manages participation but also highlights the ways in which external actors instrumentalize community spaces to perform presence and action. As Miledys, one of the coordinators of the Peaceful Process explained,

> We have realized in our work with the state institutions—and even though we are grateful for their accompaniment—that it is very different to work with state bureaucrats, who we call the *enchalecados* (the ones in vests), because they come here to *mostrarse* (to present themselves) as an organization. This is what interests the state institutions. Yes, they support our process, but it's like they are saying: "We are not only here to benefit you, but also to benefit ourselves as well by accompanying you."

Miledys unveils the ways in which public displays of state presence through "photos and signatures" are not only—or primarily—created for campesinos but more importantly used to demonstrate that the state is fulfilling its mandate. *Mostrarse* reflects the performative dimensions of state action—one that includes a disposition of self-serving arrogance. Miledys's use of *mostrarse* reflects the ways in which the state centers itself as the primary protagonist of peace through the instrumentalization of local communities. Photos, attendance sheets, meeting minutes, monitoring committees, vests, and speeches enable the state to *mostrarse*—to showcase action—often at the expense of campesino lives and livelihoods. Contentious performances, like those enacted during the land restitution ceremony, offer a critical site to analyze contested notions of peace. The land restitution ceremony exemplifies how both the state and social leaders make claims to distinct visions of peace through performances.

THE THEATRICS OF PEACE

Patterned, recurrent, and legible to grassroots actors, state bureaucrats, International Nongovernmental Organizations (INGOs), and donors alike, the theatrics of peace is not unique to Colombia but reflective of the routine practices that structure and fortify the uneven landscape of international peacebuilding across the world. As scholars working across diverse contexts of armed conflict have shown, international peacebuilding interventions routinely use photos and signatures—banners, reports, brochures, and promotional materials—to broadcast their presence and demonstrate local inclusion, even while local actors have very little impact on the actual structure, design, and management of peacebuilding processes (Autesserre 2014; Lombard 2016; Mac Ginty 2018).[5] The campesino critique of photos and signatures exposes the consequences of what Séverine Autesserre (2014) has called a "reporting culture," which pervades international peacebuilding interventions (238). Here, I extend Autesserre's analysis to show how international peace interventions use "photos and signatures" to evidence action with little regard for the actual material and political effects that such interventions have on local communities. The habitual practices associated with *fotos y firmas* confer legitimacy on international programs that claim to have conducted a "participatory" process, even when those same interventions undermine community agency and fragment local peacebuilding processes (Mac Ginty 2018).

Tania Murray Li's (2007) searing analysis of how the process of "rendering technical," which undergirds international development projects, perpetuates colonial relations of power offers comparative insight into campesino critiques of peace interventions limited merely to *fotos y firmas*. Drawing on Li, I argue that the international peacebuilding apparatus renders "peace" technical through a repertoire of performances—with grave and life-threatening consequences for grassroots actors at the forefront of building peace in Colombia. The technocratic delivery of "peace"—conceived and signed by external experts and "brought" to the territories—threatens to undermine campesino visions and practices of "real" (*verdadera*) participation, built through collective processes of *voz y voto* (voice and votes). Instead, the theatrics of peace recasts political and structural violence as a technical problem in need of a technical solution (Ferguson 1994), framing local participation as just another issue for "experts to arrange" (Li 2007, 235). As Li (2007) has shown, "rendering technical" relies on the use of external experts who "operate at a distance" (5). Built on the labor of short-term, contracted consultants who fly in and out of the territory in *chalecos* (vests) that mark their expertise, *agencias de viaje* (travel agencies) weaken the possibilities for building permanent *agencias rurales* (rural agencies). In other words, processes of "rendering technical" have resulted in the NGOization of the state, where a bureaucratic culture of reporting that privileges short-term projects has taken precedence over the creation of permanent public policies and institutional presence. Reduced to *fotos y firmas*, local participation becomes a technique of power that maintains—rather than transforms—systemic inequalities (Li 2007, 5).

How the territory is imagined and produced through state performances of peace also shapes the ways in which "local participation" is envisioned and implemented. In the land restitution ceremony, the spatial arrangements of the tent, banners, stage, podium, and bleachers symbolically reinforced the discourses that positioned campesinos as helpless beneficiaries of state care. These universal scripts construct an imaginary of the territory as deficient—apprehended only through "absence" (Williams 2017). Narratives of deficiency, common within what James Ferguson (1994) has called the "interpretive grid" of development, deny recognition for the knowledge, expertise, and ongoing processes of peacebuilding found and cultivated within local communities (xiii).[6] In rendering the territory deficient, such narratives also create structures of dependency whereby peace relies on state time frames, priorities, and mandates to determine what counts as legitimate action. Peace, in turn, becomes a deliverable commodity that can only be created and "brought" from outside the territory. Deficiency narratives foreclose possibilities for "local participation" by erasing the alternative forms of governance, collective protection, and peacebuilding efforts that have and continue to *exist* in the territory. Campesinos who, like Ciro, engage in contentious performances of peace, contest the legitimacy of state actions that emerge from false imaginaries of the campo as lacking or empty. Instead, counterperformances of peace direct attention to the wealth and abundance held within the territory.

Anthropologists working in diverse postwar contexts have repeatedly shown how the scripts of victimhood that permeate the landscape of transitional justice collapse the polyvocal experiences that people have in the midst of war, undermining fragile processes of community healing (Bolten 2012b; Hinton 2010).[7] The imposition of discursive frames onto local communities exacerbates social marginalization, ignores difference, and flattens the multiple truths that survivors of violence want to tell (Bolten 2014; Theidon 2013).[8] In *Casualties of Care*, Miriam Ticktin (2011) lucidly illustrates the ways in which "regimes of care" produce a "universal suffering victim" deemed "worthy" of care (3–5). Agentive acts of courage (Theidon 2013), resistance (Dwyer 2010; Enloe 2013), love (Bolten 2012a; Krystalli and Schulz 2022), creative world building (Nordstrom 1997), desire (Tuck 2009), and refusal (Simpson 2014) fall outside the narrow frame produced through the discourses of victimhood, raising significant questions about who can speak— and how—on the international stage of peace and transitional justice. As Roxani Krystalli (2019b) compellingly illustrates, victimhood is also a political category and a site of contestation. Those who have endured violence do not merely succumb to the labels ascribed to them but find creative ways to reclaim, rework, and redeploy the category of victimhood to access forms of reparative justice. Yet, the hierarchies reproduced through victimhood narratives also constrain possibilities for wider structural change. The victimhood/

expertise binary not only reduces participation to practices of "photos and signatures," but also obscures ongoing forms of violence perpetrated against social leaders. Those who fall outside of the state's victimhood frame are not merely rendered invisible but, instead, pathologized as deviant (Ticktin 2011).

The production of the state as a benevolent caregiver simultaneously constructs the territory as violent and in need of intervention. In proclaiming the eradication of "blood and hate" naturalized in the countryside during the land restitution ceremony, public officials located the state outside of the history of violence that has ravaged Montes de María. These practices of historical revision allow the state to abdicate its responsibility for the violations enacted against campesino communities during the war, severely limiting the possibility for the systemic changes that reparative justice demands. The land restitution ceremony illuminates how police and military officers continue to deploy the script of "law and order" to situate themselves as the defenders of the state's peace in ways that reinforce the *continuity* of military presence from times of war into times of peace. As Paige West (2019) cogently argues, "representational rhetorics" are not benign but, instead, form the scaffolding of dispossession (12). The dual rhetoric of "lawlessness" and "state absence" found in the state's performances of peace normalizes—rather than transforms—the militarization of everyday life in postaccord Colombia. These "representational rhetorics" legitimize policing and military surveillance as a vital component of the state's peace in ways that fortify the structures and practices of carcerality, historically used to criminalize grassroots social leaders across Colombia. As I outlined in chapter 1, the state invoked the rhetoric of lawlessness to repress nonviolent social protest, legitimize mass incarceration, and justify targeted assassinations of campesino leaders who threatened the power of political and economic elites throughout the course of the armed conflict. For social leaders who have endured state violence, deficiency rhetorics are not merely symbolic, but pose direct bodily threats.

VICTIMS, EXPERTS, AND THE CRIMINALIZATION OF CAMPESINO KNOWLEDGE

The case of social leader Jorge Luis Montes, who the state detained and incarcerated following the Alta Montaña's Peaceful March of 2013, lays bare the political and material effects of the hierarchies of knowledge produced through what Roxani Krystalli (2019b) has called the "politics of victim-hood." In March 2017, in the midst of the state's rollout of the peace accord implementation, a judge charged Jorge with "rebellion," sentencing him to nearly forty years in prison despite a lack of evidence. In fact, Jorge's name never appeared on the lists submitted by the FARC as part of their agreement with the Special Jurisdiction for Peace (JEP), Colombia's transitional justice tribunal. Todd Howland, then representative of the UN High Commissioner for Human Rights in Colombia, decried the sentencing of Jorge Montes as unjust, noting the ways in which his case was not singular, but rather "emblematic" of the violations that social leaders continued to face in the postaccord context (Howland 2017). In 2017, leaders of the FARC publicly declared that Jorge Montes "is not and has never been" part of their organization. While Jorge received conditional release under the JEP, his staunch insistence on his innocence has left his case in precarious limbo—sentenced by the court yet excluded from formal transitional justice procedures. While the Victim's Law recognizes assassinations, disappearances, land mines, and forced displacement as acts of violence worthy of reparations, arbitrary detentions fall outside the state's framework of victimhood. Like Jorge, thousands of social leaders across Montes de María have "open cases" as a result of arbitrary detentions, leaving them vulnerable to arrest and imprisonment in the aftermath of war (CSPP 2020; Junieles et al. 2019).

"The case of Jorge is a clear example of the state's manipulation, their strategy to disappear a process of leadership found in communities that are organized," Elmer Arrieta Herrera, a Youth Peace Provokers coordinator explained.

> On the one side, the state encourages communities to organize, to fight for their rights, but on the other side, the state is stabbing the same communities in the back, attacking leaders, accusing them of rebellion or terrorism to keep them oppressed in order to prevent the poor class or the victims from awakening to claim their rights. They want to stay in power, and if the people awaken, well, they will no longer receive votes because people will have new ways of thinking that will change the government.

Elmer's analysis underscores how highly contradictory forms of state presence operate as a technique of power and domination in rural communities across

Colombia. While prevailing discourses of "state absence" continue to drive popular and scholarly analysis of the armed conflict, the militarization of the campo coupled with the denial of basic public services produce an experience of the state as simultaneously invasive and distant.[9]

Throughout Jorge's trial, prosecutors relied on racist tropes, citing Jorge's ability to "speak well" as evidence of his participation with the guerrilla. The racist logics of campesinos as backward and unable to engage in sophisticated social analysis, which prosecutors and the national army used to justify Jorge's wrongful conviction, continue to criminalize the oratory and analytical skills that have shaped campesino intellectual traditions for generations. The politics of knowledge—who is deemed capable of holding and producing knowledge—is profoundly implicated in the particular forms of violence enacted against social leaders in Montes de María. By stigmatizing bodies and territories that have endured historic disenfranchisement as inherently damaged, the theatrics of peace fortifies processes of dispossession through the construction of knowledge hierarchies that normalize violence against campesino social leaders (Tuck 2009).

Arbitrary detentions not only repress social mobilization in the short-term but also have lasting effects, as evidenced in the case of Jorge Montes. Indeed, the representational rhetorics that the state deployed to justify the disproportionate use of policing and incarceration of Black, Indigenous, Campesino, and queer bodies throughout the armed conflict persist today, violating the accord's guarantee of nonrepetition. In the theatrics of peace, the production of a worthy, suffering victim not only dispossesses social leaders of their knowledge and agency, but more insidiously renders their political engagement in real participation through voice and votes (*voz y voto*) a criminal act. In this way, the theatrics of peace does not merely "coexist with violence," but is constitutive of it (Gupta 2012, 88).

Despite the persistence of violence in the postaccord context, however, social leaders continue to creatively flip, refuse, and transgress the state's script to make their claims to peace and dignified life seen and heard on the national stage. In 2020, under the right-wing administration of President Iván Duque, social leaders in Montes de María confronted an increasingly hostile political climate. In response to a wave of death threats and targeted assassinations of social leaders across Colombia, members of the Montes de

María Regional Space for Peacebuilding (Espacio Regional), led by Juana Alicia Ruiz and Jorge Montes, issued a "Collective Proposal for a Community Policy of Security Guarantees for Life and Territorial Protection (June 2020)." The proposal offered a searing indictment of the state's militarized approach to security and offered nonviolent alternatives for guaranteeing the collective protection of social leaders. "We exchange the bodyguards, armored vehicles, and state security schemes," write the members of the Espacio Regional, "for more democracy, more citizen participation, more coordinated state presence, and more collective work." Throughout the document, they situate Montes de María as a territory with an established and robust history of nonviolent action and community mediation. In a direct repudiation of the deficiency labels that seek to erase the long-standing traditions of territorial peacebuilding and collective organizing that have persisted in Montes de María, the proposal concludes with a final statement: "From Montes de María, a territory of reconciliation and peace, we sign this statement on the 25th of June 2020, in the times of the pandemic."

THE *ENCHALECADOS*: DISARTICULATION AND TRANSGRESSION FROM *WITHIN*

The expert/victim binary produced through the theatrics of peace obscures the various roles that both grassroots and state actors play and the multivalent ways in which they interact. As Gupta (2012), contends, disaggregating the multiple practices, relations, and scales that produce the state allows for more textured social analysis of power and violence. In the case of Montes de María, disaggregating the state also reveals the transgressive performances that bureaucrats have enacted—often at great risks to themselves—to transform unjust policies *within* various state institutions in their work to build a just and transformative peace.

On July 31, 2020, the Committee for Solidarity with Political Prisoners and the Movement of Victims of State-Sponsored Crimes (MOVICE) presented the Colombian Truth Commission with a report on the "massive and arbitrary detentions" that occurred across Montes de María (CSPP 2020). The two-hundred-page report draws on meticulous documentation, archival research, and firsthand testimonies that bear witness to the systematic use of incarceration of campesinos under the presidency of Álvaro Uribe Vélez.

Between 2002 and 2004, the state incarcerated more than six thousand civilians from Montes de María to reinforce the public's perception that the government was winning the war against the FARC by repressing campesino resistance movements (CSPP 2020). Although the report is one of the most comprehensive studies of the systematic use of arbitrary detentions in the region, public recognition for the mass incarceration of campesino leaders did not begin with the release of the report but was instead born from decades of activism led, in large part, by officials working *within* state institutions. In a single year, the ombudsperson documented 328 cases of arbitrary arrests of campesinos in El Carmen de Bolívar alone (Junieles 2017). Years of legal research and advocacy allowed for a process of trust building that enabled state actors to gather testimonies, document cases, and guard archival evidence later used to demonstrate the systematic use of arbitrary detentions under former President Uribe.

"We decided to focus our advocacy efforts on arbitrary detention," a state official explained, detailing how regional-level bureaucrats fought against national mandates intended to obscure the state's use of arbitrary detentions. "This was during the time of Uribe and 'el uribismo' had metastasized throughout the entire state and strong right-wing positions were everywhere."[10] The two fans that whirred behind us competed with the calls of street vendors selling fruit outside. A recorder sat between us on the desk, nestled between piles of books on peace and reconciliation. Taking a deep breath, the official continued to slowly detail the national and regional dynamics that shaped political violence in Montes de María: "My boss at the time banned me from making reports on arbitrary detentions. I led a defense hearing that made the front page. My boss told me in an event afterward that we could not screw our own, that loose screws could not exist, that the institutions needed to be united, and that I was a loose screw wandering around alone." The countertheatrics of this bureaucrat brought visibility to the state's use of arbitrary detentions through a publicized court hearing that undermined state performances of unity and strength. The transgressive performance also undercut attempts to erase acts of state violence from the public imagination. Such actions carried great risks for state officials willing to fight for peace from within their agencies, many of whom encountered implicit and explicit death threats, like the one intimated to this official.

"There was a directive that prohibited us from making declarations for victims of the army, victims of these detentions," another bureaucrat recalled, reflecting on the decades of internal struggle and external activism by groups like MOVICE that allowed for greater recognition of state violence. "A big fight ensued over this, and they finally allowed us to take these statements [from victims of the military]." The official took a sip of water and leaned back in their chair before continuing, "But, some of those lineages still exist, and there are bureaucrats on the inside of state entities that still maintain this posture, who still will not record statements from the victims of violations committed by state actors." The official paused briefly before concluding, "You see? It is violent."[11]

The intense struggles that took place *within* the state formed a significant part of the political work that opened a space for survivors of state violence to make claims to reparations. For this bureaucrat, the struggle for political transformation within the state has not ended. As they make clear, tensions within the state persist as some officials uphold practices that feed a culture of impunity while others work for change from within. Despite the highly uneven power dynamics at play in the erasures of state violence, sustained pressure from outside organizers as well as transgressive actions by state officials have resulted in important gains, including public recognition and policies capable of holding state actors more directly accountable for violence committed against civilians. As Gupta (2012) underscores: "The dichotomy of collaboration and resistance is unhelpful in thinking of strategies for political struggle . . . what is at stake is nothing less than transformation in the manner in which the state comes to be constructed. It is a struggle that problematizes the historical divide between those who choose to do political work within the state and those who work outside of it" (108). The commitment of some bureaucrats to engage in political work within their institutions has and continues to open possibilities for alliance building capable of reimagining and reconstructing the state itself.

Close attention to how public officials narrate their own experiences of failed state policies also reveals insight into the more mundane practices and internal dynamics that perpetuate bureaucratic violence. The lack of budget lines needed to guarantee the material implementation of reparation agreements, burdensome bureaucratic regulations and procedures, and miscommunication between regional and national offices have led to burnout and high turnover of those who work within the state agencies tasked with victim's advocacy. The state officials that I interviewed repeatedly drew on the discourse of "disarticulation" to explain the barriers to implementation they faced and their sense of powerlessness within the wider system. Disarticulation, here, refers to the fragmented structure of the state, where the construction of isolated, individual agencies with narrowly defined mandates undermines coordination and knowledge-sharing between state programs so that no entity is responsible for the consequences of state (in)action.

"For me, the problem of the Victim's Law is the problem of articulation," a former state official from the Victim's Unit reflected. "The National System for Victims was supposed to integrate the fifty-four entities, but this has not worked. And there is not a single mechanism to correct this." As this bureaucrat laments, rather than evaluate and address the failures of previous transitional justice mechanisms, the state created new postconflict agencies, further perpetuating disarticulation across the agencies charged with implementing the peace accords. Across dozens of interviews, bureaucrats underscored the problem of disarticulation as one of greatest impediments to the current implementation process. "Disarticulation" is not merely the result of incompetency but rather a product of rendering peace technical. Consultants and low-level bureaucrats often work on short-term contracts, rather than salaried positions. They are overworked, underpaid, and occupy precarious professional positions that require them to find new employment every six months. The power disparities and biases embedded within the hierarchical structuring of national, regional, and local offices only further exacerbate burnout among bureaucrats who work in the peripheral regions of the country. High turnover rates, the dissolution of old agencies, and the creation of new ones creates a fragmented system, which further undermines fragile processes of trust-building between local communities and state institutions, a key element necessary for lasting peace (Appleby and Lederach 2010; Burnyeat 2021; Ricigliano 2012).

"There is an immense disarticulation between the institutions in charge of the peace [accords] and the power play is very big, even more so right now since the elections are approaching," an official from the Office of the High Commissioner for Peace reflected as we sat, drinking fresh orange juice from a nearby Bogotá vendor, taking in a few moments of sunshine on an outdoor park bench. When I asked for a concrete example of disarticulation, they discussed, at length, the process of co-constructing a peacebuilding project with a coalition of social leaders in one of the territories prioritized for implementation. "We co-created a budget, a proposal, and a strategic plan," the bureaucrat explained. Unfortunately, miscommunication *between* competing state agencies and distrust *within* the regional and national offices resulted in the termination of the project. "This [disarticulation] fractures social processes because people start to have desires, desires that are very legitimate, and this is *grave*." The official paused before continuing to explain the effects of disarticulation: "And now, what are people in those rural communities doing? Well, the other day there was a massive land grab and people were killed. What I am saying is that the fracture is so deep, Angela, that people are dead. It is not just that the [state] has fractured the social fabric, people are dead. This disarticulation is perverse for peacebuilding, it is perverse."

State performances of unity mask the violent effects that disarticulation has on the lives of those most affected by the armed conflict. Such performances limit—rather than expand—the possibilities for more transformative and democratic approaches to participatory peacebuilding. Short-term electoral cycles, fiscal calendars, report deadlines, and the use of contracted consultants fragment the implementation process with *grave* and life-threatening consequences for those living at the epicenters of postaccord peacebuilding. Here, disaggregating the state across various locales and agencies exposes how *disarticulation*—rather than unity—works as a technique of power in the theatrics of peace.

THE CITIZENS FAIR

On March 25, 2017, the state hosted a Citizens Fair (*Feria Ciudadana*)—in El Carmen de Bolívar, which purported to bring public services to the rural municipalities of Montes de María. In the preceding weeks, flyers and radio announcements declared that all of the major state institutions would be present for the one-day fair, replete with state promotions (*ofertas*).[12] The National Fair for Citizens Services was not unique to the region. The state hosted similar fairs across the rural territories following the signing of the peace accords.[13] People traveled from the surrounding municipalities to El Carmen to meet directly with state institutions in charge of health insurance policies, school enrollment, ID cards, and victim's reparations. Even though the Citizens Fair did not begin until eight in the morning, a line of people extended across the city center by six, wrapping around a charter bus emblazoned with the governor's slogan: "Bolívar Advances!" The idle line of people waiting next to the bus offered a poignant repudiation of the governor's shallow performance of *cumplimiento*—the fulfillment of its mandate.

Once inside, another line wove around the borders of the tent as people waited to meet with the Victim's Unit. The vast majority of those waiting in line were elderly—individuals prioritized for reparations but for whom the main offices located in the capital city remained inaccessible. Representatives from eighty different local, regional, and national institutions meandered through the tents in their multicolored vests (*chalecos*). Various newspaper, radio, and television stations broadcasted the event across the country—with interviews with state officials about the Citizens Fair, who claimed that the event "articulated" the institutional offerings across the state's municipal, regional, and national offices. The brochures and banners that lined the tents declared the state's "presence" in the territory, reinforcing the state's assertion and image as a "government of results" committed to bringing services to the rural areas. "This is disrespectful," one of the leaders of the Alta Montaña lamented. He shook his head with disgust as I approached him. We caught up on recent community events as he waited for his turn to meet with officials about his pending land restitution claim. "They are not going to solve anything here. This is pure *politiquería* [politicking]." Throughout the day, many people described the fair as a "production," "pure chaos," and "more photos and publicity"—just another manifestation of state politics as usual.

Later that afternoon, in the quiet patio of the Sembrandopaz house, the theme of participation emerged during an interview with Dionisio Alarcón. "Citizen participation is an effective tool if it would be taken into account as something fundamental," Dionisio reflected. "But they [the state] approach citizen participation like it's a bandaid. We have these tools that the Constitution gives us so that we can claim our rights, but every time we claim our rights there are obstacles and this becomes like a knot that prevents us from advancing. But the state is still able to say that they have given people this tool." Dionisio paused, gathering his thoughts, before continuing, "For example, what is happening here, today. This morning, all of these 88 institutions providing services to 14,000 citizens will appear on TV in all of the newspapers, all around the country." He looked down at the weathered notebook that lay open on the table. Years of handwritten poems and stories holding the living memories of his community spread out before us. "Everything that one lived there," Dionisio continued, shifting his gaze toward the Montaña,

> And all that is still happening, in reality, is something else. But what the
> press is going to show to the country is something different. The government
> is putting on this production, has called the news media so that they can
> come and take photos so that the rest of the country sees that the government
> is doing something, while the rest of us are here in the heat, in the chaos.
> There are no solutions here.

As Dionisio underscores, these performances are not *for* communities affected by the war but rather produced for a wider national and international audience as a way for the state to *mostrarse*—to showcase itself. He makes direct connections between what "one lived there"—the violence carried out against civilians during the armed conflict—and "what is still happening"— the false promises and the state's perpetual denial of the campesino right to basic public services.

Throughout this chapter, I have argued that the repertoire of performances found in the theatrics of peace plays a central role in the construction of Colombia's "postconflict" state. This chapter offers ethnographic insight into the effects that performances—as a form of state action—have on communities that have endured the devastating consequences of war. Following campesino social critiques, I contend that the state's—and international community's—use of *fotos y firmas* (photos and signatures) to perform presence and action denies campesinos meaningful participation in the co-construction of policies as envisaged by the accords. Instead, the instrumentalization of campesino communities as props used by bureaucratic agencies to *mostrarse*—showcase themselves—perpetuates social inequality, violates human dignity, and deepens distrust and resentment toward the *institucionalidad*. By training the spotlight on the state as the primary protagonist of peace, such performances also locate campesinos as helpless recipients of state care, undermining possibilities for political participation.

The theatrics of peace, which delineates clear roles, draws on specific scripts and casts the spotlight on the state as a benevolent caregiver, further masks the multiple, punctuated, and discordant ways social leaders experience the state as oppressor, enforcer, occupier, arbiter, *acompañante*, provider, and defender. In producing a caring and unified nation against the backdrop of the lawless and violent territories, the state reinscribes hierarchical power relations between "experts" and "victims." The emblematic case of Jorge Montes illustrates the ways in which the representational rhetorics that render Montes de María and its inhabitants deficient—and in need of intervention—not only undermine campesino agency but more insidiously, criminalize social leaders' political participation in community peacebuilding. In this way, close attention to the material practices and political effects of the patterned performances that state agencies engage in postaccord contexts offers significant insight into the processes and discourses that produce the uneven landscape of peacebuilding—one played out across the world's stage.

Performances are also sites of contestation, negotiation, and refusal. The dynamic interactions that occur within and between actors engaged in claim-making through contentious performances offer critical insight into the everyday practices that constrain—or strengthen—alliances between local, national, and international peacebuilding processes. While the narrow frame produced through the theatrics of peace threatens to erase multigenerational processes of territorial peacebuilding, I have sought to show how local actors appropriate, rework, transgress, and refuse global mechanisms of "participation" and "peace" on the ground through counterperformances. Social leaders appropriate the state's stage to recast the public spotlight on the fertile lifeworld of mud found in the campo as that which gives rise to peace "from and for the territory."

CHAPTER FOUR

TOO MUCH *PRISA*

The Temporal Dynamics of Violence and Peace

"*AMIGA!*" I HEARD OMAR'S VOICE before their long, lean arms held high in an open greeting came into view. The emblematic yellow church that stood in the middle of El Carmen's plaza formed the picturesque backdrop for our reunion. A prominent leader for the *comunidad diversa* (diverse community) and outspoken advocate for LGBTQIA+ rights across the Caribbean coast, I sought Omar's perspective on the implementation process, which had been underway for nearly two years. After we spent time catching up, I asked Omar about the implementation of the *enfoque diferencial* (differential focus), which included important measures for their ongoing work. Rather than respond to my inquiry with specific examples, Omar offered a reflection on the state's general approach to implementation. "They are running with too much *prisa* (hurry)," Omar responded, shaking their head in disapproval. "The times are distinct."

As implementation of the peace accords unfolded in Montes de María, social leaders repeatedly asserted that state institutions were operating with "too much *prisa* (hurry, haste)." Like Omar, social leaders argued that "the times" posed one of the greatest challenges to building territorial peace. The widespread circulation of campesino critiques made in the temporal register of *prisa* raises significant questions for anthropological inquiry into war and peace: What practices, technologies, and relations shape the temporalities of *prisa*? What does *prisa* feel like for those on the receiving end of external peace interventions? In this chapter, I ground these questions in an ethnographic case study of the 2017 ñame (yam) crisis that led to a series of negotiations between the Peaceful Process and the state institutions responsible for implementing collective reparations. Close attention to the everyday interactions between campesino leaders and state actors reveals the multiple layers of meaning embedded within the critique of *prisa*. When social leaders claim that the implementation is being carried out with *hurry*, they are not suggesting that the peace accords are being implemented rapidly. As I will show with ethnographic detail throughout this chapter, the experience that campesino communities have of state implementation is one of deferred action. The discursive frame of *prisa* (hurry), therefore, reveals a distinct social theory of time—one that moves beyond quantitative measurements limited to speed, progress, and efficiency—and toward a "felt theory" of time as relational, affective, and embodied (Million 2008).

Campesino critiques of *prisa* unveil the temporal dynamics that render oppressive intervention practices an inevitable good within the wider system of international peacebuilding. In particular, ethnographic attunement to how campesinos experience *prisa* illuminates the multiple and discordant temporalities that naturalize shallow performances of peace, which limit action to *fotos y firmas* (photos and signatures). In doing so, this chapter affords insight into the temporalities that perpetuate harm in the name of peace by casting an ethnographic lens on the discourses and practices of *prisa*.

THE 2017 ÑAME CRISIS

During the 2013 negotiations that followed the nonviolent march in the Alta Montaña, the Ministry of Agriculture rejected the Peaceful Process's demand for subsidies for the avocado; instead, the state institutions responsible for agricultural production and commercialization offered a series of "productive projects" that included the promotion of ñame—yams—in the region. The state provided "certified" ñame seeds at a reduced cost to campesinos who, in turn, were responsible for the physical labor required to prepare the land, plant the seeds, and harvest the crop. To participate in the program, campesino families took out bank loans from financial institutions that partnered with the state for the ñame project in order to purchase the certified seeds. In contrast to the avocado, which had ensured food sovereignty, the ñame project increased campesino dependence on the state—and the lending institutions that benefited from the agricultural project.

Ñame is a culturally significant food staple on the Caribbean coast; campesinos traditionally cultivated it for subsistence—and not commercialization—clearing and burning small plots of land to prepare the soil for the yams. With the state's large-scale ñame project, however, campesinos began "slashing and burning" large extensions of land that had been left barren in the wake of the death of the avocado. The fires that burned across the mountains where avocado forests once flourished filled the air with a hazy smoke as families prepared their farms to receive the state's certified ñame seeds. "I prefer not to burn too much," Héctor reflected. We stood at the edge of a cliff overlooking the ashen hillside, smoke still billowing from the ground, "but, this was the only way to prepare the soil in time to receive the [ñame] project."

After the first season of planting, campesino farmers succeeded in producing an abundant harvest. Unfortunately, the state project had not taken into account the impact that an overproduction of ñame would have on local market prices. In April 2017, as ñame flooded the local and regional markets, the price of the crop plummeted to historic lows. Without an insurance policy or clear plan for commercialization, campesinos across Montes de María began to sound the alarm about an impending economic crisis. They warned the state institutions responsible for the project that the *deflated* value of ñame coupled with the *inflated* interest rates on the bank loans would generate profound economic insecurity in their communities. Social leaders across the region wrote letters, made phone calls, and established meetings with state officials in order to alert local authorities to the long-term consequences that defaulting on the bank loans would have on the families who had participated in the state agricultural project. With few concrete responses from the state, social leaders issued public statements warning national and local authorities that, if left unresolved, the ñame crisis would result in massive economic displacements, violating the right to dignified return as promised in the accords. The state met their appeals with silence.

As a palpable fear spread across the communities in the Alta Montaña, the coordinators of the Peaceful Process organized an "extraordinary assembly" to discuss their options in preparation for an upcoming *mesa de seguimiento* (monitoring committee meeting) with the institutions responsible for implementing their collective reparations plan. Although the state had implemented a few of the reparation measures, the vast majority of the agreements remained only on paper.

"The value of ñame has crashed," a community leader reflected. "Women are displacing to the cities to look for domestic work."

Así es (that's right), collective affirmations rippled across the open-air meeting space as another leader detailed the consequences of the ñame crisis in their community. "The ñame is being left to rot in the ground. The cost to harvest the ñame is greater than its value. The ñame has gone *pa' bajo* (crashed). We are eating ñame with ñame," he concluded, emphasizing the severe poverty and hunger produced by the state's monocrop project, planted at the expense of other subsistence crops in the region. The heavy weight of the unfolding ñame crisis settled around the communal meeting house as each leader continued to share their grievances and fears.

"I have been analyzing this situation. In other regions, when the coffee farmers had a crisis, the state provided subsidies," Aroldo Canoles, one of the coordinators, reflected, turning the discussion toward concrete actions that could stave off economic devastation. "I propose that the government buy this ñame from us. In the Guajira, there is hunger, there is a water crisis. There, in the [transition] zones where the FARC are, I hear they also need food programs."

"*Sí, señor*," several campesino leaders punctuated Aroldo's analysis in a show of support, propelling the conversation forward.

"Our school food programs serve bread wrapped in plastic," Miledys, a teacher and coordinator of the Peaceful Process, interjected, adding to the proposal. "This generates waste, and it is not sufficient. Here, we do not eat bread. Here, we are used to eating ñame. Why can't we use ñame for our school food programs instead?"

A renewed energy filled the meeting space as leaders drew on one another's analyses to develop a set of concrete solutions to the crisis. After several

hours, the coordinating committee reviewed the suggestions and established
a plan for the upcoming *mesa de seguimiento*. They would propose that the
government buy the ñame for state-led programs in the Caribbean region
including school lunch programs, food distribution programs in the Temporary Rural Zones of Transition and Normalization for demobilized FARC,
and disaster relief efforts in the Department of La Guajira. Since all of these
state-led food programs were located and administered along the Caribbean
coast, they reasoned, using a locally sourced crop like ñame would be a more
sustainable and culturally appropriate alternative to the potatoes and packaged bread shipped from the capital city.

"Over these last days, I have been thinking," Ciro Canoles reflected, after
each of the points of the proposal had been defined, "I think that we should
show them [our harvest]—let's bring sacks of produce with us, those who still
have avocado can bring that, too—let's deliver this to the state." The proposal received enthusiastic support as leaders began organizing the symbolic
action, identifying who could bring ñame and avocado to present to the state
bureaucrats. With the late afternoon sun beginning to set, the leaders shook
hands, said their goodbyes, and began their long journeys home—some by
foot, others by mule, and others by moto—to the various communities of the
Alta Montaña.

In April 2017, campesino leaders from the Alta Montaña traveled to the
urban center of El Carmen de Bolívar for another *mesa de seguimiento* with
state officials. Since 2013, the coordinating committee had engaged in dozens
of *mesas* to guarantee the implementation of their collective reparations plan.
This time, the Office of the High Advisory to the President on the Regions
(translated as Alta Consejería) convened the meeting in the auditorium of
the University of Cartagena's satellite campus in El Carmen. The large stage,
colonial architecture and decor, and stadium-style seating replete with red
theater chairs contrasted sharply with campesino assemblies held in open-air,
communal meeting houses. State bureaucrats placed the governor's banner
announcing, "Bolívar Advances!" next to a long, narrow table covered in a
white cloth at the front of the stage. Name tags for each of the directors of
the state institutions lined the table. As campesinos arrived, they stored the
sacks of ñame and avocados they had carried with them at the back of the
auditorium before taking their seats in the red velvet chairs below the stage.

Bureaucrats and government employees filed into the auditorium from their respective cities, each wearing different colored *chalecos* (vests), marking their institutional expertise. In addition to state bureaucrats, invited journalists from various radio, television, and newspaper outlets also lined the sides of the auditorium with their microphones and cameras ready to capture the state in action. By the time the meeting started, the red velvet seats were almost completely full of spectators from the media, universities, NGOs, and government entities.

A bureaucrat from the Alta Consejería facilitated the meeting, allocating time for representatives from each of the state institutions to speak first. Once the state bureaucrats finished speaking, campesino representatives from the distinct monitoring committees were given time to respond. The state representatives had a name tag and seat at the table on the stage. The Alta Consejería provided only two seats at the main table for representatives from the Peaceful Process. The vast majority of campesino leaders presented their reports from their auditorium seats, located below the stage.

When the discussion finally turned to the agricultural committee, Ciro opened with a carefully constructed speech. He detailed how the state refused to provide subsidies for the loss of the avocado, which formed the Peaceful Process's primary demand during the 2013 march. As an alternative, Ciro explained, the state created a productive project focused on promoting ñame. "We have provided the physical labor," Ciro continued, underscoring that campesinos in the Alta Montaña had successfully fulfilled their part of the project, producing a robust harvest of ñame. "Unfortunately, the overproduction of ñame in the local markets has driven the value of ñame down," he continued, noting the ways that the state's project had left the very communities they intended to serve in a situation of acute economic insecurity.

"Doctor," Ciro directed his speech (*discurso*) to the national director of the Alta Consejería, "We have a proposal we want you to take to President Santos. We propose that the government buy this ñame for schools, for their programs in La Guajira, and for the FARC camps as they have done in the past for the potato farmers and coffee farmers." He then outlined previous precedent for the proposed response to the impending agricultural crisis. "Here, we do not eat potatoes. For campesinos, potatoes are not food. Bread is not food. What we eat here is ñame, is yucca. We are not satisfied until we have our ñamecito with a small piece of *quesito* (cheese)." Laughter and applause erupted from below, as people nodded in agreement. Ñame, he argued, was more culturally appropriate, local, and sustainable than shipping potatoes and packaged bread from the cold, Andean regions to the northern, Caribbean coast.

"This region is known for its avocado—for producing the biggest and best avocado in the country, maybe the world." Ciro continued, making explicit the connection between the impending ñame crisis and the death of the avocado. "Today, we have very few avocados left." As Ciro spoke, several leaders from the Peaceful Process walked down the long, steep aisle with bright green, football-sized avocados in their hands. "In 2013, we initiated a process of reconciliation and we marched and we signed agreements with the government because of the death of the avocado. Here, we present you with the few avocados we have left, so that you may taste the rich abundance of the Alta Montaña." Ciro then motioned toward the back of the auditorium, where one of the campesinos walked down the auditorium stairs and toward the stage with a heavy sack of ñame over his shoulder. "Tell President Santos," Ciro continued, "that here, there is an abundance of ñame ready to be sold, to be exported." Ciro took the large, plastic sack full of freshly harvested ñame and placed it onto the white tablecloth directly in front of the state representatives. "And that the government should buy this ñame from us," he concluded triumphantly. A flood of camera flashes filled the auditorium as more campesinos walked onto the stage, extending their gifts of fresh avocados and ñame to state officials.

In contrast to the Land Restitution ceremony, where campesinos held out the state's "gift" of land titles, here, high government officials held the gifts of bountiful produce from campesinos out for an unexpected photographic moment. Social leaders from the Peaceful Process flipped the state's script, inverting the donor-beneficiary relationship to situate campesinos as the expert producers and providers of Colombia. The carefully planned performance conveyed multiple layers of meaning: the symbolic action centered campesino expertise, celebrated the gift and solidarity economies central to campesino life and livelihoods, and made visible the direct connection between the death of the avocado and the state's failed ñame project, intended as a form of reparations.[1] Through this symbolic performance, social leaders declared to a wider national and international audience that the *campesinado* had successfully upheld their end of the agreement for the state-led ñame project by producing an abundant harvest. Now, it was the state's turn to respond.

In the weeks that followed, however, the state did not offer concrete solutions. Instead, the Alta Consejería convened another meeting (*mesa*)—this time in the capital city of Bogotá. Although the Alta Consejería had raised the possibility of sending a delegation to Bogotá, the final confirmation for the meeting did not come until several days before the trip. The coordinators of the Peaceful Process responded quickly—sending out WhatsApp messages and making late night phone calls in order to identify representatives who could travel to Bogotá. In late May, I accompanied representatives from the coordinating committee of the Peaceful Process to Bogotá. We left El Carmen before dawn, arriving at the capital city by plane in time for a full day of meetings. Dressed in heavy coats, scarves, and winter hats, we took the stairs to the third floor of a high-rise building located in the bustling, historic center of Bogotá.

Inside the conference room, a middle-aged woman with thick-rimmed glasses and a blue vest sat at the far end of the long, rectangular table. The vest, emblazoned with the image of two hands holding a dove, indicated her institutional affiliation with the *Defensoría del Pueblo* (ombudsperson). The leaders greeted her warmly. She opened her laptop and reviewed the notes that had been sent from the regional representative who was present at the last meeting. She listened attentively as the leaders detailed their increasing concerns about the ñame crisis. Drawing on the institutional memory she had accumulated over years of accompanying victims of the armed conflict, she reiterated the leaders' concerns about the direct connection between the death of the avocado and the ñame crisis. Such recognition, from a state official, bolstered their confidence as they went over their talking points in anticipation for the day's meetings.

Soon after, a representative from the Alta Consejería entered the conference room. Dressed in a crisp, white, collared shirt and leather shoes, his attire contrasted with the vest he usually brandished during "field visits" to the regions. The bureaucrat welcomed the leaders to Bogotá and then proceeded to outline the agenda for the day on a large flip board. From ten in the morning until five in the evening, the leaders had one-on-one meetings with representatives from the institutions responsible for the Alta Montaña's collective reparations plan. While the agenda included meetings with all of the institutions responsible for implementing collective reparations, the campesino leaders had traveled to Bogotá with the explicit aim of negotiating a constructive response to the impending ñame crisis. The morning session, which included representatives from the Ministry of Agriculture, the Colombian Agricultural Institute (ICA), and the Colombian Corporation for Agricultural Research (CORPOICA) was, therefore, the most pressing meeting of the day.

The state officials arrived in a small group, placed their briefcases and laptop bags on the table, and greeted the campesino leaders in the room as they took their seats. In addition to the state institutions initially charged with implementing the agricultural measures during the 2013 march, representatives from the three new postconflict agencies were also present, including the National Land Agency (ANT; Agencia Nacional de Tierras), the Rural Development Agency (ADR; Agencia de Desarrollo), and the Territorial Renovation Agency (ART; Agencia de Renovación Territorial). The facilitator introduced the representatives from each of the state institutions responsible for rural development and agricultural measures and then turned to the leaders of the Peaceful Process to outline a progress report on the implementation process.

"We signed accords with the state after the 2013 march, agreeing to receive productive projects directed toward the avocado," Ciro began, situating the ñame crisis within a wider series of failed interventions in his opening remarks, "Unfortunately, the drought killed all the avocado they sent."

"The projects that have come to the zone are *proyectos huérfanos* (orphan projects)," Jorge Pérez, who sat next to Ciro, interjected. "They arrive suddenly and then they disappear. There is no assistance, and many projects have arrived during times when there is no rain. It requires planning according to *los tiempos*, the times when we are able to plant trees. Now, all of the seedlings have died. Why? Because there was no participation." Ciro and Jorge proceeded to underscore the ways in which the unexpected and uneven arrival of orphan projects not only undermined the integral reparations espoused in the Victim's Law but had further exacerbated social and economic tensions in the Alta Montaña. Jorge continued to emphasize the state's lack of attention to the times (*los tiempos*), which he argued had resulted in flawed project designs. For rural communities that do not have irrigation systems, reservoirs, greenhouses, or storage facilities, seasonal knowledge, close attention to weather patterns, and changing waterways are vital for farming. In contrast, "the times of the state" operate according to electoral and budgetary timelines rather than the seasonal and place-based times of the campo, necessary for successful agriculture in the Alta Montaña. "We need real (*verdadera*) participation" Jorge concluded, "and we need to look deeper to see what is really going on."

"During the march, we proposed a subsidy for the avocado," Aroldo's voice rose from the other end of the table. "But [the state] brought this 'renovation project' and now over 80% of what they brought has died because of the heat." Echoing Jorge, Aroldo outlined the material effects of agricultural projects guided by the times of the state. "When there is technical assistance, it is for short time periods, but it is not something *permanent*," he paused, reiterating Jorge's critique of "the times,"

> We are waiting for the legalization of our land so that we can begin other projects focused on health, education, and agriculture, but it all depends on legalization [of land]. The processes of land restitution are complicated and there we see the inequality. And now, we have an excessive production of ñame. The agrarian bank loans have high interest rates. What is the relationship between the state and the entities that give bank loans? These projects are going to lose money again. Take it from this old man, we are going to see history repeat itself.

"Sixty families received restitution in November," Ciro added, "But, the vast majority of families remain without titles." As Ciro spoke, Jorge reached into his bag and pulled out a stack of papers. He carefully unfolded the documents and began reciting the names of each of the farms in the Alta Montaña still awaiting legal land titles. When he finished, Jorge explained that campesinos have to rely on intermediaries because the state has not yet formalized their land. Without land formalization, Jorge explained, campesinos are not eligible for agricultural projects that allow them to engage in the direct commercialization of their produce.

"This is not just an issue of agriculture," Miledys's voice rose from across the room. Dressed in a bright red shirt with a matching scarf and shoes, she connected each of the previous points to issues of education and health. "I am a teacher. We are holding classes under a tree because the roof is collapsing in on us." She then proceeded to explain that someone in the community had donated a plot of land for the new school building, but they could not move forward with the reparation measure because they lacked a formal land title. Without land formalization, fulfillment (*cumplimiento*) of the reparation measure was simply not possible.

"What we are asking," Aroldo concluded, "is that we please work in a way that is equitable and integral." Rather than treat each item as a discrete problem, the leaders carefully wove together the death of the avocado, land titles, and the ñame crisis together. Situating his final remark within the language and framework of the Victim's Law, Aroldo also sought to hold the state to account for the lack of an "integral" approach to collective reparations as mandated in the Victim's Law. Rather than provide a subsidy for the avocado—which would have placed decision-making power in the hands of campesino farmers—the state delivered a series of flawed "orphan projects" that arrived "suddenly" to the campo, with little consideration for the place-based and structural conditions needed to ensure successful implementation. As a result, campesino communities in the Alta Montaña now found themselves in the midst of a severe economic crisis—one produced by the state in the name of repair.

A state official from the Colombian Corporation for Agricultural Research (CORPOICA), the institution responsible for the avocado renovation project, was the first to respond to the concerns raised. Rather than address the social leaders directly, the bureaucrat turned, instead, toward the administrative assistant in charge of taking the official meeting minutes. "Since 2013, CORPOICA has been present in the territory," they began. "We are not an agency that provides technical assistance beyond the technological materials that we deliver," the bureaucrat glanced briefly across the table at the social leaders. "For the record," the official stated, making eye contact with the administrative assistant taking the official minutes once more before proceeding, "We have concluded our part of the agreement. It is important that it be made clear that since 2013 until now we delivered avocado plants in two phases and we have fulfilled the agreement that we made." The official paused, waiting for the administrative assistant to finish recording the statement. "It is very sad that the ñame couldn't be commercialized, but this agreement is completed (*esta cumplido*)." With their statement recorded, the official rose and excused themselves from the meeting.

For the state official, the primary objective of the meeting with social leaders from the Alta Montaña was not to fulfill victim satisfaction through the implementation of integral and equitable reparations but, instead, to establish a clear, written record. As the bureaucrat made clear, the recorded documentation of the speech act, *esta cumplido* (completed), constituted the state's fulfillment of the agreements signed with the Alta Montaña, regardless of the project's effects. *Fotos* (photos), *firmas* (attendance sheets and reports), and *mesas* (negotiating tables) are performative acts of *cumplimiento*—the fulfillment of the state's responsibilities through the paper trail of proof left in the wake of endless cycles of meetings and "orphan projects."

Throughout the negotiations that took place surrounding the ñame crisis, campesinos repeatedly appealed to state actors for more meaningful forms of direct participation that would draw on their deep knowledge of the land, their understanding of the historical processes that have produced economic crises in the campo, and their attention to place-based and seasonal conditions to inform agricultural policies. The national peace accords, notably, include the transversal value of participation because the historic exclusion and disenfranchisement of Campesino, Afrodescendant, and Indigenous communities from political decision-making is widely considered one of the root causes of the armed conflict. However, the theatrics of peace allows the state to perform their compliance with a participatory process, even as negotiations, meeting minutes, and project reports consistently undermine campesino agency. Careful scrutiny of the patterned performances that the state engages, therefore, exposes how the state masks perpetual *incumplimiento* (lack of compliance) through "participatory" consultations—what Francisco Gutiérrez Sanín (2020) refers to as the Colombian state's "*ciclo de incumplimiento* [default cycle]" (471).

In *Red Tape*, Akhil Gupta (2012) illustrates the ways in which the reporting culture characteristic of state bureaucracies naturalizes structural violence. Gupta argues that excessive writing and audit trails have become the primary "form of everyday state action" in ways that mask and render invisible the structural inequalities that generate social suffering (143). Social leaders extend this analysis by drawing attention to the temporalities that structure and maintain the harmful effects of what Gupta calls "everyday state action" and which campesinos refer to as the *institucionalidad*. For social leaders, "true participation" requires attention, first and foremost, to "the times (*los tiempos*)." Critical, temporal attunement reveals the ways disarticulation within the state allows bureaucrats to abdicate responsibility for the harmful effects of poorly designed interventions by limiting knowledge and action to narrowly defined roles and mandates. Throughout the negotiations in Bogotá, campesino leaders from the Peaceful Process outlined how "the times of the state (*los tiempos del estado)*"—the sudden arrival of fragmented and orphaned projects—resulted in repeated cycles of failed interventions, perpetually extending reparations to an abstract future. As they make clear, the times of the state not only produce ineffective projects but also deepen inequality under the auspices of participatory peacebuilding.

RUNNING FAST AND PERPETUALLY DEFERRED: THE TEMPORAL REGIME OF *PRISA*

Between April and August 2017, the leaders of the Alta Montaña engaged in six more rounds of formal negotiations with state officials in an effort to prevent—or at least minimize—the economic losses incurred as a result of the ñame overproduction. As each meeting led to yet another round of negotiations, trust in the state began to erode and frustration mounted. Economic desperation led women and youth to displace to urban cities in search of domestic work and informal employment. Many people left their ñame to rot in the ground because the cost of harvest exceeded the crop's market value. Those who harvested the ñame, stored the yams under the open-air, thatched roofs of communal meeting houses as they waited for a response from the state. As each day passed, however, hope for a constructive solution receded—and along with it, community trust in the Peaceful Process also faltered. After months of negotiations, the Ministry of Agriculture finally approached the coordinators of the Peaceful Process with a concrete response: the multinational company Market Foods had agreed to buy the ñame through a public-private alliance.

After three months of ongoing negotiations, representatives from Market Foods traveled to the Alta Montaña. They spent a day sorting and classifying the ñame for export to Miami. In total, Market Foods took 1,160 sacks of harvest worth 35.000.000 pesos (approx. $10,000USD) with them to the port city of Barranquilla. They did not compensate campesinos for the transportation costs used to get the ñame from their rural and isolated communities to the paved road, nor did they offer any payment for the produce. Instead, representatives from the company explained that payment would come in full once they exported the ñame to Miami. With no other alternatives, the leaders agreed to the terms and conditions set through the state's alliance with Market Foods.

Several weeks later, Market Foods informed the Peaceful Process that the ñame had gone bad and was no longer adequate for exportation. Therefore, they could not pay for the "rotten ñame." Rather than return the harvest to the Alta Montaña, Market Foods had, instead, burned all of the ñame. The loss of the ñame and the lack of accountability for the state's role in the failed alliance with Market Foods intensified the dire economic situation in the Alta Montaña. The fragile trust that had been painstakingly built across the divided communities began to unravel as false rumors spread suggesting individual leaders had pocketed the money.

In the aftermath of the fallout with Market Foods, the Peaceful Process prepared, once more, for a *mesa de seguimiento* (monitoring committee meeting) with the Victim's Unit to discuss the implementation of collective reparations. "They robbed us," a campesino leader reflected softly, his voice more resigned than angry. We had placed our white, plastic chairs at the edge of an overlook, allowing the steady breeze and stunning views of Montes de María to pour over us as we waited for the state officials from the Victim's Unit to arrive. "The only way we can guarantee our rights in this country is through nonviolent mobilization. It is obvious that there is no political will."

State officials arrived at the open-air meeting house, located at the edge of the paved road in the Alta Montaña, by midmorning. They emerged from the SUV wearing blue vests, "The Unit for Attention and Integral Reparations for Victims" etched in red on the back. The main facilitator had flown in from the capital city of Bogotá the night before. Campesino leaders, in contrast, arrived by foot or mule—waking at dawn and walking for several hours—to attend the meeting. They scraped the remnants of the thick mud off their tall rubber boots as they waited for the meeting to begin.

After passing around an attendance sheet, the state official who had flown in from Bogotá opened the meeting by stating that campesinos needed to "ground in reality" what they had "dreamed up" over the last several years. While the official acknowledged that these "dreams" had emerged as the result of meeting after meeting that their own institution had facilitated since 2013, they eschewed all responsibility for the flawed process. Instead, they cited institutional changes that were out of their hands—namely, that the Victim's Unit was now under new direction with different mandates that corresponded to the new agencies being formed to implement the peace accords. Despite the fact that the primary mandate of the Victim's Unit is to articulate the various state institutions charged with implementing "integral reparations," the official never once discussed the six meetings that had taken place over the last two months. In fact, they made no mention of the ñame crisis or the dire economic situation in which campesino communities in the Alta Montaña—the "subject of collective reparations"—found themselves. Instead, they reprimanded campesino leaders for demanding too much and failing to understand the legal constraints and budgetary procedures of the state. In order to solve the stalled reparations process, they asserted, campesino leaders needed to "ground" themselves in reality. The state representatives were there to help manage these unrealistic dreams of roads, schools, and health clinics into realizable projects. Participation amounted to little more than a signed attendance sheet.

The piles of ñame that surrounded the open-air meeting space made materially present the long laundry list of failed state projects and broken promises. Palpable frustration spread across the room as representatives from the distinct state agencies proceeded with business as usual, presenting feasible projects to satisfy the reparations measures. Eventually, the meeting turned to a discussion focused on agriculture and rural development. A state bureaucrat, brandishing a Ministry of Agriculture vest, introduced himself. He explained that he had been recently contracted to carry out a new agricultural project in the region. "I have a very exciting offer for you today," he began with nervous enthusiasm. "We have established a new alliance to develop ñame projects in the region." Audible sighs of frustration and anger swept across the room as the official continued to lay out the terms and conditions of the project, clearly unaware of the significance that the piles of ñame that surrounded him held.

"Here, we do not need more ñame," a campesino leader interrupted. "Here," he gestured toward the piles of ñame that framed the meeting space, "we are eating ñame with ñame. Some of us have even left our ñame to rot in the ground because the market value does not even cover the cost of harvest."

Other leaders joined the conversation. One by one, they retraced the events that had led to the current ñame crisis, dating back to the state's initial ñame project, which purportedly served to repair the loss of the avocado. They detailed each of the negotiations that had taken place with various state institutions over the last several months, ending with the failed partnership with Market Foods. The consultant, clearly unaware of the ñame crisis and the negotiations that had taken place between his own institution and leaders from the Peaceful Process over the last three months, struggled to formulate a response. He feebly remarked that he would make a note about their concerns for his supervisor at the regional office. A wave of disgruntled sighs and side comments once again spread through the meeting space.

"It is clear there is no intention here," one of the leaders remarked. "I think it is time that we consider ending this reparations process." Others nodded in agreement.

"We have had meeting after meeting and what have we gained?" Elmer Arrieta, a youth organizer added. "The only thing we have learned throughout this process is that the state just wants to *mostrarse* [showcase itself]. They take our *firmas* [signatures] and leave."

As more leaders began to express their genuine intentions to end the reparations process, the main facilitator from the Victim's Unit intervened in an attempt to ameliorate the situation. After a heated conversation, the leaders agreed to another dialogue under one condition: The Peaceful Process would set the agenda and facilitate the meeting.

In the weeks that followed, social leaders from the Montes de María Regional Space for Peacebuilding (translated and shortened to Espacio Regional) coalition decided to take action to address the ñame crisis into their own hands. With the support of a number of journalists who participated in the coalition as "allies," they created a YouTube video to make a final plea for Colombians across the country to buy 100,000 sacks of ñame before the harvest went bad. The video, picked up and recirculated by the popular journalist Daniel Samper Ospina, went viral.[2] People across the country began calling for local and state responses to the "ñame challenge" under the hashtag #elretodelñame / #yamchallenge. The playful theatrics of the YouTube video combined with the Espacio Regional's sustained advocacy led to a successful "yam-a-thon" that promoted direct trade between ñame farmers and local buyers. Over 60,000 sacks of ñame sold in less than one week.

The national spotlight, now firmly focused on Montes de María, also forced the Ministry of Agriculture to provide a public response to the situation. On September 12, 2017, in an interview with the national radio station RCN, then Minister of Agriculture Aurelio Iragorri said that the state had attempted to support campesino ñame farmers through an alliance that guaranteed the "exportation of the product in order to decongest the quantity of ñame in the country" (RCN Radio 2017). He explained, however, that the ñame that "the campesinos included for export were rotten." The crisis, he concluded, had not emerged as a result of flawed state projects, but instead reflected the "informality of the rural sector" (RCN Radio 2017). The minister made no mention of the early warnings that campesino leaders had issued to public authorities at the end of April, nor did he situate the overproduction of ñame within the context of the agricultural projects that the state had designed as a form of reparations to victims of the armed conflict. Instead, he drew on racist tropes of campesinos as backward and uneducated, placing the blame firmly on the "informality of the rural sector." The Minister of Agriculture's public declaration not only circulated false information but also further humiliated campesinos dedicated to guaranteeing the survival of their communities. Months of endless negotiations between campesino leaders and the state in search of a concrete response to the ñame crisis had revealed the state's profound lack of political will to invest in campesino lives and livelihoods. The viral circulation of the YouTube video and the overwhelming response to the "yam-a-thon" offered a hopeful contrast by demonstrating the social will of people across Colombia to support campesino communities and economies.

Since 2013, the Peaceful Process has engaged in meeting after meeting with the Victim's Unit focused on their collective reparations plan. Yet few material measures beyond symbolic or token gestures have been implemented. On October 19, 2020, seven years after the Peaceful March of 2013 that led to the collective reparations plan with the state, movement leaders once again took their demands to the street. In a press release distributed prior to the march, the Peaceful Process cited the stalled land formalization processes, economic hardships incurred as a result of state projects that had once again resulted in an overproduction of ñame in 2020, and targeted death threats against social leaders in the region as the primary drivers for the march. In the midst of the global coronavirus pandemic and in the face of heightened political violence in the region, campesino leaders turned to organized, non-violent mobilization in order to make their claims to reparative justice visible. The state's promise of "dignified return," they declared in a public statement, continues to remain only "on paper" (*de papel*).

Attendance sheets, meeting minutes, reports, speeches, vests, and monitoring committee meetings shape the *institucionalidad* in Colombia, defining "what the state is and what it does" (Gupta 2012, 153). In her research on the production of "bureaucracies of victimhood," Roxani Krystalli (2020) directs ethnographic attention to attendance sheets as "a site of politics and an instrument of power." Following the attendance sheets from meetings with victims to the offices where bureaucrats carefully transcribe the pieces of paper into an elaborate system of verification, Krystalli details how public officials understand and use attendance sheets not only to verify "victim participation" in transitional justice processes but also to certify the fulfillment (*cumplimiento*) of the state's role and mandate.[3] Within this logic, meetings (*mesas*) are not a means to an end, but the substance of state action, carefully recorded and performed through the theatrics of peace. These bureaucratic practices reflect what Valentina Pellegrino (2022) has called "*incumplir cumpliendo* [complying incompliantly]," whereby the state generates a facade of action while "obfuscating the state's failure to achieve any of the intended changes" (4). As social leaders illuminate, *incumplir cumpliendo* also operates with distinct temporalities.

"What we have realized in all of these processes of monitoring meetings is that there is a strategy that the state uses in order to avoid *cumplimiento* [compliance]," William Jaraba Pérez said as he sat across from me in a handmade wooden chair and reflected on the collective reparations process in the Alta

Montaña, "and it is this: they [the state] change the positions of public bureaucrats in order to *delay the processes* [of implementation]. Every six months,
new people come in and we have to repeat the exercises we have been doing
over and over again" (emphasis mine). Dressed in a button-down shirt, khaki
pants, and black, leather tennis shoes, William exuded his role as a beloved
teacher. A breeze passed through the open-air living room of his *bahareque*
and palm-thatched home, located in the heart of the Alta Montaña.[4] Chickens, puppies, and children meandered in and out of the room as we talked for
several hours about the history of the campesino struggle for peace in the Alta
Montaña. Admired for his ability to listen, William's immense understanding
of the history and social dynamics of campesino organizing has garnered him
respect and trust across the region. Taking his time, he carefully detailed the
strategy of delayed implementation, drawing on the example of the avocado:
"This is connected to the avocado and to the ñame—and this is the *most
serious problem* that we have here," he began, placing emphasis on the deeply
problematic patterns that connect the death of the avocado to the ñame crisis,

> Look at the problem of the ñame. We first marched because of the death
> of the avocado and because of that, the ñame projects came. Many people
> planted ñame because the avocado had died and because the state promoted
> these agricultural projects that were supposed to respond to the avocado.
> Here, the avocado was our economy, it was our health, our education, it was
> our autonomy. And today, we are eating ñame with ñame.[5]

In outlining the direct linkages between the state's response to the death
of the avocado and the subsequent ñame crisis, William exposes the dissonant temporalities that structure the feeling of *prisa* (hurry). The state's high
turnover rates and fragmented responses result in endless cycles of meetings
that delay the implementation of reparations. Indeed, the "exciting" ñame
project that the consultant from the Ministry of Agriculture presented to the
Alta Montaña in *the midst of an overproduction of ñame* brings the uneven
temporalities and violent effects of *agencias de viaje* (travel agencies) into
sharp relief. In a context where attendance sheets and meeting minutes have
become the state's primary form of action, campesinos experience implementation as simultaneously "running fast—*corriendo rápido*" and "perpetually
delayed—*dilatado*." As William underscores, the temporal dynamics that

undergird external interventions pose the "most serious problem" that social leaders face in their collective struggle for justice and peace.

The temporal regime of *prisa*, exemplified in the 2017 ñame crisis, reflects the ways in which Miriam Ticktin's theory of "emergency time" (Ticktin 2011, 63) coproduces what Javier Auyero (2012) has called "waiting time." While Ticktin focuses on the harmful consequences of short-term, emergency humanitarian interventions, Auyero argues that "waiting time" naturalizes bureaucratic violence and reinforces state domination through the "constant deferring and the routine raising of false hopes" (148).[6] While the temporalities of "emergency" and "waiting" may seem oppositional, campesino critiques of *prisa* illuminate how they are, in fact, mutually constitutive. The state's helicopter approach to presence, high turnover rates, and the proliferation of fragmented—and changing—agencies result in an endless cycle of emergency meetings that offer a nonresponse in the guise of action, or, what Pellegrino refers to as *"incumplir cumpliendo"* (2017, 2022). The protracted experience of waiting for concrete actions in the face of urgent, community concerns that emerge from the whiplash of repeated and hastily conducted interventions structure the feeling of *prisa*. In other words, *prisa* naturalizes shallow performances of peace as an acceptable form of implementation, enacting harm in the name of repair.

Prisa and oppression share the same etymology: *premere*—to pressure, press down and press against (*presionar*), to tighten and constrict (*apretar*[7]), to oppress (*oprimir*). "Presses are used to mold things or flatten them or reduce them in bulk, sometimes to reduce them by squeezing out the gases or liquids," Sara Ahmed (2017) writes, drawing on the work of Marilyn Frye, to lift out the embodied and affective experience of oppression. "Something pressed is something caught between or among forces and barriers which are so related to each other that jointly they restrain, restrict, or prevent the thing's motion or mobility" (50). For Ahmed, oppression is the experience of feeling "pressed into things, by things, because of who we are recognized as being" (50). Ahmed does not position "force"—that which propels—as oppositional to "barriers"—that which restrains and pushes against—but instead foregrounds the relationship between "forces and barriers" as deeply "related to each other" (50). Campesino discourses of *prisa* further expose the temporal dynamics that undergird Ahmed's account of oppression.

THE INTERNATIONAL POLITICAL ECONOMY OF *PRISA*

At a bustling intersection in the heart of Bogotá, I met Camila, a bureaucrat who had attended various dialogues between the state and the Alta Montaña. Dressed casually in jeans and a worn, black leather coat, she blended in with the crowded streetscape of the *séptima*—the seventh avenue. Camila greeted me warmly with a kiss on the cheek. We passed several vendors selling used books and wool scarves before turning off into a side alley. My glasses fogged over as the door to the warm café closed behind us. After ordering aromatic teas and settling into a private window table overlooking seventh avenue, Camila began recounting her life story. She had committed decades of her life to social justice, living and working in rural areas of Colombia as an activist and, later, as a human rights lawyer. At the height of the war, she accompanied and defended trade union and campesino organizers until a series of death threats forced her to flee to the capital city.

When the Victim's Law passed in 2011, the transformative possibilities that the legislation offered for communities that had endured generations of armed conflict inspired her to advocate for human rights from *within*—rather than outside of—the state. *Activista* (activist), *acompañante* (accompaniment worker), and *funcionaria* (bureaucrat), Camila's *proyecto de vida* (life project) to defend human rights guided her work and life across multiple social, political, and geographic locations. We refilled our *aromáticas* with hot water. The mint leaves and strawberries slowly floated to the top of the stemmed, glass mug as I turned our conversation toward the 2017 ñame crisis.

"This is where you begin to realize that there is no intention here, *no hay ninguna intención*," Camila reflected, with a heavy sadness, echoing a common sentiment I had also encountered among campesino leaders. "To say that it is intentional, however, is different than to say that there is no intention, because in the end I also cannot ignore that the state, for better or worse, is making some effort." She took a sip of the infused tea before continuing, "but the question is, what are they making the effort *for* [*para que*]? Why did the [state's] productive alliance project not contemplate commercialization? You see? And apparently, these projects are not integrated into the state's market policies."

Camila looked out the window, shifting her gaze away from me and toward the crowd of people that whirred past us. We sat in silence for a while, taking in the scene. Finally, Camila spoke once more, the tone of her voice clear and thoughtful: "This is not just a problem of the Colombian state, this is also about the international political economy." She turned her attention back to me as she continued,

> For me, the ñame crisis exemplifies this problem. Here, we have a zone that is absolutely intervened in, accompanied, where the bank has given loans for state projects that are focused on ñame, and then, in the end, when they harvest a large amount [*una cantidad*] of ñame, no one expected it—not the Ministry [of Agriculture], or the state entities, or the bank that gave the loan. [No one] did the analysis to say: 1,000 campesinos in this zone have accessed credits in order to cultivate ñame. . . . How is it possible that the Ministry of Agriculture did not know that the ñame would explode? What strategies did the Ministry of Agriculture have for this kind of crisis? Not a single one. Absolutely nothing. I can't imagine the level of frustration within the communities.

Camila's voice softened to just above a whisper, "As a public bureaucrat, because that is what I am, I feel extremely exhausted and anxious to think about this." She paused, looking down at the recorder, the blinking red light flashing on the table between us, before making eye contact with me once more. "I live from this system. I pay my rent, my children's education, by working for a state that is violating the rights of others. They are exterminating the campesino population, this whole strategy is a lie, the intention is nothing more than speeches [*discursos*]."

Camila exposes how everyday state performances reduce inherently political processes of peace to discrete, technical projects with grave and life-threatening consequences for campesino lives and livelihoods. As she underscores, these practices are not unique to Colombia but instead emerge from within the wider international political economy of peace that drives the state's technocratic approaches to implementation. The use of intermediaries like *operadores* (operators), universal project blueprints, log frames, econometrics, and unquestioned costs of technical assistance have come to dominate international peacebuilding programs (Pugh, Cooper, and Turner 2008).[8] The economic model that undergirds international donor demands enables the state and INGOs to circulate resources internally through inflated technical and logistical budget lines in ways that exacerbate social and structural inequalities (Distler, Stavrevska, and Vogel 2019; Richmond 2011).[9] Short-term project frameworks that privilege technical projects also mask the wider historical, social, and political dynamics that give rise to violent conflict, resulting in cycles of failed—and unending—interventions. Photos, attendance sheets, and speeches confer legitimacy onto programs that claim to have conducted a "participatory" process, even when these interventions repeatedly fail.

Campesinos, in sharp contrast to the state, are constantly held to account, managed, monitored, and evaluated—deemed both untrustworthy and worthy of blame. To participate in the monitoring meetings (*mesas*) detailed throughout this chapter, campesinos lose a day of labor on their farm. The cost of transportation and the time and energy required to walk for hours to attend meetings is high in a context of acute poverty and economic insecurity. However, when campesino leaders request stipends to facilitate their participation, they are admonished for being "dependent" on the state and demeaned as "entitled."

The territorial gaze cast on the campo—which locates the state and international community outside of the politics and histories of violence in places like Montes de María—naturalizes the cost of private vehicles, hotel rooms, and flights as inevitable expenditures for external experts who fly in to the rural territories in order to help campesinos "ground" their dreams for schools, health care centers, and land titles into realizable projects. Yet, when these projects fail—as in the case of the ñame crisis—the burden of responsibility most often falls on the shoulders of campesino communities. For Ferguson (1994), these failures are not neutral but have profound political effects. As the death of the avocado and the subsequent ñame crisis clearly demonstrate, with each failed project, new projects emerge in their wake, further entrenching "the exercise of bureaucratic state power" (Ferguson 1994, 254). The lack of critical reflection on the effects of these failed projects produce an endless cycle of interventions despite small, feasible changes that could improve effective forms of implementation. For example, had the state institutions included campesino expertise in the design and management of the avocado renovation project, which would have incorporated skilled attention to regional and local conditions into the process, the seedlings may have taken root. By naturalizing the theatrics of peace as a legitimate form of state action, however, the temporal regime of *prisa* produces and maintains an uneven landscape of peacebuilding that forecloses possibilities for direct and sustained local participation.

"One of the complaints that I have is that the professional class looks at grassroots organizations like they are incompetent to manage resources."[10] Aroldo Canoles sat across from me in the windowless bodega that Sembrandopaz had converted into a meeting space. The fluorescent light from the exposed bulb that hung overhead flickered in the dimly lit room as evening approached. "For this reason, they rarely include us, because they say that we lack experience with *papelería* (bureaucratic paperwork)." The hum of the fan competed with the jeeps that passed in front of the house as they made their way to collect the late afternoon harvest. A large banner that declared "We Sign The Peace" (*Firmamos La Paz*), etched with the signatures of hundreds of grassroots leaders, brought vivid color to the bare, concrete walls. Over the course of several hours, Aroldo guided our conversation through stories (*cuentos*)—the theoretical scaffolding of campesino social analysis and critique—as he outlined the constraints and possibilities for building territorial peace.

"If the international community would take a closer look at the grassroots organizations, where there has been very little engagement with the actual process, they would see that those who receive the money are largely the technical operators [*operadores*]." Aroldo took a sip of cold water from the small, plastic bag that sat in front of him on the table before illustrating his point:

> There was this project and almost all of the investment came from international donors. They said that 14.000.000.000 pesos [$3,000,000USD] were invested to promote squash, create reservoirs for water access, build collection and storage centers for the harvest, and some other things. It turns out that this got implemented in a way that was, like *corriendo* [running], and in the course of two years, they had five different operators who, in the end, received the money. Nothing arrived to the communities, absolutely nothing.

Aroldo calls for the international community—and donors in particular—to "take a closer look" at the actual, material effects of technocratic peacebuilding. He specifically directs critical attention to the figure of the *operador*—the technical expert who manages the expenditures of individual projects from a distance. Aroldo outlines how the *operador* allows the state to circulate resources internally through inflated technical, logistical, and organizational budget lines. "You see," Aroldo continued, "the first weakness that the peace process in Havana had was the economic model. Here, in Colombia, this is what maintains us in this situation, where the poor will always be poor and the rich will continue to become richer. . . . This system of intermediaries is a totally diabolical model because it is exterminating the people."

Aroldo's clear-sighted analysis lays bare the violent effects of *prisa*. Echoing Camila, he points toward the constant turnover of contracted consultants and "technical operators" who "flood" the region, brandishing their vests in punctuated waves. In particular, he traces how the use of technical experts who operate from a distance coupled with short-term interventions produce an experience of the state as *corriendo* (running) while simultaneously resulting in "absolutely nothing" for the communities they are purportedly serving. Aroldo embeds his analysis of these dissonant temporalities within the international political economy of peace. "Why do international donors not trust grassroots organizations to administer the resources if this is what is happening?" Aroldo asked me, returning once more to his initial response by posing a rhetorical question, "it is the economic model."

Prisa is not unique to Colombia, but instead reflects the prevailing temporal mode for international peacebuilding. As Aroldo vividly details, the neoliberal economic model, which produces what David Harvey (2005) has called a "space-time compression," exacerbates inequalities within the postaccord landscape. In particular, Aroldo critiques the ways in which the theatrics of peace privileges particular forms of expertise and knowledge at the exclusion of others, with detrimental consequences. The routinized intervention practices that Aroldo and Camila outline make holding the state and international community accountable for *incumplimiento* (noncompliance) nearly impossible—even when such interventions are carried out at the expense of campesino life.[11] As the ñame crisis clearly illustrates, with every failed state project, new projects emerge with little reflection on the causes or consequences of failure. As Louisa Lombard has shown, liberal peace interventions that "are conceived of as short-term" produce an "accordion" effect "alternately expanding and contracting, but always necessary" (Lombard 2016, 252). The material and political effects of interventions carried out with *prisa* generate resentment toward the *institucionalidad*, unraveling the fragile processes of trust-building between campesino communities and state institutions.

Campesino critiques of *prisa* not only unmask the temporal dynamics that perpetuate oppressive intervention practices, but also gesture toward alternative possibilities for building a more liberatory peace. "The accords, for us, offer hope," William Jaraba concluded, after detailing the failures of the implementation process. "We are hopeful that they can put pressure so that the government fulfills what it has never fulfilled. Here, there is no justice. Here, there is no equity. Here, what there is, is inequality." While highly critical of the state's approach to implementation, William does not dismiss the accords altogether. Instead, he locates the peace accords as a contested site imbued with possibility.

For social leaders in Montes de María, more emancipatory approaches to peacebuilding require first and foremost a shift in "the times." Reflecting on the violence of emergency interventions, Povinelli (2011) similarly comes to the conclusion that an "otherwise" might not emerge through radical acts of transformation but may instead be found in the daily work of "maintaining a life-world under constant threat of being saturated by the rhythms . . . of another" (130). As I have shown throughout this chapter, social leaders contest and refuse harmful intervention practices within the temporal register of *prisa*. Their critiques reflect an understanding of time as relational, affective, and embodied—central to the work of building territorial peace. As Ricardo often says, "time is justice."

Part III
PAZ SIN PRISA—
SLOW PEACE

Despacio porque hay prisa—Slow down because there is hurry
   —Montemarianx saying

FIGURE 5. The Relevo Generacional (Generational Successors), Ecological Caci-cazgo 2017. Young campesinos stand in between two banners featuring their elders, created as part of the Alta Montaña's historical memory process. Photo by author.

CHAPTER FIVE

THE TIMES OF
SLOW PEACE

"OUR TIMES ARE NOT THE same as theirs," José Macareno Acosta repeated, shaking his head as we walked out of the meeting room where a heated and emotionally charged monthly dialogue facilitated by the Montes de María Regional Space for Peacebuilding (translated and shortened to Espacio Regional) had just concluded. The dialogue had generated frictions after representatives from a private foundation presented a proposal for a rural development project. The content of the proposal addressed widely held concerns throughout the territory, including water shortages, access to clean drinking water and health care, inadequate school facilities, and the lack of agricultural infrastructure. The process, however, generated a sense of shared indignation among social leaders who criticized the shallow "participatory" exercise as a form of instrumentalization aimed at receiving a territorial stamp of approval from the "base" with little substantive input from grassroots representatives in the actual design and management of the project.

As the funding sources for the project became clearer, tension in the room mounted. Namely, the corporate sponsors of the project included companies with ties to land dispossession in Montes de María. Cloaked in the guise of social responsibility, these foundations continued to drive the expansion of the agroindustrial complex in Montes de María through the more palatable discourses of "sustainable development."[1] One by one social leaders expressed

profound concerns about the project's organizational structure, which con-
ferred decision-making power on actors responsible for past violence in the
region at the exclusion of grassroots representatives. Several members recalled visceral and intimate experiences of forced displacement, describing
the weight of the bodies of loved ones they carried on their shoulders as they
fled their homes. Others pointed to wider structural patterns, carefully outlining how the forced displacements of their communities mapped onto the
expansion of agroindustries in the region. The fact that these companies now
sought to form a public-private alliance in the name of rural development
raised deep suspicions.

While tense, the transparent and detailed discussion reflected the *confianza* (trust) that had been built between social leaders and allies (*aliados*)
from the private sector, creating a safe space for a frank assessment of the project. However, the representatives of the private foundation seemed caught
off guard by the negative response and sought to reiterate, once again, how
each of the actionable items in the project responded to shared, territorial
priorities. Attempting to explain the rift that the proposal had exposed, they
juxtaposed their role as technical experts with the wider political work of the
Espacio Regional and underscored the upcoming fiscal deadlines for the project. Any substantive changes, they concluded, might unravel the project—
and with it, access to urgent necessities like water, schools, and roads. As the
dialogue came to an end, José Macareno sought to find the right words that
could explain the clash (*choque*) in vision and approach to peace. Gravity and
exacerbation tinged his voice as he concluded with a final statement: "Our
times are not the same."

In the weeks that followed, grassroots members of the Espacio Regional
held a series of internal dialogues in order to identify a constructive response
to the rural development proposal. They agreed that regardless of the coalition's role, the project would inevitably arrive, raising several, important
questions: Should they continue participating in the construction of a project
in order to mitigate harm, or should they refuse? What hidden agendas drove
corporate sponsorship? How could they accompany the project without becoming co-opted by powerful actors in the region? What alternative structure
could they propose to increase the possibility for more substantive participation in the design and management of the project? The dialogue exposed

the multiple—and competing—theories of change that existed across the grassroots movements in the region. "Sometimes we criticize," a representative from one of the women's movements reflected, "but we do not propose things. We remain silent. If we could develop a serious proposal, it could have an impact." While some agreed, taking a similarly pragmatic stance, others expressed a more profound distrust in the project, reflecting on past experiences with similar interventions in the region: "We have been here before, we cannot let history repeat itself." Tension accompanied the dialogue as people attempted to express themselves across different locations, experiences, and positions.

Over the next two weeks, the coalition met multiple times before eventually coming to a consensus. The Espacio Regional would continue to participate in the project with one caveat: representatives from various grassroots organizations based in the region needed to form a majority of the board of directors. The members also concluded that a smaller dialogue needed to take place with allies from the private sector to situate the project within the wider history of external interventions that had enacted harm (*acción con daño*) against the territory. "The times are not the same [*Los tiempos no son lo mismo*]," José Macareno reiterated: "The objectives of the international community are distinct. They do not think in terms of building a process, but rather focus on market competitiveness. . . . We have to have this clear and begin the dialogue from there. Our times are distinct." In this chapter, I take up Macareno's assertion that any dialogue about peace must begin with critical analysis of "the times." I unpack the layers of meaning embedded within the distinguishing narratives about "the times" that circulate widely across Montes de María. I contend that social leaders theorize time as historically situated and relationally constituted, rather than quantitatively measured. Drawing on the embodied practices, narratives, and social analyses of campesino social leaders, this chapter advances an ethnographic theory of slow peace.

THE TIMES OF SOCIAL LEADERS

Based on their agreed-on action points, a small delegation from the Espacio Regional organized a follow-up dialogue with representatives from the private sector in order to put forward an alternative proposal for the organizational structure of the project. As the representatives entered the room, they immediately expressed their genuine surprise and concern for the negative responses that the project had received. They reiterated that while they remained personally committed to the Espacio Regional, they could not engage in "the political" work of the coalition but only provide "technical support." Ricardo motioned for the representatives to take a seat and waited for the room to become quiet before opening the dialogue. "With any project, we must first locate ourselves [*ubicarnos*]," he began, shifting both the tone and framework of the conversation. "And, in order to know where we are going, we must first understand where we have come from," he tilted his head slightly to one side, a smile forming in his eyes as he focused his attention on the representatives from the foundation. "In this region, there have been many projects that have caused harm. The question is: How do we make sure that what happened doesn't repeat itself?" He paused, allowing time for people to sit with the question. "There is a struggle between the technical and the political," he continued. "The technical is always operating within the limits of certain time frames, and sometimes technocrats [*los técnicos*] become impatient and make decisions in order to meet the deadlines. So, where you really feel the struggle between the technical and the political are in the times. The times are distinct."

The foundation representatives nodded to express their understanding of the tensions between "technical" and "political" approaches to peace. "But," one of the representatives interjected, returning once more to the pending project deadline, "do you really think that people want to wait until there is consensus so that children can have water?" The rhetorical challenge cast doubt on the efficacy of the lengthy deliberations that collective processes demand, including the additional time that this particular dialogue had added to an already tight schedule. The representative's response revealed what Viveiros de Castro (2004) has called an "equivocation," which he defines as "not just a 'failure to understand' but a failure to understand that understandings are necessarily not the same" (11). In response, José Macareno once again attempted to explain what, precisely, they meant by "the times." "*Ancestralmente* (ancestrally), the territory has continually suffered from interventions, and it is marked by this," he began, situating his account of the times within the history of the territory:

The context must be clear. We are talking about the dispossession and recuperation of land, we are talking about the experience of slavery, we are talking about the role that elite landowners have played to always maintain these structures. What you say is lacking—water and schools—emerges from this, from this lack of participation by the people. Interventions have caused much harm, and that is the dialogue that we want to have. The times for us, social leaders, are not the times of the foundations. We must understand this and begin the dialogue from there.

Amilcar Rocha González, seated next to José Macareno, spoke next, adding context to "the times." "Every time we try to claim our most basic rights, we receive death threats," he explained. "The ñame is going bad, the roads are not adequate to transport our harvest to the market, and we do not have sustainable commercialization of our agricultural products." He paused, ensuring that the representatives understood that he shared their concerns for the pressing issues that the development project sought to address. "We lack articulation with the state. What can we do so that the state doesn't see us as terrorists but as citizens? If we can achieve this, we would have guarantees of security," he continued, marking a clear departure from depoliticized technical analyses to make clear the constellations of power that generate the interlocking experiences of political and economic insecurity:

> We have had fifty years of formation that have taught us that the state is the enemy. So, there is this disarticulation and it emerges from abandonment and bureaucracy, and this is *political*. The *institucionalidad* does not want to work within a collective process. We are asking, when they refuse to work with our collective processes, is it because they can't or because they lack political will? The times are distinct.

Amilcar challenges the foundation's framing of "rural development" as solely an issue of "technical" concern, separate from other forms of direct violence against social leaders. Instead, he begins by outlining how a half century of state violence has eroded trust between campesino communities and the *institucionalidad* to lay bare the ways in which water shortages and ñame crises are cut from the same cloth as death threats, arbitrary detentions, and state abandonment. Like many social leaders across Montes de María,

Amilcar invokes the term *institucionalidad* to encompass not only state institutions but also the alliances created between the state, the private sector, and international community. Here, *institucionalidad* is not limited to the fixed entities of state institutions but instead gestures toward the long shadow cast by the institutional structure of interventions that have fundamentally shaped territorial relations in Montes de María.[2] Rather than separate the technical from the political, Amilcar's explication of the times exposes the linkages between mundane, bureaucratic practices and the criminalization of social leaders. Amilcar's admonishment is not abstract. While there is widespread public concern for the alarming increase in the targeted assassinations of Afro-Colombian, Indigenous, and Campesino leaders, the state has taken little, if any, concrete actions to prevent such violence, demonstrating a lack of political will to protect the lives of those engaged in the defense of territorial peace. In making visible the multiple and uneven forms of state presences and absences in the territory, Amilcar calls into question the dominant temporal formations that create the pretext for the state and private sector to refuse collaboration with grassroots processes as an inevitable outcome— rather than a political choice. In doing so, he illuminates the ways in which "the technical" is always shot through with "the political."

Amilcar, José Macareno, and Ricardo's attempts to explicitly address the temporal disjuncture that emerged in response to the proposed rural development project crystallize how social leaders theorize "the times" as a plural, embodied, and historically constituted site of power. The correctives they made to interpretations of time as limited to speed and duration trouble the false binary between the urgency of daily survival and long-term processes of movement-building. In tracing the history of harmful external interventions that have taken place in the region, they challenge the premise that issues of rural development—the lack of water, schools, and health care—emerge from deficiencies that are endemic to the campo, situated as merely technical problems in need of technical solutions.[3] Instead, they contend that the erasure of "the political"—the history of decision-making processes, political economic structures, and relations of power—from technical interventions in Montes de María not only obscures but also perpetuates cycles of harm enacted against the territory. By widening the temporal lens, they historicize the multiple forms of violence that rural communities face in Colombia's postaccord context. Beginning with colonization and enslavement, they trace the long history of interventions that have led to current socioeconomic inequalities and expressions of political violence. Addressing the multiple forms of violence that threaten campesino life, they insist, requires close attention to "the times."

In contrast to "technical times" that flatten and erase the history of political violence, "the times of social leaders" recasts the territorial gaze away from the campo and toward the *institucionalidad*, offering a critical interrogation of approaches to the accords' territorial focus that treat the campo as isolated, bounded, and backward. Instead, social leaders direct analytic attention to the political and temporal dynamics that have generated processes of deterritorialization and reterritorialization in Montes de María, implicating the state, the private sector, and the international community as key participants in the violent interventions that have shaped—and continue to shape—territorial relations. For leaders, the transformation of entrenched forms of social and economic inequality requires close attention to the temporal continuities that buttress political violence across times of war and into so-called times of postconflict (*posconflicto*). In this case, their critical analysis of the times exposed the ways in which the private-public development project *reproduced* structural inequalities and disenfranchisement, which had given rise to violence in the territory for generations.

Temporal contestations also bring the ancestral histories of campesino organizing and *resistencia* into sharp relief. In *Beyond Settler Time*, Mark Rifkin (2017) argues that Indigenous temporalities, tied to "particular territories, to the ongoing histories of their inhabitance in those spaces, and to histories of displacement from them" have the capacity to unsettle dominant temporal formations that undergird continued forms of colonial violence (3). Drawing on Indigenous scholarship and practice, Rifkin interrogates the dominant temporal formation of "settler time," taken as self-evident and universal. "Exploring what constitutes the background for marking and experiencing time," Rifkin contends, "draws attention not only to the . . . context for thinking and feeling time's unfolding but also to the taken-for-granted processes through which temporal dynamics are figured" (12). In contrasting the embodied dispositions of haste that the calendared times of technocratic peacebuilding produce with the deliberative times of social leaders, Ricardo echoes Rifkin, offering a theory of time that is not fundamentally grounded in clocks, but in relations. "Many say that the times of the state are not the times of the community, that the times of the private foundations, the times of the NGOs, and of the agencies are not the times of the community," he began when I asked him to explain the critique of "the times" that circulates among social leaders in Montes de María,

> I think they are talking about the difference between projects and processes. From the community, from here, you focus on the collective process, that process is not easy, it is a long process, it is an integral process, it is a process that is continuous—one that *does not have a measured time*. In contrast, people who come with projects, well, the project operates with specific times that move from points A to B, C and D. So, for me, that is where there is a clash [*choque*] because people who come from outside the region, who come with projects, they are also the ones with resources, and they set the requirements . . . and these projects with these times are different from a community process that does not have that time. (emphasis mine)

Ricardo's incisive analysis of the temporal contestations that shape the field of peacebuilding in Montes de María reflects what Sarah Sharma (2013) has called the "politics of uneven time" (214). Rather than situate the clash as merely the result of competing understandings of time, Ricardo interrogates the ways in which the privileging of certain temporal frameworks, taken as universal and self-evident, produces an unequal landscape of peacebuilding that limits possibilities for just and transformative approaches to peace. For Ricardo, territorial peacebuilding "does not have a measured time," but is, instead, a permanent and open-ended process that is responsive to the relational dynamics found within communities that have resisted and worked to transform violence across multiple generations.

In a follow-up interview, José Macareno Acosta similarly positioned his theory of "the times" against the backdrop of the wider international political economy, which drives the theatrics of peace on a global scale. "Look," he explained, shifting his weight on the plastic chair as he leaned into the recorder, "the international community, which is permeated by economic globalization, cares more about results that demonstrate their assistance through photographs and publicity than about building a process of *resistencia* in the territory." He leaned back in his chair and took a sip of coffee. "For example," he continued, offering a concrete illustration, "The times of BID (InterAmerican Development Bank), which contributes money to the different INGOs, are not the times of the Espacio Regional. The foundations have to respond to the times of BID, which are framed within grant proposals and resource allocations." He paused once more, placing his cup on the tile floor next to his chair, before proceeding,

> But the times of social processes are the following: A social process means building trust and that *confianza* is translated in truly empowering people within the territory and from the territory. A social process means preparing people who have spent their whole lives in the territory, who know the territory, who share it, so that they have the opportunity to continue that labor. *Building a process* transforms the country politically and economically. . . . But if we bring a bunch of people from Bogotá, who are in charge of some BID project through a foundation, those are not the times of the territory. That is why I say, this is not operating with the times of the Espacio Regional because they are not the times of our history, they are not.

José Macareno critiques the temporal order of *prisa*, which objectifies peace as a finite project that limits participation to shallow performances enacted through "photos and publicity." In contrast, "the times of the territory" emerge from the continuous, daily work of tending relations of trust and solidarity as the groundswell for building peace. For José Macareno, peace must begin with "people who know the territory." Trust is built through an immersion into everyday organizing in the campo in ways that also shape how time moves, feels, and becomes embodied. When I asked Ricardo what it would look like if international agencies took seriously the times of social leaders, he elaborated on José Macareno's description:

> External agencies would not create projects limited to three year time frames, but would commit to a minimum of ten years. And they would not require this method of identifying the logframe [*marco lógico*]. We would not have to work within a framework where we ask the community how the project meets the requirements [of the logframe], but rather we would ask, first, how their collective process is going. You see? To work in a way so that the com-

munities can identify, first, how these projects support their processes, so
that the projects are done in such a way that they do not interrupt the process
but rather support a wider, social process.

Quantifiable measurements created for the purpose of monitoring and evaluating peace based on isolated indicators too-often fragment, obscure, and
erase the daily work of territorial peacebuilding as an integrative and relationally grounded process. The times of social leaders offer a stark alternative
to the calendared times of technocratic peacebuilding, where the rhythms of
project deadlines, annual reports, and bureaucratic protocols erode relations
of care and interrupt community processes of social healing and *resistencia*.

Social leaders engage in a "critical understanding of time" as a plural
and embodied site of power that shapes social relations and political action
(Sharma 2013, 315). There is a profound urgency in the call to interrogate
the dominant temporal order of *prisa* that naturalizes the continuation of
violence in Montes de María. Following Sharma (2013), I argue that social
leaders' acute attention to and explicit interrogation of "the times" as a key
locus of power has the potential to "alter and transform some of the most
normative categories and practices of political life, and . . . ethical relations
with others" (314–15). Indeed, I contend that "the times" are at the heart of
the campesino struggle for liberation, raising significant questions for ethnographic inquiry: What everyday practices, relations, and geographies shape
the times of social leaders? And what possibilities for building peace *otherwise*
become visible through close attention to the temporal dynamics that contour grassroots organizing in the campo?

THE TIMES OF THE CAMPO

We flagged down several motos from the main highway that connects Cartagena to the lower region of Montes de María. Naún and I had presented
at a peace studies conference hosted by the University of Cartagena the day
before. We left the city before dawn in order to beat the morning traffic, arriving to the outskirts of Maríalabaja just in time for breakfast at the corner
gas station. Naún gave my moto driver directions as I hopped on the back.
We soon turned off the main highway and onto a small, gravel road, leaving
the buzz of traffic behind us. Endless extensions of palm oil trees, planted in

neat rows, surrounded us as we ventured farther down the dirt road. Kids played in the cool, murky waters of an irrigation stream to our left, built explicitly for the palm oil plantation. The moto eventually crested a steep hill, giving way to a breathtaking view of a reservoir, cradled in the valley of the Alta Montaña.

Naún hopped off the moto, calling out a greeting to the boat driver who waited for us below the steep bank. We scrambled down the rocky hillside to the water's edge. The narrow motorboat swayed back and forth as we stepped in and took our seats. As we made our way across the body of water, and toward the mountains of the Alta Montaña, otherwise imperceptible communities came into view. Naún named each of the communities that we passed, orienting me to the place names, histories, and stories that have shaped his life. "When we were younger," he explained, "we paddled across the reservoir to attend high school every morning." He nodded emphatically, a broad smile extending across his face in response to my uncontained look of surprise. The boat eventually docked at the far edge of the reservoir. I grabbed my backpack; the water bottle and hammock that hung from each side swayed back and forth as I stepped awkwardly out of the rocking boat.

We followed the narrow footpath through a small palm oil plantation that sits at the water's edge, making our way inland toward Naún's home. Over the course of the thirty-minute hike, the landscape changed dramatically. The increasingly dense forest shielded us from the intense sunshine and provided cool, protective shade. The soundscapes of Naún's community enveloped us long before his house came into view: birdsong, the soft sound of the flowing arroyo, the slight rustling of the wind in the canopy, and the distinctive cries of a donkey greeted us. "¡Ay-o!" Naún yelled across the valley as a palm-thatched *bahareque* home came into view. "¡Eee-o!" the neighbor, unseen across the distance, returned Naún's greeting with a *grito* (shout).

The donkey's ears flicked back and forth when we approached the entrance of Naún's home. Hogs, hens, dogs, and cats roamed in and around the patio of the house. Ignacia González Jiménez emerged from the open-air kitchen located on the backside of the house, where a silver cooking pot sat over the small fire. The aromas of fresh coffee wafted from the kitchen, greeting us at the entrance of Naún's home. Ignacia's smaller stature disappeared under her tight, strong hug and exuberant welcome. The same broad smile that I had come to associate with Naún spread across her face as she led me to the living room. She offered me a wooden chair with one arm while effortlessly lifting the backpack off my shoulders and onto the table nearby with the other. Rice hung, drying, from the rafters above our heads.

An older woman—with seemingly unending reserves of energy—Ignacia had single-handedly raised six children, including Naún, throughout the course of the war. Her contagious laugh and joyful spirit belied the violence and loss she had endured throughout her life. She handed me a cup of hot coffee, which she had carefully prepared without sugar just for me, knowing my preference for *tinto amargo* (bitter coffee). "I don't use sugar either," she encouraged, putting me at ease while I sipped the tailor-made brew. "Bitter coffee is healthier, it keeps me strong and active." Her father, she explained, had similarly taken his coffee without sugar. He had lived many years and remained healthy and strong until the day of his death. "The day he died, he harvested avocado in the morning, returned home to fix the chicken pen in the afternoon, and then passed away in the evening." She smiled, adding, "He had the strength of the campo."

Ignacia eventually returned to the kitchen to finish preparing ñame, yucca, and rice for lunch. Naún and I moved from the wooden chairs to the hammocks that hung between two beams at the edge of the patio. "Do you know why they gave me the nickname Salvador (rescuer, savior)"? Naún leaned his head over the brightly woven hammock, craning his neck slightly to make eye contact. A smile tugged at the edges of his mouth. "Salvador?" I asked, encouraging him to continue the story, which I had not heard before. He swung his body around in the hammock to face me and recalled the events surrounding his birth. "The day of my birth, they [the guerrilla[4]] arrived at eight in the morning to assassinate my aunt and my cousin." He leaned forward, balancing his weight in the taut hammock. The guerrilla, he explained, held Ignacia and her sister, Angelina, at gunpoint. I had heard pieces of this story before, told by Angelina, whose experience with the war I detailed in chapter 2, but I had not connected the experience to Naún's birth. Under intense emotional and physical stress, Ignacia unexpectedly went into labor. The surprise of a laboring woman coupled with the onset of a torrential rainstorm led the guerrilla rebels to put down their weapons and join community efforts to reinforce the palm-thatched roof against the high winds, providing protective covering for Ignacia. She gave birth to Naún a few hours later. When the rains subsided, the guerrilla left the community. "And that is why they call me Salvador," a full smile broke out across Naún's face as he relaxed back into the hammock.

The armed conflict pervades Naún's entire childhood. Soon after Naún's birth, the paramilitaries also invaded the community, this time targeting his father as well as his aunt, Angelina. As the primary manager of the motorboats that the community used for transportation, Naún's father had access to the key corridor that connected the mountains to the lower region of Montes de María. The paramilitaries burned all the boats and searched, unsuccessfully, for Naún's father. Repeated near-death experiences with the paramilitaries eventually forced his father to displace to the city. He never returned. Ignacia became the head of the household, remaining resistant along with her children in their beloved community throughout the course of the war. The saliency of Naún's identity as a *constructor de paz* (peacebuilder) is intimately tied to his past experiences with violence and collective *resistencia*. As Naún's birth story makes clear, intergenerational relations of solidarity fashion Naún's sense of self and belonging in the aftermath of war.

With the heat of the midday sun in full force, Naún and I wandered back to the house where we met his brothers for lunch. Heavy white sacks filled with harvested produce hung on both sides of the donkeys who accompanied his brothers as they descended from a nearby hill. They unloaded the day's harvest, greeted me warmly, and then left to bathe in the river behind the house before returning for lunch. "She has the sharpest memory of anyone in this community," Naún said proudly, motioning to Ignacia as we sat down to eat. "People come here to remember. She can recall the exact dates of each community event—like a living book. Ask her anything." A lively conversation of *echando cuentos* (swapping stories) ensued as we posed various questions about the history of the community to Ignacia until the peak of the afternoon heat finally subsided and Naún's brothers returned, once more, to tend to their farms.

The late afternoon sun transformed the neatly swept, dirt patio from a light brown to a burnt orange. Ignacia shooed us away from her kitchen, dispelling us of any notion of helping with the dishes. Instead, we wandered behind the house, where a handful of cows were grazing. As we gently herded the cows into the pen for the evening, Naún explained that Ignacia plays an integral role as a mediator in the community. While she has never had interest in occupying a formal leadership position, Ignacia's daily work to strengthen the social fabric of the community has been crucial for collective well-being. When I asked him to explain what community mediation entails, Naún explained that Ignacia attends fiestas and gatherings to ensure no fights or disputes break out. "There are some people who have returned, who have been reincorporated" he explained, carefully introducing the sensitive subject of community reintegration of former combatants.[5] "She was one of the first to reincorporate them, to welcome them, to make sure they had food, and land to farm. We sometimes watch their kids." Despite direct acts of harm that the former combatants had carried out against the community, Ignacia worked to ensure that they had what they needed to rebuild civilian life. The Community Action Council (abbreviated JAC; Junta Acción Comunal) and key leaders of the community also supported their return, knowing that doing so would reduce the possibility of continued violence and restore the relations of solidarity central to life in the campo. "She has done the same for the Venezuelans," he added, referring to several families that had arrived recently, seeking refuge from the increasingly volatile political and economic situation across the border.

Ignacia exemplifies the often invisible and gendered labor of grassroots organizing found in the *cotidianidad*—everyday life in the campo. As an elder, who holds the wisdom of the community's history, she plays a fundamental role in trust-building, strengthening community relationships, and facilitating processes of social healing. She also explicitly chooses to engage in those practices outside of more visible leadership positions. Peacebuilding, for Ignacia, involves the everyday work of tending relations of care in the campo. Daily house visits lay the groundwork for trust, which is vital for community reintegration. Shared cups of coffee, childcare support, farming opportunities, and forms of economic stability make the collective value of solidarity, which guides the community's governance structure, concrete. Such gestures also solidify the community's expectation that those seeking to reintegrate adhere to the same values.

In the early evening, after Naún and his brothers had stored the day's harvest, cleaned and sharpened their machetes, and unsaddled their mules, we journeyed across the community. We walked deliberately through the land-scape of Naún's home. He pointed out the different trees, watering holes, and historical markers along the way. We crossed a small footbridge and made our way up a steep hill to Angelina's house. She and Geovaldis greeted us warmly. We pulled our chairs to the edge of the veranda overlooking the valley below. "You will never want to leave the clean air of the campo!" Angelina declared with excitement. She brought us each a cold drink and took a seat. The long braid that nestled between her shoulder blades swayed back and forth as she detailed the events that transpired during the community's recent patron saint festival. After an hour, Naún stood, motioning that it was time to move on. The sun reflected off Angelina's red, wire-rimmed glasses. She held my hands in hers for an extended goodbye. "I'm so proud of Naún," she said. "The way he has learned to speak, his love for the campo," she paused, tears welled slightly in her eyes, "it moves me deeply."

We stopped at the house across from Angelina to greet and talk with the neighbors. After introductions, Naún inquired about their families, the *cosecha* (harvest), expectations for rainfall given wider seasonal patterns that had emerged over the last several months, and the health of the soil. Naún's community is one of the few places in the Alta Montaña that has remained largely untouched by the *Phytophthora cinnamomi* fungus—yet the commu-nity has remained alert to the possible spread and presence of the fungus. Eventually, Naún turned the conversation toward the collective reparations process, upcoming integration events and actions organized by JOPPAZ, and reminded everyone about the final focus group conversation for the Alta Montaña's historical memory process. He also provided a brief update on the continued process to become officially recognized by the state as an "ethnic, Afrodescendant community." As he talked about the various collective ac-tions and efforts taking place across the Montaña, Naún seamlessly wove spe-cific stipulations from the peace accords into the conversation, grounding the negotiated text in the everyday life of the campo. He provided ample time for questions and listened carefully to the concerns and suggestions that emerged over the course of the conversation until the room grew quiet, at which point, he stood and extended his hand. "*Nos vemos* (we will see one another)," he said, offering a characteristic, open-ended campesino goodbye before moving on to the next house visit.

After repeating similar conversations in multiple homes, I began to realize that Naún was not merely visiting neighbors, but more importantly fulfilling his role as a social leader—as both the youth representative of JOPPAZ and president of the Community Action Council. He had invited me into the daily work of campesino organizing—or what social leaders more colloquially refer to as *llevándolo a la base*—taking their work to the grassroots. Our walk extended over the course of several hours. Flashlights guided us back to the house, where the flickering light of the fire welcomed us to a *criollo* (organic) meal of fresh rice, chicken, tomatoes, and yucca. With full stomachs, we pulled out our blankets and strung our hammocks between the beams of the house. I rocked my hammock slightly, allowing the mountain air and depth of the evening's darkness—far from the lights of the city—to envelop me in sleep.

Around four in the morning, I heard Naún's brothers once again saddling their burros and mules, clicking their tongues as they climbed the steep hill toward their farmlands, ready for another day of work. At the edge of the house, Ignacia stood feeding the chickens and hogs, calling them each by name. The fire in the kitchen was crackling and I could smell fresh coffee brewing on the pot. When morning light finally broke, I rolled out of my hammock and folded it carefully into my backpack. After consuming a hearty meal of fresh scrambled eggs, boiled yucca, and homemade cheese, we started our journey up and over the peaks of the Alta Montaña and toward the urban center of El Carmen. As we walked through the hillsides of the Montaña, we made brief stops at different communities along the way, passing on handwritten messages (*razones*) about the upcoming meetings, the final focus group conversation for the memory process, and the Peaceful Process's monthly assembly. We arrived in El Carmen several hours later where we met Jocabeth at the Sembrandopaz house. Jocabeth had also left her community early that morning in order to attend the workshop on human rights and the peace accords, scheduled to take place in El Carmen that afternoon.

With a few hours to spare before the meeting, we sat in the open-air kitchen discussing the upcoming workshop. Jocabeth and Naún sat side by side across from me on a worn, black futon. A small fan pulled in fresh air from the large, gated doors that connected the kitchen and living room to the outdoor patio. I took my recorder out and placed it on the white, plastic chair that sat between us. "For the campesino, the city is a prison," Jocabeth began, reflecting on the experience of forced displacement and the accords' promise of dignified return: "Many of our elders who displaced, died in the city—and not from hunger or anything like that—many died because of pure imprisonment. The campesina is used to breathing fresh air, riding her donkey, walking through the countryside, greeting neighbors, and interacting with other people. The displacement was like a kidnapping that killed many of our elders."

Naún nodded, further describing the social unraveling and relational reconfigurations that occur in the wake of forced displacement. "We are not used to the dynamics of the city. The trust, friendship, and love within the family is lost [in the city]. One of the most important things for a campesino is to live with the love of their families and neighbors. In the city, that relationship is lost."

"We notice the difference just by how someone in the city walks and how a campesino walks," Jocabeth interjected, a smile spreading across her face. Naún laughed, nodding emphatically in agreement while Jocabeth continued. "They are two very different styles, ehm," she paused, looking for the right words to explain the difference, "A person in the city is like running, like walking very, very fast. But, in contrast, the campesino walks slowly [*despacio*], to be able to look at the birds, or to notice the color and changes in the soil, to see whether the soil is healthy or not, and to greet one another on the journey," Jocabeth paused again. "You see," she concluded, the tone of her voice once again serious, "these are the things that make a campesino."

For Naún and Jocabeth, time is not grounded in calendars, but in relations. In campesino farming communities, time is shaped by seasons, weather conditions, geography, and social and ecological relations—necessary for the well-being of a community. Although most people have individual plots of land, the campesino economy is sustained through networks of support, trade, and collective care—or, in Naún's words—"through love." Reflecting on the experience of forced displacement from the campo to the city, Naún and Jocabeth underscore how the "dynamics of the city" shape an embodied experience of time as *running*, fleeting, and scarce, depleting the reserves needed for the relational labor central to life in the campo.

Walking slowly (*despacio*), in Jocabeth's account, is not a form of lethargy limited to notions of speed, but rather a way of inhabiting the world. Life in the campo requires a constant wakefulness to the multiple relations that compose the wider ecology of the territory. As Jocabeth explains, the keen ability to notice the color of soil, subtle changes in foliage, and shifts in waterways and sedimentation are vital to the survival and well-being of rural communities. In contrast, the frenetic pace of "running," of "walking very, very fast," forecloses the relationships of love that emerge from the placemaking practices that shape how campesinos are "alive to the world around them" (Basso 1996, 106). Time is not treated as a unit of measurement but rather understood and experienced as an embodied way of living that contours how people relate to one another and their *entorno*. Time moves differently, is felt in the body differently, and organizes social life in distinct ways. The ways people inhabit time inform divergent notions of what counts as "doing," what is measured as "action," and what is disregarded as idleness. Resonant with theories of "crip time" within disability studies, different embodied ways of living challenge Western temporal orders that privilege progress and efficiency over human flourishing and social justice (Taylor 2017, 131).

In stark contrast to Jocabeth, bureaucrats from the city frequently ascribed emptiness to the times of the campo, translating the relational gestures of handshakes at the beginning of a meeting, shared meals and coffee, as well as the daily labor of community organizing, as time "lost"—deemed peripheral (and detrimental) to "the event" of peace, verified through attendance sheets and meeting minutes. With little attention to the relational practices that ground the times of social leaders, bureaucrats failed to see key moments of trust-building and substantive forms of campesino peacebuilding as such—translating significant acts of care into time "wasted" and devoid of meaning. The everyday—and often gendered—labor of grassroots peacebuilding embodied in the daily lives of Ignacia, Naún, and Jocabeth, too often remains invisible to those far removed from rhythms of the campo. "Un-seen," Carolyn Nordstrom (1999) reminds us, "equates to un-exist" (81).

In a context where "relationships are lost"—frayed and untethered by forced displacement and distrust—daily house visits, shared land for farming, and the ability to listen deeply to the collective concerns and needs that emerge within particular communities form an integral part of the struggle for peace. Territorial peacebuilding requires temporal attunement to the everyday rhythms of the campo that give rise to relations of solidarity. In critiquing "the times," social leaders call into question the inevitability of linear and progressive temporalities that render their relational practices of peace a stagnant form of inertia, where circling around is perceived as never moving forward—an experience of time as lost, empty, and stuck.[6]

The careful, attentive, and relationally centered ways that Jocabeth and Naún move through the territory also inform how they orient themselves toward a future horizon. Sara Ahmed (2006) writes that orientations "not only shape how we inhabit space, but how we apprehend this world of shared inhabitance" (3). For Ahmed, orientations reflect wider processes of social belonging—"how we come to feel 'at home'" (7). Imagined futures of dignified life take shape through the repetition of everyday placemaking practices found in the work of campesino organizing and territorial peacebuilding, revealing how orientations are simultaneously "emplaced and emplacing" (Rifkin 2017, 45). Building on Ahmed, Rifkin (2017) contends that the "feeling of where one is going" is also the "substance, feel, and force of time unfolding" (3).

Jocabeth and Naún offer a distinct account of slowness as a form of presence and practice of attention. The material practices of farming with a machete, transporting harvest by donkey, cooking over an open fire, storytelling, and community organizing create what Tim Ingold calls "taskscapes" (2000, 154). The everyday taskscapes of the campo shape how people enter into and experience time as embodied and relational. The deliberate ways people move through place, tending multiple relations of care in the campo are, in the words of Jocabeth, "what make a campesino." Walking slowly, here, is not stagnant or empty, but rather intimately tied to the "making of worlds" (Ahmed 2006, 20).

PAZ SIN PRISA: TOWARD AN ETHNOGRAPHIC THEORY OF SLOW PEACE

During a dialogue between members of the Espacio Regional and key national and international actors charged with the implementation of the peace accords, the issue of time emerged once again. After a long discussion focused on identifying measures where the content of the accords overlapped with the coalition's territorial priorities, Andrea shifted the conversation away from the specific, isolated, and measurable stipulations found in the text. "The real challenge for territorial peace," she asserted "is the clash [*choque*] in the times." Several members of the Espacio Regional nodded fervently in agreement. "Here, we do not work with *prisa* [hurry]," Andrea explained, "And maybe we have not done a lot of things, but what we have done, we have done with *cuidado* [carefulness]. In contrast, the implementation of the government operates with certain time frames, and those times are not our times. They are running with *prisa*."

In juxtaposing *prisa* with *cuidado*, Andrea situates an understanding of "the times" as relationally grounded, rather than quantitatively measured. Here, *prisa* is not limited to notions of speed but also includes the affective valences of carelessness (*sin cuidado*), haste (*premura*), impatience (*impaciencia*), and flippancy—a form of action without reflection (*ligereza*). Andrea invokes *prisa* as an antonym to *cuidado* (care). By embedding the dual meaning of *cuidado* as both an act of "care" and a form of action characterized by "carefulness," Andrea offers a relational understanding of slowness that includes attentiveness, reflexivity, and intention. *Prisa*, in contrast, is a form of erasure (*invisibilización*), action without reflection, and carelessness. In locating the clash between the times as one of the gravest challenges that social leaders face, Andrea positions her call to slowness as an urgent matter of life, vital to the work of territorial peace.

Several recent ethnographies that detail the experience of marginality characteristic of late liberalism provide accounts of a different kind of slowness than the one articulated by social leaders in Montes de María. The listless temporalities of waiting time and bureaucratic inertia (Auyero 2012; Jaramillo 2012), of lethargy and boredom (O'Neill 2017), of exhaustion and enduring (Povinelli 2011), and of environmental violence (Nixon 2011) gesture toward the stagnation and loss that accompany gradual and violent processes of letting die (Foucault 2003, 241). As I sought to understand the multivalent claims that social leaders made in the temporal register of slowness, however, I repeatedly came up against the conceptual limits of slowness circumscribed to the confines of measured time, understood merely in terms of acceleration and deceleration. While Sarah Sharma asserts that becoming "temporally attuned" to oppression requires analysis beyond the registers of "fast" and "slow," I argue that social leaders articulate a more textured and relational understanding of slowness as a way of inhabiting the world and a mode of attention (Sharma 2013, 315). Social leaders advance an understanding of slowness as subjectively experienced and relationally ordered through the everyday practices of living memory, solidarity, and community organizing that exist within the territory. Following Daisy Tam (2008), I contend that building *paz sin prisa*—peace without hurry—engages a "praxis of 'slow'" where the daily labor of caretaking socioecological landscapes marred by violence give "time its quality" (213).

In *A Watched Pot*, Michael Flaherty (1999) argues that social practices, context, and subjectivity shape the feeling of time in motion. "To experience the passage of time," writes Flaherty, "is to make something of one's immediate circumstances" (9). When social leaders, like Andrea, contest the times of the state and the international community, they expose the continuation of violence enacted against campesino ways of life through routinized intervention practices that reinscribe harmful, colonialist relations of power. "At stake in these rural communities' struggles is not the right to idleness," writes Kristina Lyons (2020), reflecting on the work of grassroots soil practitioners in the coca-growing region of the Colombian Amazon,

> But the right to another kind of work, another kind of dream, and a world that does not run only on the inevitable and structurally designed market-based time and velocity. . . . It is necessary to slow down and ask what kinds of questions emerge from an ecologically relational world that not only obliges different strategies for how to keep on enduring in the face of a war machine that proposes peace through poison, but that strives to cultivate different socioecological, economic, and political realities. (135)

The theories, narratives, and embodied practices of peacebuilding that I have traced throughout this chapter fashion an ethnographic theory of slow peace. The times of social leaders challenge the calendared times of the *institucionalidad*, where the rhythms of project deadlines, annual reports, and bureaucratic protocols carried out with *prisa* disrupt and erode relations of love and solidarity. In contrast, slow peace emerges from a wider historical and collective struggle for liberation, rooted in relationality and connection to place. In the aftermath of generations of violence and in the face of continued stigmatization, leaders in Montes de María reconstruct themselves and their territories as ethical subjects, worthy of dignified life through inhabiting a mode of slowness. "There are forms of time," writes Zoe Todd (2019), "that shape the world and refuse its current accretions of hate, violence, violation." By embodying a quality of attention, care, and intention (*cuidado*) for one another and their territory, slowing down allows social leaders to work against the compounding forces of political and environmental violence. The cyclical, indeterminate, and place-based temporalities that shape the practices of slow peace also allow campesinos to build collective power, recentering community agency in an implementation process that is too often dominated by elite interests.

Slow peace recasts the work of peacebuilding as part of a multigenerational, multispecies, and continuous struggle for liberation. Peace, here, is not understood as linear, sequential, or measured, but rather actively and continuously built in the everyday (*cotidianidad*). Becoming "temporally oriented" requires "ways of inhabiting time" that disrupt the temporal workings of power and oppression (Rifkin 2017, 2). Slowness reconfigures the present as a "site charged with multiple durations, pasts, and possible futures" (Koepnick 2014, 4). In rupturing the veil that masks the temporalities of *prisa* as an inevitability, social leaders open possibilities for building liberatory peace "from and for the territory."

Campesino theories of slowness resonate with the surge of "slow" movements that have arisen across the world in response to the "space-time compression" wrought by rapid globalization and neoliberal extractivism (Harvey 1994, 2005). The "partial connections" (Strathern 2005) forged across slow movements amplify the pressing need to interrogate the dominant temporal formations that render bottom-line, cost/benefit, and growth-driven frameworks inevitable—deemed the only possible option for global engagements—at the expense of certain lives and livelihoods (Berg and Seeber 2016; D'Alisa, Demaria, and Kallis 2015; Honoré 2005; Koepnick 2014; Livingston 2019; Parkins and Craig 2006; Petrini 2007; Tasch 2010). The translocal call to slowness illuminates embodied ways of living that work against the global processes and economic structures that produce an experience of time as fleeting, impatient, demanding, and rushed.

Social leaders' call to slowness challenges the temporal dynamics that frame collective processes of deliberation as a form of protracted action. Slow peace does not negate the exigencies of the collective struggle to build peace in the face of death threats, dispossession, and environmental degradation, but, instead, offers a forceful antidote to persistent forms of violence.

"You know, during the times of ANUC, when we were in the process of recuperating land, we would meet together, sometimes 100, 120 people." Seated across from me in the open patio of his house, José gestured animatedly with his hands as he spoke. "I would go to the meetings with my friend, my best friend, who they killed, here, in my town," he took a deep breath and rested his hands on his knees. "He was the last land claimant that they killed here," he explained, his voice softening to a whisper. "We would go on foot toward Bogotá. We would eat what we could find, but we would always go." Shifting his weight in the chair, he paused, before returning to the present struggle. "Today, with all these NGO interventions and with the international community, well these are different times." His voice lingered on the word *tiempos*. "Before," he continued,

> We acted with more solidarity. It was easy to go anywhere, because wherever we went, people would welcome us with yucca and coffee. Today, this is not the same, solidarity has been lost. People no longer dare to challenge or contradict certain ideas out of fear of offending the *institucionalidad*. They take on a position that is wrong just to avoid contradicting the foundations. We are not against the foundations; We are against the *form* in which they are doing things.

As José makes clear, the *form* in which external agencies operate erode the legal orders and relations of solidarity that govern collective campesino life in Montes de María. In privileging the production of paper over the patient and continuous work of tending relations of care, José argues that external interveners lack what John Paul Lederach (2016) calls a "quality of presence" (*calidad de presencia*), necessary for nurturing community well-being in the aftermath of violence.

Temporal formations also contour divergent forms of political participation. Ricardo contends that building a healthy and democratic political culture requires recognition for institutions that operate outside of the "times of the state." Government officials who work within state institutions form what Ricardo calls the "official institutional framework." Charged with policy making and "governability" (enacting laws and policies), "the times" of these institutions are shaped by short-term, electoral, and budgetary cycles that circumscribe possibilities for building transformative peace. For Ricardo, therefore, peacebuilding requires forms of political engagement and governance that move beyond the "official institutional framework." In particular, he points to the promise and strength of "the institutional structure of civil society," which holds the distinctive possibility for engagement in permanent processes of organized political action.

"This institutional structure is not *just* civil society," Ricardo explained during one of the Espacio Regional's monthly dialogues, "but represents an *organized* civil society, a civil society that is *active*, one that is *articulated*." Formed through permanent processes of community organizing that bring together social and community leaders from schools, churches, grassroots organizations, associations, and trade unions, the institutional framework of an organized citizenry has the power of *gobernanza* (governance), distinct from the governability (*gobernabilidad*) of the state. For Ricardo, peacebuilders must be attentive to *both* of these temporal frameworks and learn how to work strategically *within and between* them. This requires an understanding of the law and how "official" institutions (ought to) work as well as deep engagement with local, municipal, and national electoral politics. Understood as an inherently political process, peacebuilding includes the creation of grassroots civic forums and broad-based coalitions that can hold elected officials accountable to shared, territorial priorities. Slowing down works against the rushing currents of the political context through continuous and collective organizing. By doing so, slow peace opens possibilities for the transformation of entrenched structural inequalities while simultaneously remaining responsive to emergent threats of political and environmental violence.

Campesino theories of time offer insight into the temporalities that structure multiple and compounding forms of violence—as well as the temporalities that undergird the practice of freedom. Slow peace reconfigures peacebuilding to foreground care and attention, movement and placemaking, memory and urgency, abundance and pleasure against the backdrop of logframes and project timelines, dispossession and uprootedness, amnesia and inertia, abandonment and loss. "We have to unlearn hurrying," admonishes Robin Wall Kimmerer (2013), reflecting on possibilities for creating more sustainable ways of living, "this is all about slowness" (233). Understood as a set of embodied and relational practices, slowing down forms a vital part of the regenerative struggle to build peace "from and for the territory" in Montes de María. Slowness fashions an expansive present where ancestral memories and future horizons meet, giving rise to campesino resurgence.

CHAPTER SIX

VOICE AND VOTES
Building Territorial Peace

THE MONTES DE MARÍA REGIONAL
SPACE FOR PEACEBUILDING

Nearly thirty social leaders and a dozen allies (*aliados*) from various state, academic, nongovernmental institutions and private foundations sat in a circle under a shade tree in the back patio of the Sembrandopaz house. Members of the Montes de María Regional Space for Peacebuilding (shortened and translated to Espacio Regional) continued to arrive throughout the morning from different municipalities. As people entered, they took time to go around the circle, shaking hands and greeting one another. Ricardo invited everyone to hold a moment of silence, opening the space of dialogue. A rooster crowed in the background as the circle grew quiet.

"I am reminded of a story," Ricardo began, breaking the silence after several minutes had passed. "A family built a new room in their house. The walls were smooth and ready for a new color of paint. Everyone agreed that they should paint the room green. But," he paused, building toward the crux of the short story, "there are many shades of green. The eldest daughter preferred a light sea green, but the parents suggested a deep forest green instead. The youngest disagreed with all three, opting for bright, fluorescent green." Ricardo looked down at the black and white *vueltiao* hat in his lap. "You see, the difficult question was not whether they should paint the room green. The difficult part was deciding what shade, out of all these different shades of green, to choose." Silence fell over the room as we reflected on the story. "We are at a key moment," Ricardo continued,

> The peace accords have been signed. On the one hand, the government, under Santos, has agreed to fulfill what the state has never fulfilled. On the other hand, after fifty years of fighting, the FARC has decided that what they have not been able to achieve with arms they will now pursue through peaceful means. . . . They are organizing themselves into a political party and they have begun moving to the transitional zones. But these two groups, the government and the FARC, what they have known for the last fifty years is war and what they have agreed to in Havana is to end the war. But ending the war is not peacebuilding. *Guerreros* [fighters] do not know how to build peace. Peace is built by the people [*pueblo*]. Those of us here, we have spent many years working to build peace in our communities, and we are at a key moment when we can gather all of this wisdom, all of our accumulated knowledge, to support these accords and continue our work for peace. Soon, many people, many organizations will be arriving in their *chalecos* [vests] to the territory. How can we make sure that what we build will continue to come from here? How can we make sure that we will not be swayed by the rushing currents of the political context [*coyuntura*]? And that is why we are here, to strengthen our processes. We must sit together, discuss, have a dialogue about what kind of peace we are building.

The Espacio Regional gathers each month for a sustained dialogue process that aims "to reunite" grassroots movements that were fragmented by the armed conflict. As a movement of movements, the base of the coalition includes representatives from Afrodescendant, Indigenous, Campesino, women's, youth, religious, and LGBTQIA+ social processes dedicated to the work of peacebuilding in Montes de María. The sustained dialogue process exemplifies Anna Tsing's (2005) notion of "friction" as generative of social change through "awkward, unequal, unstable, and creative interconnections across difference" (4). Over the course of my fieldwork, I found that people expressed the greatest satisfaction with dialogues marked by friction, where everyone had a chance to bring their distinct—and often competing—perspectives into conversation. These dialogues rarely, if ever, ended in resolution. Yet,

moments when people could "speak clearly" and honestly across difference reflected a profound shift away from the collective experience of mass violence
that had generated a climate of repressive silence over the course of the war.

The Espacio Regional's commitment to the guiding principle of *intercul-*
turalidad (interculturalism) affords close analysis of the different ways people
have experienced—and continue to experience and resist—violent conflict
in Montes de María. Sustained dialogue, rooted in *interculturalidad*, opens
possibilities for what Veronica Terriquez (2015) calls "intersectional mobilization" where "the recognition and activation of multiply marginalized identities at various levels of collective identity formation" catalyze transformative
approaches to peace (314). Rather than collapse or erase difference, "speaking
clearly" widens social leaders' collective analytic frame, allowing the coalition
to identify, creatively respond to, and transform the multiple and compounding violence enacted against the territory. In a context of social fragmentation
produced by repressive silence and fear, the Espacio Regional's open-ended
commitment to intercultural dialogue is an imaginative act of world-building
(Nordstrom 1995).

In sharp contrast to the theatrics of peace, which relies on distant intermediaries and fleeting interactions to create a facade of neutrality, members
of the Espacio Regional advocate for an understanding of peace as an inherently political process—one that requires sustained proximity. To this end,
the Espacio Regional also facilitates "improbable dialogues," bringing actors
who wield influence in the region together with grassroots social leaders.[1]
As the conveners and facilitators of these spaces of "encounter," the Espacio
Regional's approach to dialogue destabilizes the "victim-perpetrator-expert"
distinction that typically inflects transitional justice mechanisms. Over the
last six years, the Espacio Regional has facilitated dialogues with military
generals, paramilitary commanders, members of the FARC's 35 and 37 Front,
and proprietors of multinational corporations. Coalition-building through
sustained dialogue generates collective agency and social power, evidenced
in the Espacio Regional's ability to organize negotiations, grassroots truth-
telling processes, and improbable dialogues with "unlikely actors" on their
own terms.[2]

In this chapter, I outline how the Espacio Regional's commitment to a
permanent process of sustained dialogue offers a radical departure from the

temporal order of *prisa*.[3] While the theatrics of peace circumscribes participation and perpetuates harm through the practices of *fotos y firmas* (photos and signatures), I argue that the indeterminate temporalities that shape the Espacio Regional's approach to peacebuilding as an active and continuous social process of "learning by doing" ushers forth a vision of political participation rooted in *voz y voto* (voice and votes). For social leaders who have endured the crushing experiences of "being silenced" and rendered invisible as a result of violence and historic disenfranchisement, creating and holding a space for voice and votes is a political act, rooted in the work of grassroots peacebuilding. I draw on oral life histories with members of the Espacio Regional to analyze how collective deliberation, coalition-building, and sustained dialogue offer insight into the praxis of slow peace.

PARTICIPATORY PEACEBUILDING AS *VOZ Y VOTO*

At the beginning of each new year, the Espacio Regional holds a multiday intensive retreat. The retreat offers a focused space where members of the coalition can deliberate and build a collective agenda together. Over several days, members reflect on the areas of convergence—as well as divergence—found across the diverse agendas of each of the social movements they represent. The creation of a shared platform, built through consensus and collective deliberation, works against the push and pull of political trends and the seduction of spectacular single events—or, in Ricardo's words, "the rushing currents of the *coyuntura*." Collective reflection on areas of divergence also illuminates different experiences of violence enacted across the axes of gender, sexuality, ethnicity, race, class, and generation in ways that crystallize the wider aims and territorial priorities of the coalition. Drawing on the Freirean pedagogy of "learning by doing," the Espacio Regional begins each monthly dialogue with collective analysis of the current political context (Freire 1970). Members situate their analyses of social and political issues within the particular contexts and lived experiences of the communities they represent. Iterative processes of social analysis orient collective action in a way that is *responsive* and *anticipatory*, rather than *reactive*, to the urgent crises that emerge in the territory, a central tenet of conflict transformation (Lederach 2003).

While *aliados*—allies—from universities, state institutions, INGOs, and private foundations also participate in the monthly dialogue, they do so in a supporting role that aims to amplify and articulate territorial priorities within the spheres of influence they inhabit. The tensions that have inevitably arisen during the Espacio Regional's sustained dialogue process have led to debates about power and process. In clarifying their role and acknowledging their positions of power and sources of influence, committed *aliados* have contributed to the Espacio Regional's vision and practice of territorial peacebuilding. Concretely, they have provided critical support for media and public communications, developed pedagogies for applying the legalistic and burdensome text of the peace accords to territorial priorities, provided pro bono legal support for incarcerated social leaders, and facilitated simulations in preparation for formal meetings and negotiations with the state. They have also mobilized institutional support and visibility for nonviolent marches and symbolic political actions—a key strategy to ensure collective protection for those at the forefront of organizing nonviolent marches in a context where the state continues to criminalize and violently repress social protest. Over the last decade, the monthly dialogues coupled with concrete expressions of solidarity have cultivated *confianza* (trust) among those dedicated to the Espacio Regional, creating a safe space where difficult conversations and organized political actions can take place. Always partial and never complete, the indeterminacy built into the Espacio Regional's commitment to a permanent process of dialogue has allowed understanding across difference to deepen.

The Espacio Regional offers an alternative to depoliticized approaches to dialogue where a focus on the resolution of interpersonal conflicts can obscure—and, in turn, reinforce—the structural, historical, and material conditions that produce and naturalize inequality. Instead, members of the Espacio Regional embrace Dr. Martin Luther King's (1963) understanding of conflict as generative of nonviolent social change. "Creative tension" for King as well as members of the Espacio Regional forms a necessary mode of engagement, capable of making visible and disrupting subtle instantiations of structural and political violence. In *Letter from Birmingham Jail*, King (1963) exposes the facade of "negative peace" espoused by the moderate, white Christian pastors to whom he is writing. The empty rhetoric of "negative peace," devoid of structural analysis and political transformation, further perpetuates the continuation of injustice. While "negative peace" veils and maintains the status quo, King argues for a commitment to "positive peace" founded on the presence of social justice. Johan Galtung (1969) popularized King's distinction between "positive" and negative "peace" within the field of peace and conflict studies. Galtung asserted that limiting theories of peace to the absence of war ignored the continuation of other forms of violence. Developed alongside his theory of "structural violence," Galtung contends that "positive peace" requires the transformation of systemic injustices that impede the full flourishing of human life.

Peace studies scholars have further illuminated the generative dimensions of "creative tension," arguing that such a focus requires a shift away from conflict resolution and toward conflict transformation (Lederach 2003; Zapata-Cancelado 2020). In particular, peace researchers have highlighted the long-standing practices of nonviolent, civil resistance that grassroots communities in Colombia have engaged in order to prevent violence and create spaces of peace in the midst of armed conflict. Rather than position strategic and ethical approaches to nonviolent direct action in an oppositional binary, this literature reveals how contentious—and defiant—expressions of collective resistance go hand in hand with the creation of alternative and cooperative spaces for collective life amid war (Burnyeat 2018; Hernández Delgado 2012; Hunter-Bowman 2018; Kaplan 2017; Masullo 2015; Rodriguez 2012). Versed in the theory and praxis of nonviolent direct action and positive peace, members of the Espacio Regional similarly situate dialogue as a political practice—one that is central to their struggle for building territorial peace.

"For peace to be *positive*, it needs to be political," Ricardo explained, echoing King and Galtung. "This whole process is political. If it is not political, it is not a process. Now, this does not necessarily mean partisan or electoral, but it has to be political." A steady breeze from the Caribbean rolled over us as we talked late into the evening at an outdoor table in the city of Cartagena. Sembrandopaz had convened a two-day dialogue on reconciliation as part of their work with the Citizen's Commission for Reconciliation and Peace in the Caribbean (shortened to Citizen's Commission)—a coalition that connects grassroots leaders, social movements, educators, and human rights defenders across the northern coast. Following the signing of the peace accords, the Citizen's Commission drew on their extensive engagement in grassroots peacebuilding to facilitate informal dialogues between civil society and members of the FARC in the Zonas Veredales Transitorias de Normalización (Transitory Rural Zones for Normalization). Through an iterative process of dialogue, they established a strong foundation for the difficult work of trust-building. That the FARC had made special travel accommodations to participate alongside representatives of victims' organizations reflected the significant groundwork the Citizen's Commission had been able to lay in a relatively short period of time. Yet, this dialogue process, which took place outside of formal state reincorporation efforts, remained largely invisible to wider national and international audiences. Despite the extensive, relational network and context-based knowledge that the coalition had accumulated over ten years of building peace in the midst of war, their primary donors did not renew their funding, deciding instead to channel resources toward formal implementation efforts. In contrast to the donors' focus on "negative peace," members of the Citizen's Commission did not see the peace accords as the *end* but rather as the *continuation* of their work to build peace. The dialogue in Cartagena provided a space for members of the coalition to reflect on the lessons they had learned over the last decade at a critical juncture in the nation's history—with particular attention focused on how to continue the work they had advanced without guaranteed funding.

"These are structural transformations and that is why peacebuilding requires political action, why communities must learn how to engage in political advocacy, to generate real political participation." Ricardo moved his open palm in small circles as he spoke,

> It is through a political process that transformation takes place. To participate is not just to be informed. Participation is not being told, "we have a project here." No, one must be invited to participate in the idea, to produce the idea, to discuss it, to be included in such a way that they now feel that they have given birth to this. For me, this is what political means.

Resting his hands on the table, he smiled and tilted his head slightly to the side, before concluding, "It is not easy, and I am not telling you that we are completely doing this, but this is the vision, this is how it ought to be."

Ricardo distinguishes between "the political (*lo político*)" work of peacebuilding that aims to transform structural inequality and "*la politiquería*"—partisan performances of action that rarely, if ever, move from vacuous discourses to practice. The linguistic shift that takes place between *la poli-tiquería* and *lo político* mirrors social leaders' critique of instrumental forms of participation reduced to photos and signatures (*fotos y firmas*), which they juxtapose with real participation, rooted in voice and votes (*voz y voto*). Partic-ipatory peacebuilding through "voice and votes" takes seriously the forms of governance that exist outside of state structures, where collective deliberation and community organizing emerge from and connect to the shared values, needs, and desires of the territory. Consistent with Gandhian approaches to active nonviolence, the coalition strives to embody and create spaces for *voz y voto* through the work of everyday peacebuilding (Cortright 2009; Gandhi 1948; Hallward, Masullo, and Mouly 2017; Hallward and Norman 2015).

Like Ricardo, members of the Espacio Regional do not claim to have fully realized their vision for peace. Instead, a prefigurative praxis underpins the Espacio Regional's understanding of peace as a continuous and active social process where imagined futures are brought into being through their present actions. The articulation of prefiguration offered by proponents of what Angela Davis (2005), drawing on W. E. B. Du Bois has called "abo-lition democracy," is most resonant with the Espacio Regional's approach to sustained dialogue (Gossett and Spade 2014; Kaba 2021; McLeod 2019).[4] Indeed, Ricardo's commitment to nonviolent direct action emerged alongside his formation within the Anabaptist theological tradition. His engagement in abolitionist praxis, including conscientious objection to obligatory military conscription, shapes and is shaped by a particular political theology that es-pouses an eschatological framework attuned to the "now of the not yet." This framework refuses the false binary of ethical and strategic nonviolent action to see the two as deeply enmeshed in the practical work of ushering forth the "Kingdom" here on earth. The temporalities of prefiguration, embedded within the political theologies that animate many social leaders' dedication to peace in Montes de María, reflect what Deborah Thomas (2019) has called "prophetic time," which she juxtaposes over and against Western liberal tem-poralities.[5] Drawing on the work of Anthony Bogues, Thomas writes about the long "*prophetic redemptive tradition*" found among Afro-Caribbean lead-ers (89). "Prophetic time," Thomas contends, "validates the expectancy of and faith in a future in a way that creates a sense of an already existing freedom rather than one that is always one or two steps away" (126). For Thomas, "it is this sense of expectancy, this reframing of space, and this epistemological approach that prophetic approaches to temporality generates within Black Atlantic contexts" (126). Rooted in the temporalities of prefigurative praxis, sustained dialogue is not merely a means to peace but the substance of peace unfolding.

RECLAIMING THE WORD

"I have been in the campesino struggle since '71, searching for and generating life," Catalina Pérez Pérez, a member of the Espacio Regional, explained when I asked how she became involved in peacebuilding. "I started very young," she continued, with a bright smile spreading across her face,

> I am one of the women who participated in the 800 land recuperation actions on February 21, 1971. Working with campesina women has been most significant for me, because campesinas have always been relegated, denied education in the campo, and we, the women, have been mistreated. But when women organize themselves, we are also a force. When the Agrarian Reform Institute [INCORA] began issuing land titles, women were not included in the process, so there was this need for us to organize. . . . For us, the land is life and peace because this is our territory. And, in this way, we have been building peace for a very long time.

Like Catalina, members of the Espacio Regional narrate their work for peace as part of the multigenerational campesino struggle for land and life. Although today these organizations may wield different names, have a slightly different composition, and include new areas of engagement, social leaders graft the Espacio Regional coalition into the long history of collective *resistencia* that began before and continued throughout the armed conflict.[6]

Catalina's participation in the ANUC in the early 1970s informs her vision and practice of peacebuilding as a process of "generating life." Catalina does not romanticize the campesino movement but instead focuses on the evolution of campesino social and political organizing. In particular, she notes changes in the patriarchal organizing structures of the early campesino movement as well as local governance systems that denied women participation, education, and legal access to land. Catalina played a pivotal role in organizing the feminist wing of the ANUC. As I discussed in chapter 1, the women's association not only shifted representation within the ANUC but also had a significant impact on public policies that previously deprived women of access to land—and, therefore, life. Catalina and other campesina organizers within the ANUC successfully advocated for a reformulation of land rights that recognized "rural women" as "political subjects," independent of their relationships with men. For Catalina, peacebuilding emerges from the daily practice of caretaking land and territory.

Catalina's early engagements in territorial peacebuilding, however, also posed a threat to local and national elite political structures. "I was removed from my territory, taken out of my country to *destierro* [exile]. I was organizing a campaign when they took me, put me in jail, and accused me of being guerrilla. The police accused me, the army brigade accused me," she paused, transported momentarily through the landscape of her memories. "Well, many things one has suffered in this life," she concluded, shaking her head as her voice grew quiet. "My organization was destroyed by the violence, the social fabric destroyed. I felt like I had nothing. Everyone must belong [*pertenece*] to something." Tears welled in Catalina's eyes, but her voice did not waver. "Today, I am rehabilitating the organization with my fingernails so that I am not left *invisibilizada* [invisible]." She brushed a tear away from her cheek before returning once more to the significance of the Espacio Regional, "I see myself reflected in this space." A smile spread across her face once more. "Despite it all, *amiga*," she asserted, the characteristic exuberance returning to her voice, "I *trust* [*confío*] in peace, I *trust* in the struggle, I *trust* in the social organizations, and I *trust* that it is possible to make a different country."

Incarcerated and exiled, Catalina's experience of state violence typifies the criminalization of campesino organizing that marked the arrival of the armed conflict to Montes de María. Catalina's use of *destierro* (exiled, without land), rather than *exilio*, reveals the ways the state's systematic use of incarceration not only operated as a form of repression but also dispossession. Catalina understands the work of the Espacio Regional as part of a wider, grassroots process to "build a different country"—one that is inextricably bound to cultivating and defending dignified life in the campo. In particular, she ties the practices of "voice and votes" found in the Espacio Regional's monthly dialogues to visibility. *Pertenencia*—or social *belonging*—emerges from regenerating relations of solidarity that disrupt the forces that render campesino

life invisible, and therefore, disposable. Drawing on ethnographic research
in New York City, Symone Johnson (2019) outlines the ways in which Black
healers "make, hold, and guard structures of belonging" as a vital part of their
practice for "healing justice." Catalina echoes Johnson's (2019) theorization of
belonging as a "relational practice of placemaking" that affirms life as well as
a form of "sovereignty, a claim to one's self and the place where that self rests."
The Espacio Regional does not provide "mere context" for social leaders to
reflect on the work of community peacebuilding but is instead a significant
site of collective healing in the wake of violence.

"For me and for many women," Catalina explained, turning our conversation toward the peace accords,

> the most important aspect of this peace process is that we have active par-
> ticipation in the decisions of the peace process, that they are not made from
> above, that it is not between the guerrilla or the government, but that the
> *pueblo* [the people], the women, the youth, the children, the social organi-
> zations, are also included—*that we exist*. . . . But, sometimes I see this peace
> process as something that is very shallow. Why? The only thing that has
> been put in practice is the disarmament of the guerrilla, and disarmament
> is not peacebuilding, disarmament is only one small part of peacebuilding.
> (emphasis mine)

Catalina critiques "negative" approaches to peace, limited only to formal
processes of disarmament. Instead, she advocates for an understanding of
peace as actively and continuously built from the knowledge, lives, and relations that exist in the territory. Without the active participation of *the pueblo*
(the people) in the design, management, and implementation of the accords,
the peace process remains "very shallow"—yet another promise that remains
only on paper. Catalina's articulation of participation stands in stark contrast
to the practices of photos and signatures that entrench the binary between
experts and victims and erase the wisdom found within rural communities.
"The Espacio Regional, for me, it is like a school," Catalina concluded.

> Wisdom, for us, is not only in the schools or universities, but also found in
> traditional knowledge, ancestral knowledge, knowledge born from the terri-
> tory. Wisdom emerges from our cultural roots, where there is much knowl-

edge [*muchos saberes*]. I am an intellectual in my *campo* [field]. Each one [of us] is an intellectual in our field, so they cannot devalue me just because I am a campesina. But, today, people are still afraid to speak. It is necessary that we open our mouths, that we not be afraid. Fear is what they invented, precisely to repress us, to eliminate us, to take our territory away from us, to remove us from our territory, our life, which is the life of the campo.

Participation understood as voice and votes, ruptures the criminalization of campesino knowledge that produced a widespread fear of speaking in rural communities throughout Montes de María. In the face of imminent violence and threats of incarceration, Catalina buried her precious books in the ground before fleeing, entrusting the land to protect, hold, and guard campesino wisdom traditions. By situating the Espacio Regional as a school, Catalina reveals how the continuation of campesino *saberes* (knowledges)—frayed and buried, but *not* eliminated—animate the practices of territorial peacebuilding. Invoking the plural form of knowledge—*saberes*, Catalina also underscores the territory as an intercultural space that holds and generates multiple forms of wisdom. By creating participatory spaces of *voz y voto*, members of the Espacio Regional reclaim stigmatized bodies and territories—and the polyvocal knowledges that emanate from them—as worthy of dignified life.

"I began working in peacebuilding in 2009. As a woman, it has been difficult, because at the time, the campesino movement was 99% men and only 1% women," Yolyz Correa reflected, echoing Catalina's critique of the patriarchal organizing structures that inflected early iterations of the campesino movement. We had just finished eating *sancocho* (stew) after the monthly Espacio Regional dialogue. Buoyed with fresh cups of coffee, we sat together in the back patio of the Sembrandopaz house, where Yolyz recounted her lifelong commitment to the campesino struggle:

> We reinitiated the Mesa Campesina [campesino working group] as a way to reactivate the Asociación Nacional de Usuarios Campesinos [ANUC], which was stigmatized at that time. We could not even talk about the ANUC. . . . I became involved in peacebuilding, mediating between the men and the women, to see what problems we had in common, what proposals we could create together, and to reclaim the use of the word.

Confronted with death threats and stigmatization, finding courage "to reclaim the use of the word" constituted a radical act of social repair and transformation—one that helped cultivate a more plural, grassroots movement in Montes de María. "Even in 2009, we did not dare to speak," Yolyz continued,

> There was still fear in the territory, fear that you might notice still exists today. To be a campesino was synonymous with guerrilla, with insurgency, so when one raised their voice in a public place, in a space like what we have here [referring to the Espacio], to dare to say what was happening in terms of forced displacement and land dispossession, this was met with stigmatization, and they would send you death threats saying "shut up or your children will be orphaned."

Yolyz turned her head toward the guayabana tree at the edge of the patio. We watched the sun dance across the leaves to the rhythm of the afternoon breeze. "No one could speak alone," Yolyz explained, "we had to surround ourselves with other people, other groups, other organizations, and this helped us reclaim the use of the word, where we could sit before the administration and demand that they fulfill their obligations." Yolyz paused, taking a sip of her coffee. "You see," she continued, "before, as a woman, to dare to speak to an administrator *and to do so alone*," her voice trailed off momentarily. "Well," she continued, "A lot of displacements happened because we dared to speak [*nos atrevíamos a hablar*]."

Catalina and Yolyz position the historical significance of *voz y voto* against the backdrop of the dual experiences of social marginalization and state violence that produced a widespread "fear of speaking." Coalition-building and collective action formed part of a wider repertoire of nonviolent protection that campesina women used to reclaim the word in the face of political and gendered violence (CNMH 2011; Lederach 2019). Catalina and Yolyz place particular importance on the plurality of the knowledges born from the gendered and embodied labor of care and *resistencia*.

Here, voice (*voz*)—or reclaiming the word—requires close attention to the multiple vectors of violence that move fluidly across times of war into so-called times of peace. Catalina's and Yolyz's accounts demand more textured analysis of participatory peacebuilding across the axes of gender, generation, race, class, and territory (Dwyer 2010; Theidon 2009; Riaño-Alcalá 2006). They point toward the ways in which the affective comportments of grief, love, and care that people express in their everyday lives illuminate different modalities of voice, including refusal and embodied forms of expression, which constitute fundamental political acts of self and world-creation (Cox 2015; Das 2007; Dwyer 2010; Mahmood 2005; Ross 2003; Simpson 2014; Theidon 2013). Rather than limit *voz y voto* to verbal expression, reclaiming the word emerges from the collective practice of *interculturalidad* as part of a wider "decolonial paradigm" for peacebuilding (Mignolo 2005, 120). Yet, gendered expressions of voice and agency too often remain invisible to national efforts, with dire consequences for grassroots approaches to territorial peacebuilding.

Cynthia Enloe's provocative question, "where are the women?" is not one that merely seeks to identify women's absence, but is, instead, a call to reframe the lens of research and analysis on the lives, actions, and spaces that women inhabit and create (Enloe 1990). Over the course of my research, state, (I)NGO, and private sector actors frequently invoked the tropes of the *machismo/marianismo* binary to describe campesino movements as male-dominated and campesina women as submissive, effectively erasing the multiple modalities of political agency and forms of participation that campesina women engage in their communities. In her work with disenfranchised youth in Medellín, Pilar Riaño-Alcalá (2006) writes against "the bipolar concepts of *machismo*—hypervirility—and *marianismo*—a female archetype of purity and submissiveness" to uncover the ways in which the reductive binary also maps onto gendered notions of violence and peace (143). As Carol Cohn (2010) has effectively shown, gender hierarchically structures social relationships by ascribing power to specific practices and roles in postaccord contexts throughout the world. The meanings "attached to each category are not neutral," writes Cohn, "rather those coded as masculine are consistently valorized over those coded as feminine" (7). Campesina organizers like Yolyz and Catalina subvert depoliticized and devalued caricatures of rural women to locate the home as a significant site of *resistencia* in the context of dispossession. As Cherríe Moraga and Gloria Anzaldúa (1981) assert in their introduction to *This Bridge Called My Back*, "the revolution begins at home (xxvi)." Indeed, in the aftermath of forced displacement, the relations that women forge through their daily labor in the campo forms the backbone of the collective struggle for land, life, and dignified return.

"Territorial peace is when there is no more uncertainty in the territory," Yolyz explained, "so that when I lay down to sleep, I know that I am going to wake up well, because no one will attack me at night or detain me arbitrarily—that I sleep well, that my children can go outside peacefully." In weaving acts of state violence like incarceration seamlessly together with gendered experiences of violence that take place in the home, Yolyz offers a more capacious theory of territorial peace beyond the release of arms. Yolyz and Catalina outline the multiplicity of violence, threat, forms of resistance, and political agency that campesina women experience in the midst and aftermath of war. Their accounts of territorial peacebuilding also demonstrate how the Espacio Regional's approach to sustained dialogue expands possibilities for "intersectional mobilization" by laying bare hidden forms of violence that perpetuate social exclusion and produce differential experiences of violation (Terriquez 2015, 343). With a commitment to "learning by doing" and intercultural dialogue, the Espacio Regional both envisions and cultivates alternative forms of collective living, capable of guarding and sustaining the fragile webs of relations that breathe life into the territory. Situated as an ongoing process of collective action and reflection, the pedagogy of "learning by doing" allows the coalition to refine their strategies for building peace in order to remain responsive to unexpected expressions of violence that emerge within the territory. The Espacio Regional's commitment to a permanent process of community organizing generates collective agency in a context of deep asymmetries, offering insight into the temporal formations of resurgence.

THE TIMES OF REFUSAL AND RESURGENCE

As the implementation of the peace accords unfolded in Montes de María, the Espacio Regional initiated a series of dialogues with the new postconflict agencies in an effort to advocate for and ensure a more participatory process. In one particular dialogue, a state bureaucrat for the Agencia Nacional de Tierras (ANT; National Land Agency) traveled from Bogotá to meet with the Espacio Regional about the specific measures focused on land restitution. While the coalition sought to address the land measures as a *collective*, the bureaucrat's approach to restitution resulted in a fragmented process based on the state's discrete, legal categories of identity. Rather than approach the "territorial focus" and "differential focus" of the accords as coimbricated, the agency parsed these "transversal threads" into separate offices for ethnic, campesino, and gender-based land claims. As a result, the official from the ANT office insisted that he could only address the particular measures for land rights developed for campesinos at the exclusion of Afrodescendant, Indigenous, and gender-based restitution processes. The ANT's structure—and the forms of interaction that proceeded from it—not only threatened to undermine the coalition's collective agenda but also dispossessed Afrodescendant and Indigenous leaders of their identity as campesinos. In particular, the disarticulation within ANT undermined the territorial vision of the Campesino Reserve (*zona reserva campesina*) as an *intercultural* space for cooperative and solidarity economies that necessarily brings together Campesino, Indigenous, Afrodescendant, and women-led movements.

"The state works in a way that fragments social processes," a member of the Espacio Regional reflected as we exited the room following the dialogue. The statement echoes Charles Hale's (2006) critique of neoliberal multiculturalism. As Hale (2006) contends, "proponents of neoliberal governance reshape the terrain of political struggle to their advantage, not by denying indigenous rights, but by the selective recognition of them" (35). While the state offers some forms of recognition, it does so within controlled frameworks that reinforce essentialist stereotypes built on notions of authenticity. Neoliberal multiculturalism works through—rather than transforms—the restrictive binaries of modern/traditional, progressive/backward, and changing/timeless that undergird the persistence of racist and colonialist intervention practices. Recognition framed by and for the state erases *prior*—and *continued*—forms of organizing social and political life in territories across Colombia (Alfred 2005; Coulthard 2014; Dest 2020; Simpson 2014). Drawing on the work of Carlos Duarte (2016) and the Center for Intercultural Studies at the Javeriana University, Kristina Lyons (2020) furthers this critique, noting how "*desencuentros territoriales* [territorial disagreements] are, in part, a consequence of the way multicultural constitutional reforms in 1991 introduced a differential and asymmetric framework of rights and social protections" (143). Rather than address shared forms of "social exclusion and agrarian-based violence" across "heterogenous interethnic territorial configurations," multicultural neoliberalism shores up state power and social control through fragmentation (Lyons 2020, 143).

Against the backdrop of neoliberal multiculturalism, coalition-building through sustained and intercultural dialogue generates collective power, creating the necessary conditions for a "politics of refusal" (Simpson 2014, 12). "Coalitions are key, they are necessary," Ricardo reflected as we curved around the bends in the road that traverse the mountainous landscape of Montes de María on the way to a follow-up dialogue with members of the *base* (grassroots). "Coalitions are also very complicated and never easy." The tensions and questions that remained following the visit with the National Land Agency had prompted a series of internal dialogues for social leaders aimed at reflecting on the deeper divisions the encounter had surfaced. Negotiating a careful balance between the internal work of movement-building and the external work of connecting multiple social movements together—without flattening their distinct political aims—is one of the most difficult challenges for coalitional organizing (Lichterman 1999; Shange 2019).

As we made our way across Montes de María to attend the dialogue, Ricardo explained that years of community organizing had allowed him to identify five key "ingredients" for effective coalition-building. "First, and most importantly," he reflected, "coalitions must allow each movement, each social process to maintain their distinct identities, to allow for difference." To do so, Sembrandopaz prioritizes the daily accompaniment—not of the coalition—but, instead, of each of the social processes that form the base of the coalition. Rather than ask how each of the social processes strengthen the coalition, Sembrandopaz flips that question on its head to ask: How does the coalition care for, strengthen, and contribute to the distinct aims, challenges, and visions that grassroots members hold? The orienting question for coalition-building, in other words, begins with careful and nuanced attention to the particular needs espoused by grassroots social processes—"the *base*." In addition to Sembrandopaz's approach to accompaniment, the Espacio Regional has a facilitating committee that not only provides logistical and organizational support but also attends to the internal dynamics and concerns of each of the social processes. This framework for coalition-building is rooted in a commitment to cultivate a participatory political culture through *voz y voto*—one that recognizes the power that an organized and intercultural citizenry holds for transforming violent conflict.

"Second, for a coalition to function," Ricardo continued, "it must create a space where all of the members can participate and feel heard." For Ricardo, only when coalitions create a space where each of the members feel fully represented can the third ingredient follow: "Coalitions must celebrate small victories. This creates a sense of *confianza* [trust]." Closely connected to the third ingredient, Ricardo also emphasized the need for coalitions to generate public visibility. While this fourth ingredient can lead to the obfuscation of the everyday labor of community organizing—the backbone of large-scale protests—public recognition both affirms and produces a sense of collective agency.[7] "All of these four ingredients," Ricardo concluded, before turning to the final, foundational element of coalition-building, "require a commitment to a *permanent* process of learning by doing [*aprender haciendo*]."

As the late afternoon sun shifted into evening light, casting shadows across the palm-thatched, circular meeting house, Ricardo returned to the conditions that allow coalitions to thrive. By that point, the dialogue had circled around for several hours, giving each individual time to express their concerns and highlight the priorities, agendas, and current actions of their distinct social movements. While at times tense, the open discussion instantiated trust among grassroots members, who offered honest assessments of the different forms of exclusion and disenfranchisement that their communities faced. In doing so, social leaders reiterated a shared concern for one another's struggles and underscored the collective challenges that the state's "sectorialized" approach to implementation posed to their work for territorial peace. As the dialogue came to an end, the group returned to their collectively constructed territorial agenda as a way to frame and guide the next dialogue with the National Land Agency. The Espacio Regional's permanent process of dialogue allowed social leaders to reassert the accords' "territorial" and "differential" foci as interlocking principles.

"If someone yells here and another person yells over there no one will be heard. But, if we all yell at the same time, they will hear us," Ricardo reflected, after everyone had finished speaking. "The only way to continue forward is to unite our forces. But this does not mean that we lose our identities. We must strengthen ourselves from within, but we also must do this in a way that articulates with others." People nodded, punctuating Ricardo's words with "*así es*" (that's right). "This is the invitation, that we join in political action together. We must permanently create and open spaces that allow us to do this—that they *be permanent*, so that we can generate trust, where we can ask difficult questions and dialogue across our differences."

The next month, members of the Espacio Regional gathered once more in El Carmen for another dialogue with representatives from the National Land Agency. A brightly colored burlap banner with "Espacio Regional de Construcción de Paz" painted against the backdrop of the Montemariana range enlivened the meeting space. Rain pounded loudly on the tin roof, drowning out the whirring sound of the fans. As the rain dissipated, Ricardo began the dialogue with a moment of silence. A deep quiet enveloped the meeting space. After a few minutes, Ricardo opened the space for collective deliberation. One by one, social leaders expressed their concerns about the effects that "disarticulated," rather than "integral," approaches to implementation have for grassroots peacebuilding. In concluding remarks, Andrea gathered the concerns expressed across the members of the Espacio Regional into a brief summary, ending with a call to action: "What we have planted here implies a challenge for the National Land Agency," she began,

> Here, we work with an intercultural dynamic, and this must be understood and reflected by the Land Agency. We cannot be sectorialized—this only creates internal conflict. What you see here is not the work of one day, but of many years where we have sat together—Afro, Indigenous, Campesino, Women, and Youth—to look at the issue of the land in an integral way. And that is how we are here today. The Agency, similarly, must work in an integrated manner. In our next meeting, the Agency must attend to us in a way that reflects how we organize ourselves here.

The Espacio Regional's commitment to a permanent process of dialogue created the conditions necessary for the coalition to refuse the state's divisive and fragmented approach to implementation. Instead, members of the Espacio Regional reasserted the primacy of their collective agenda as central for territorial peace, demanding that state agencies shift their practices to reflect the intercultural commitments and organizational structures found within the territory. In doing so, the Espacio Regional shifted the territorial gaze of the accords away from a focus on the campo, to demand, instead, structural changes within the *institucionalidad*.

In *Mohawk Interruptus*, Audra Simpson (2014) distinguishes between resistance—which works within the framework of the state—and "refusal," which interrupts the operations of state power by denying the legitimacy of state-centric policies and practices. Taiaiake Alfred (2005) similarly contends that Indigenous resurgence emerges from a radically different ethics and politics than resistance frameworks that limit collective action "strictly in opposition to the colonizer" (130). Alfred argues that resurgent political praxis "defeats the temptation to stand down, to take what is offered by the state in exchange for being pacified (151)." For Alfred, only through a commitment to an ongoing, "regenerative struggle" can "the preconditions for a peaceful coexistence" emerge (151–52). In this case, the Espacio Regional did not sever their engagement with the state but instead shifted the grounds and conditions on which political negotiation and alliance-building in the name of peace took place. The coalition's space for "real" participation, built through *voz y voto*, did not exclude state actors but rather brought the postconflict agencies into the territorial framework of *interculturalidad*.

"It is easier to build from the vision of the communities than to impose things on the communities," Amilcar Rocha González, a social leader committed to organizing Black community councils across the coast later reflected,

> If the state thinks that imposing things from the cities of *cachacolandia* and
> *paisalandia*[8] on Montes de María is going to build peace, it could be well
> intentioned, but it will not stick in the territory. . . . That is why we are in the
> Espacio, because we have been deepening our shared vision with one another
> to weave together this territorial network. . . . Only in spaces like this one
> can you explain to the foundations the importance of the territory, of the
> environment, to bring them in, so that they can know our culture, to see its
> importance, the importance of what we are doing. And maybe they fall in
> love [with the territory] or this human sensibility awakens in them. That is
> why the Espacio Regional is different, because it comes with the vision that
> we have to contribute to be able to live peacefully in the territory.

Collective processes of "voice and votes" regenerate campesino legal orders built through "love," capable of awakening the "human sensibility" of respect for the wisdom and beauty held within the territory.

"What we want is for the territory be respected, based on what we have built," José Macareno Acosta added, building on Amilcar's reflection,. "This is what it means for me to [build peace] from, with, and for the territory. The end of the armed conflict is to silence the weapons, but that is not peace. . . . Peacebuilding is integral respect for the territory . . . the social, the political, the environmental. Integral respect is respect for nature and respect for human beings. For me, that is peacebuilding." José Macareno flips the state's deficiency script on its head to insist that building peace "from, with, and for" the territory requires "integral respect" for the knowledge that exists in the campo. Notably, he situates the territory as living and animate—a key collaborator in the collective struggle for peace. The regeneration of multispecies relations of mutual care guarantees the full flourishing of the territory, which he understands as socially, politically, and environmentally constituted through solidarity and care.

Taiaiake Alfred (2005) similarly advocates for an understanding of peace grounded in *relations* rather than colonial systems of *order*. "Space must be created—intellectually and socially—for peace," writes Alfred (2005), "There must be a connection made between people, there must be a demonstration of respect, and love must be generated. Then and only then can 'issues' and interests be spoken of sincerely and resolved. This is what a commitment to coexist means (266)." Like Macareno and Rocha, Alfred's theory of peace operates within a framework of relationality, troubling the linear and progressive temporalities that undergird "simplistic notions of peace such as certainty and stability" (Alfred 2005, 27). Relationality embeds indeterminacy and repetition—rather than "certainty and stability"—into the practice of peacebuilding. Right relations do not emerge independently or in isolation but must be actively tended and nurtured. "An egg is delicate and fragile," the late Kenyan peacebuilder Dekha Ibrahim Abdi (as cited in Marshall 2011), who spent her life tending landscapes marred by ethnic, gender, and political violence, liked to say. "But given the right conditions, it gives life. You have to nurture the fragile potential for peace. Negotiations and peace agreements are just the beginning. Like a newly laid egg, we must nurture glimmers of peace and support and sustain them." *Voz y voto* arises from the sense of belonging that comes from genuine respect for the territory, where an immersion into the *cotidianidad* (everyday) illuminates and sustains the glimmers of peace found within the campo.

As social leaders across Montes de María work to organize and create a space for "voice and votes," they reclaim ancestral wisdom and traditional practices of peace in their contemporary struggle. For members of the Espacio Regional, dignified life stems from the roots of ancestral wisdom, buried deep within the regenerative soils of the territory. "If we talk about reuniting and articulating all of the social processes in Montes de María that we have been building for so many years," José Macareno concluded, "if we would be able to bring them all together to one meeting point, all of these things that we have prepared." He held his arms in the air to emphasize the depth and breadth of wisdom accumulated from decades of grassroots peacebuilding: "Well, then we would find ourselves saying to the *institucionalidad*, 'look, here, this is not a place where you all come and do [things]. NGO, you are not the one that brings this here, *because it is already here.*' Here, this is already built, synchronized, enthroned with all of our ancestry."

THE TIMES OF COALITIONS

For members of the Espacio Regional, peace is not understood as an empty signifier defined merely by war's absence, but rather an active, social process—one that must be continuously cultivated and nurtured within the territory. The times of coalitions work against the "rushing currents of the *coyuntura* [context]" that shape and are shaped by electoral calendars, development projects, and emergency interventions. Indeed, members of the Espacio Regional locate the "clash in times" between social leaders and external interveners as one of the gravest challenges they face in their work to build peace. Through a commitment to permanent movement-building, the temporalities that give rise to *voz y voto* also create the conditions necessary for social leaders to refuse the temporal regime of *prisa* as they work to collectively "reclaim the use of the word" in the face of violence. In *The Moral Imagination*, John Paul Lederach (2005) connects voice to a deep sense of purpose and belonging. "Voice," writes Lederach, "is located where breath dies and is born, where what is taken in gives life, where what has served its purpose is released anew.

Voice is located at the source of rhythm, the internal drumming of life itself"
(166). The recursive temporalities embedded within this notion of voice reflect the fragile processes of slow peace that members of the Espacio Regional
have created in the wake of violence.

As the Commission for the Clarification of Truth, Coexistence, and Non-
Repetition (CEV) in Colombia sought to carry out its mandate in the midst
of the global coronavirus pandemic and in the face of new waves of state
violence, CEV director Francisco de Roux similarly reflected on vulnerability
as a site of grounded hope and possibility.[9] "To live with the enormity of vulnerability is to live authentically, in solidarity and interdependence," de Roux
wrote in March 2020, "because only there will we understand that we are all
carried by each other, protected by each other." Peace, embraced as a fragile
and unfolding social process, shifts the sociotemporal lens away from the
times of projects and toward the times of movements.

"What I have found here is a space where I can freely express my thoughts,"
Yolyz reflected. "Where I can build something with other people from other
organizations, where we can rebuild the social fabric of the territory." She
paused, searching for the words to explain the significance of the Espacio
Regional.

> Look, here it is possible to have dialogue, where we can speak about the prob-
> lems, about peacebuilding, about reconciliation, you see? So that when you
> find yourself in the *Espacio,* it's like it is carrying you down the path that you
> always wanted to find, and that is where you're going, right? I like it because
> we don't all think the same, but what does exist, and what there is, is respect.
> Since we have met here, Indigenous, Afrodescendants, Campesinos, women,
> youth, there is respect, despite the fact that maybe some speak in different
> tones. Sometimes we are energized, others are grounded, but we all continue
> waging peace. What is it that allows this respect? That there are people who
> have experience that they carry with them in everyday life, which is not
> only what they are living today, but what they lived before. And there is also
> projection. . . . For example, Naún has a broader projection than I have. . . .
> So, there is also this vision, there is vision, and we must contribute to that.

The multiple perspectives, lived experiences, and forms of expression held
within the Espacio Regional bring memory and projection together through

a regenerative struggle for peace. The multigenerational and indeterminate temporalities of coalition-building and sustained dialogue reflect an understanding of peace as an active and ongoing social process. Indeed, as scholar-activist Angela Davis (2016) reminds us, "Freedom is a constant struggle."

In the aftermath of decades of war and in the face of continued stigmatization, the intermingling of plural voices across difference constitutes a radical act of hope that lies at the heart of the decolonial peace praxis found in Montes de María. "Despite it all," social leaders continue to wage peace, trusting, as Catalina does, that it is "possible to make a different country." By referencing themselves differently from prevailing state-centric narratives, they locate their daily work for peace within a wider, temporal framework that emanates from the wisdom born of the ancestral struggle for liberation. Against the backdrop of forces that seek to render campesino life disposable, the Espacio Regional's approach to participatory peacebuilding through "voice and votes" recenters territorial agency to make visible and valuable that which already exists—the lives, relations, and wisdom—enthroned within the ancestry of the territory. In doing so, social leaders reclaim the accords as the fruit of their decades-long labor, "imperfect" and ripe with possibility (Roux 2018).

"This is not Santos's peace, this is my peace, this is your peace, this is the peace of people in the Alta Montaña and also people who live at the mouth of the river," Yolyz asserted toward the end of our conversation. "Territorial peace is when I believe in myself and in my territory, when I believe that everything is possible," she paused, momentarily. "You see," she proceeded, her voice quiet and intense, "The territory is everything that I have. From here," she placed her hand on her chest before gesturing outward, "*p'lante* (outward). All of the space where I can move. All of this *pedacito* [little piece] is also the territory." She rested her hand on her chest once more before concluding, "The first territory is my body, my position, that is where my territory starts—and it must be respected. Where I respect myself and they respect me, this is territorial peace, where we can live together widely [*convivir ampliamente*]."

CHAPTER SEVEN

VIGÍAS OF HOPE
Slow Peace and the Ethics of Attention

Vigil, *n. 1*

Etymology: < Latin *vigilia*, watch, watchfulness, wakefulness, < *vigil*, awake, alert

1. A devotional watching, *esp* the watch kept on the eve of a festival or holy day.
    b. In the phr. *to keep (a) vigil* or *vigils*.
    c. *pl.* Prayers said or sung at a nocturnal service, *spec.* for the dead.
2. A wake.
3. A place from which watch was kept.
4. A wakefulness.
6. A peaceful demonstration in support of a particular cause, often lasting several days, which is characterized by the absence of speeches or other explicit advocacy of the cause, and frequently by some suggestion of mourning.
    —*Oxford English Dictionary*

VIGILANT ATTENTION: ON SEEING ABUNDANCE IN SPACES OF ABANDONMENT

The coffin took up most of the living room. Flowers, photos, and candles surrounded the open casket as the wake continued throughout the night. People from the Alta Montaña had come down to the urban center despite the muddy roads to keep vigil throughout the night. Friends of the family who lived in El Carmen had offered their home for the wake. I stepped outside with Medasculo to let others enter. The cool evening air that met us at the door contrasted with the intense heat produced by the bodies assembled inside the small, concrete house.

I leaned back in my plastic chair and settled in for an evening of storytelling. Medasculo and I began the ritual of swapping stories (*echando cuentos*) of our friend, still alive in our memories. A skilled community organizer, Amalfy was someone who "knew how to mobilize." With young kids and a lively spirit, her death came as a surprise—an unjustly common experience for people who live in communities where the state has failed to provide access to basic health care. A group of men carried her body out in a hammock—the dirt roads too muddy for motos or jeeps to pass. She fell into a coma and eventually passed away in the hospital. Medasculo situated his grief within the equally potent experience of solidarity. "All of the leaders have been calling, *toda la Montaña* [the whole mountain]." He grew quiet and then added with assurance, "Her legacy will continue."

Our stories meandered throughout the night—as they tend to do during clear, slow evenings in Montes de María. Swapping stories is a favorite pastime when the sun goes down—a form of campesino social analysis that deepens affective relations of *confianza* (trust) and solidarity. We talked about the consequences of the avocado and the current ñame crisis that had led several women from Medasculo's community to displace to the city in search of domestic work. Medasculo reflected on the challenges of negotiating with a state that lacks the political will to support the campesino economy. He also noted the power of collective action and the hope that the "yam-a-thon" had given his community—especially the confirmation that a demand for campesino products exists in cities like Cartagena. In each story, he reflected on Amalfy's leadership throughout the last months of advocacy, negotiation, and protest.

Eventually, Medasculo turned back to his own biography. He entered community leadership at a young age. "Leadership is in my blood," he asserted. When the military and paramilitaries arrived in the region, Medasculo became a target and was forced to flee. Rather than heading to the city he ventured farther into the mountains to farm the land of a relative. "I don't have much. I don't even have my own land" he reflected, "*pero vivo bien, vivo sabroso* [I live well, I live deliciously]. The campo is a blessing. Here, we live with *abundancia* [abundance]."

Medasculo's claim to a blessed and abundant life in the midst of death reflects the decolonial praxis at the heart of the campesino struggle for peace in

Montes de María. Drawing on the discourses of *buen vivir* (good living) and *vivir sabroso* (living deliciously), Medasculo's critical retrieval of the campo as a blessing exemplifies how social leaders understand peace as embedded within their daily practices of territorial caretaking that allow life to flourish in the wake of violence.[1] Medasculo's fierce insistence on life in the face of violence reflects what Butler (2015) has called a "paradoxical condition" that creates "a form of social solidarity both mournful and joyful, a gathering enacted by bodies under duress or in the name of duress, where the gathering itself signifies persistence and resistance" (23). In this chapter, I ask: What is seen—and made possible—when we widen the frame and focus the lens on life and abundance, rather than limit our field of vision to death and social suffering in contexts of war? I argue that the daily and patient struggle to build slow peace derives from—and deepens—an ethics of attention. The Oxford dictionary defines attention as a practice of noticing, which stems from the Latin word *attendere*: to attend, to be present, to go regularly to, to accompany, to wait, to tend.

The practices of slow peace examined in this chapter, including accompaniment, reforestation, river mapping, and living memory shape an acute capacity to notice, affirm, and tend life in the wake of violence. I argue that these practices embody what Christina Sharpe (2016) has called "wake work" (13). As Sharpe notes, the multiple valences of "the wake as a conceptual frame" hold collective mourning together with attention. For Sharpe, "the wake" destabilizes the temporalities of "the past as past" and focuses the frame, instead, on the "still unfolding aftermaths of Atlantic chattel slavery" (2). For social leaders in Montes de María, the collective campesino struggle for territorial liberation that has persisted across multiple generations in the wake of slavery, colonial violence, and armed conflict forms the groundswell for grassroots peacebuilding. I place Ricardo Esquivia's vivid insistence that peacebuilders must become "*vigías* of hope" in conversation with Sharpe's (2016) notion of "the wake" to outline how social leaders cultivate moral dispositions attuned to life amid violence through intergenerational processes of regenerative peacebuilding. Rooted in the Latin word for "vigil," the figure of the *vigía* conjures up and weaves together collective mourning, remembrance, protest, and vigilant wakefulness as contestatory and imaginative acts of grounded hope that usher forth campesino futures. Slowing down disrupts the oppressive temporal regime of *prisa* that threatens to erase territorial histories of *resistencia* and campesino agency. Slowness, as a practice of presence and mode of attention, cultivates moral dispositions attuned to the multiple lives, sources of wisdom, and grounded hope held within the territory.

BECOMING *VIGÍAS*: THE TIMES OF ACCOMPANIMENT AND THE TENSE OF HOPE

"Accompaniment is really hard for me most of the time," reflected Lani Gomez Pickard, a Sembrandopaz *acompañante*, as we walked together to attend a wake for a community member who had been assassinated earlier in the week. The perpetrator's identity and intentions remained opaque, but the incident resurfaced memories of the armed conflict and sparked fears of a return to *aquellos tiempos* [those times].[2] Lani, who was born in North America, had spent the last several years accompanying and living in rural communities across Montes de María. As we neared the concrete home, bright blue paint chipping from the sides, she elaborated on the challenges of accompaniment. "I'm someone who likes to *do* things, so I had to work on that and most of the time I struggled to find the right balance. Being present at wakes, though, that was one space where I have always felt the closest to understanding accompaniment." Lani paused before knocking on the door. Taking a deep breath she added, "I have been to so many wakes."

Sembrandopaz *acompañantes* participate in the daily life of the communities they live alongside. Tasked with listening carefully to and walking alongside the community, rather than executing specific projects, *acompañantes* recast peacebuilding as an ongoing practice of presence and attention. In this way, Sembrandopaz offers an understanding of peacebuilding as dynamic, open-ended, and emergent in daily living—built on a framework of relationality that centers being with rather than doing. The work of accompaniment demands close attention to the experiences and relationships found at the limits of life, affording insight into what Veena Das (2007) has called the "eventfulness of the everyday" (218).

"Rather than empowering people, we must *pontencializarla*," Ricardo reflected when I asked him to describe Sembrandopaz's approach to accompaniment. The term *potencializar* carries multiple meanings that suggest actions that seek to promote, strengthen, build from, reinforce, and support that which already exists. "It is in this *potencialización* that we generate wealth [*riqueza*]. To do this we have to support people to make their dreams possible. That is why our slogan is 'we make possible *proyectos de vida* [life projects].' " Much of the daily—and less visible work—of the *acompañantes* focuses on creating safe spaces for people to share their desires, fears, and hopes in wake of violence. In addition to daily accompaniment, Sembrandopaz works to connect community desires to wider regional, national, and transnational networks.[3] The temporal framework of the life project locates peacebuilding as a permanent process of supporting human *becomings* (*potencialización*).[4]

Ricardo often draws on the metaphor of a bird to explain Sembrandopaz's vision of peace. The two wings of the bird are (1) political culture and (2) an economy of *buen vivir* (good living). The bird also has two feet upon which it stands: (3) ethics and spirituality and (4) art and aesthetics. Taken together, the bird offers a holistic approach to peacebuilding. The Sembrandopaz team gathers every two weeks in the central office in Sincelejo to brainstorm creative ways to respond to the concerns and opportunities that arise from living alongside communities profoundly affected by violence. For the team, peacebuilding requires noticing, nurturing, and growing the *riqueza* (wealth) that already exists in the communities they accompany. "Money [*dinero*] is not wealth [*riqueza*] and if money is not wealth, then the lack of money is also not poverty," Ricardo explained. "Poverty is more than a lack of money. Money might serve to buy things or provide services, but it is not wealth. *La riqueza* is what the community holds, what is found within the community."

The legal name of Sembrandopaz, Sowing Seeds of Peace (*Sembrando Semillas de Paz*), reflects an image that the team uses to gesture toward the wide temporal horizon that shapes their daily work to build peace. To plant the seeds of a mango tree requires the capacity to imagine that from the tiniest of seeds, a great tree will grow. Despite the fact that the sowers never have full control over the elements, they are intimately tied to the seeds' becoming, dedicating their lives to sheltering, watering, and attending to the seeds' growth. Although they themselves may never rest in the full shade of the tree or take a bite of the sweet, juicy mango, they continue to care for the tree, trusting that their great-great-grandchildren one day will. The daily process of growing the tree enables the sowers to notice subtle changes and potential threats that remain invisible to the untrained or distracted eye. In this way, caretaking brings the tree into being within the present. The metaphor of the tree illuminates the prefigurative praxis that animates Sembrandopaz's approach to peacebuilding, which prioritizes ongoing social processes over finite projects.

Sembrandopaz's name is not merely a metaphor but a central part of the organization's work. In 2000, Sembrandopaz purchased a plot of land on the outskirts of Sincelejo. As a result of the armed conflict, Sincelejo underwent rapid population growth, receiving the highest number of forcibly displaced people in Colombia at the height of the war. When Sembrandopaz purchased the land, the farm was completely barren, ravaged by years of war and cattle ranching. Sembrandopaz has since planted over three thousand trees. The Villa Barbara farm sits on a hillside overlooking Montes de María. On a clear day you can glimpse the shimmering light that emanates from the Caribbean Sea.

"I see a world of hunger," Ricardo explained as we meandered through the young forest of fruit, medicinal, and native trees that form Villa Barbara. "With climate change and the destruction of the environment, well it is not here yet, but I see a world of hunger. So, my idea was to plant trees that people can eat from, that give people life. These are all trees that before, in past generations, people cultivated and subsisted on." Ricardo locates tree planting not only as a future-oriented act, but also as a form of regenerative care that draws on the deep wisdom of ancestral memory to enact futures of good living (*buen vivir*). Reflecting on the work of Kenyan Nobel Laureate Wangari Maathai, Nixon (2011) argues that tree planting works against the "high-speed piratical plunder" of extractive violence by embracing "the *longue durée* of patient growth for sustainable collective gain" (133–34). Tree planting is a radical act of hope—one that operates within a "subversive time frame (134)." To plant a tree "is an act of intergenerational optimism," writes Nixon, "a selfless act at once practical and utopian" (133). Like Maathai, Sembrandopaz's commitment to environmental caretaking works to transform "the forces of incremental violence" through the "forces of incremental peace" (Nixon 2011, 136–37).

As we walked slowly along the narrow footpath, Ricardo stopped frequently to recount the stories tied to each of the trees that form a vital part of the young forest. Mango, lime, papaya, guayabana, hibiscus—each with a history, a contribution, and role to play in cultivating an ecology of life. "This is *sacha inchi*—a nut that our Indigenous ancestors used." Ricardo opened one of the star-shaped pods dangling from the branches of a large bush. He rolled the seeds in his hand before offering them to me. "Wherever I go, I collect seeds." He paused and then added, "seeds and stories." Farther down the path, he pointed out one of the taller trees. Moringa, he explained, not only produces "superfood" foliage, but is also known as a hardy tree that can withstand the harsh and arid conditions that increasingly characterize the rural outskirts of Sincelejo, which has experienced severe drought in recent years due to climate change.

"When I look out across this valley," Ricardo reflected, "I know that it is possible for it all to be green again. I can imagine it with trees planted all across those hills over there," he gestured toward the rolling hills before us. "This whole area can once again be planted with fruit trees. We have to re-build what we have destroyed." He paused momentarily, taking in the view. "This," he said, motioning once more to the Montemariana range, "is the promised land." He lowered himself to the ground and gathered dirt into his hand. "All of this," he continued, reaching out an open palm filled with soil, "is sacred land."

With pink hues streaking the evening sky, I gathered my things in preparation for my return to the city. We sat in rocking chairs on the front porch of the small cabin, taking in the view. "You see," Ricardo concluded as we waited for my moto, "the work of the *base*—the grassroots—is to see, feel, and grow the tree held within the seed." He paused, bending down to let his fingers drift over the earth, "to be so close to the ground that you can feel the grass grow." We sat in silence for several minutes in quiet reflection. "We have to find ways to become *vigías*," Ricardo continued, "The *vigías* are the ones who are always watching," he explained, guiding me through the metaphor. "We need to *vigilar*, to watch out for and be able to see where there are little signs of *esperanza*," his voice lingered on the word hope. "As peacebuilders, we must *become* this. We must become *vigías de la esperanza*, *vigías* of hope."

Over the course of my research, Ricardo frequently returned to the vocation of peacebuilders as, first and foremost, *vigías de la esperanza*—the ones who guard hope. *Vigía* does not find easy translation in English but shares an etymology with the Latin word for vigil, carrying the multiple valences of alertness, attention, devotion, mourning, and protest in its meaning. To be a *constructor de paz* (peacebuilder) is to be continuously wakeful to the possibilities and glimpses of hope found in the "weave of life" (Das 2007, 9). The practices of slow peace emanate from an acute capacity to recognize, to attend, and to affirm life amid violence.

In the essay "Arts of Inclusion; or, How to Love a Mushroom," Anna Tsing (2011) places the capacity to notice more-than-human lives as the central starting point for ecological resurgence. "Next time you walk through a forest, look down," Tsing urges, as she guides her readers into the dense world of soil, roots, worms, and fungi, before concluding the opening journey with a final appeal: "Reach down and smell a clot of forest earth: it smells like the underground city of fungi" (5). Tsing positions the underground city of multispecies entanglements over and against agroindustrial plantations founded on practices that "coerce plants to grow without the assistance of other beings." The language of the plantation found in Tsing's essay recalls the violent processes of dispossession and enslavement that gave rise to agribusinesses in places like Montes de María. In contemporary agroindustrial plantations, crops are managed, contained, and controlled with chemical fertilizers, extracted from wider multispecies worlds just as the filaments of the webs that hold the underground city below our feet are torn asunder. For Tsing, these processes of "letting die" emerge from a willful ignorance, a refusal to notice (Foucault 2003, 241). "One of the many extinctions our development projects aim to produce," Tsing (2011) contends, "is the cosmopolitanism of the underground city. And almost no one notices, because so few humans even know of the existence of that city" (6).

Like Tsing, Ricardo insists that learning to notice the wealth and emergent potentialities for peace found in everyday life requires a permanent process of accompaniment-close-to-the-ground. For Ricardo, the work of grassroots peacebuilding requires the cultivation of dispositions attuned to the otherwise imperceptible lives and relations that grow in spaces of abandonment and death. The recursive temporalities embedded in Ricardo's vision of peace resonate with Kristina Lyons's (2020) articulation of the "robust fragility" found in the microbial life that thrives amid decay (40). "I was led to think carefully about the way life slowly grows in the midst of poison," writes Lyons, reflecting on her work with grassroots ecologists in southern

Colombia, "and the temporal dynamics between moments of visibility and frenetic energy and periods of latency and imperceptibility" (40). Following the *conocimiento vivo* (living knowledge) of soil practitioner Heraldo Vallejo, Lyons contends that the processes of "vital decomposition" stand in sharp contrast to "progressivist, future-oriented temporalities" (42). Whether in the foraging of mushrooms, the regeneration of soils marred by poison, or the struggle for peace, the cultivation of an "open yet focused attention" (Tsing 2011, 10) generates modes of action and forms of relating that deepen what I call an *ethics of attention.*

"What one needs is a mathematics of the minimum, of the residue," Ricardo explained when I asked him to further elaborate on the significance of the *vigía.* "As you multiply, it still continues to grow, right?" he asked rhetorically. "We need to have that residue, that residue mathematics, so that wherever we go, we are able to see what is good. We cannot only see what is bad, but we must also look for the good," he paused, waiting for me to finish writing in the notebook that lay open on the table between us. "What our people need are practical things that allow them to see that it is possible, that, *yes*, this can be transformed, that this *can* change. That is why that saying is key: 'if it exists, it's possible.'" I had become accustomed to hearing the peace studies scholar Kenneth Boulding's (1978) self-proclaimed "First Law," outlined in the book *Stable Peace*, repeated across campesino communities in the Alta Montaña. Now Ricardo connected the saying to the work of the *vigía*, weaving territorial wisdom into Boulding's framework for peace. "Where we can see this is what the chicken does with its chicks." Ricardo continued, enlivening the theory with a metaphor. "If the chicken reaches the patio and there is a little garbage, they're still able to find the worm in the middle of that garbage and feed the chicks." A smile formed in his eyes, "We need to be able to do the same here in Montes de María. We need to be able to dig through all of this," he made circular motions with this hands, "to dig out this little piece of goodness, of *esperanza* [hope]." He paused, before concluding, "A people [*un pueblo*] without hope does not function. For there to be dignified life, and I believe it is possible, we need hope and what gives me hope are these small things, which is why I say that it is possible, it's possible . . . maybe I will not see it, but I believe we will achieve it, this is the hope, and we embody it."

Hope—as a conceptual and social category—has recently come under anthropological scrutiny (Crapanzano 2003; Kleist and Jansen 2016; Zigon 2009). While some scholars locate hope as the grounds for collective action (Appadurai 2013; Kirksey 2012; Solnit 2016), others take a more critical stance, arguing that the abstraction of hope to a distant future can result in a permanent deflection of responsibility, contributing not only to "sublime despair" but also "sublime indifference" (Haraway 2016, 4). In the essay "What It Feels Like to Be Free: The Tense of Justice," Naisargi Dave (2018) argues for an ethics found in "a refusal of the future anterior." Dave concludes that the refusal of the future anterior, of what could be, is also, necessarily, a refusal of hope. Instead, Dave writes, justice is felt in "love without future, a kind of fullness of being (a beauty) in every moment" (Dave 2018).

In contrast to Dave, Paulo Freire (1994) locates hope in the present progressive tense, as an ongoing and indeterminate practice. For Freire, hope is concrete, born through the collective struggle for justice. "The essential thing is this," writes Freire, "hope, as an ontological need, demands an anchoring in practice . . . hope needs practice in order to become historical concreteness. That is why there is no hope in sheer hopefulness" (2). Freire warns of the inaction that is born from despair (*desespero*) as well as from the complacency produced through naive hopefulness. While seemingly opposed, Freire argues that both affective registers materialize as a result of hope's absence (2–4). To work against inaction, Freire insists on a pedagogy of hope anchored in practice. Only through an immersion into the everyday struggle for justice does hope "become historical concreteness" (2). Freire's distinction between "hope" and "hopefulness" reflects a shift in the tense of hope—one that permits a reading of Dave's critique of hope as an obstacle to justice alongside Esquivia's insistence on hope as necessary for and generated through the struggle for justice. For all three, "justice, like art, is a practice" (Dave 2018). Or, in the words of abolitionist Mariame Kaba (2018), "hope is a discipline and . . . we have to practice it every single day."

The practices of building *paz sin prisa* reconfigure hope's tense in the "dynamic present" (Freire 1970, 84), where ancestral memories shape what sociologist Ann Mische (2009) has called "futures in action."[5] Peace arises from the patient and daily work of tending territorial relations, where people can feel the tree's becoming. Slowness, as a practice of presence and a way of relating to the world, cultivates a sense of grounded hope in the wake of violence. Like the mushroom foragers at the center of Tsing's research or the hen in search of nourishment in Ricardo's story, building slow peace requires an ability to walk purposefully, with care and intention—taking in and holding together the complex worlds underfoot. This slowness is not defined by protracted action (Auyero 2011; Jaramillo 2012), lethargy, or boredom (O'Neill 2017), but rather by constant vigilance.[6] Slowing down to notice has at its center a profound urgency in the defense of life—one felt in each step taken on the soft underground world.

ECOLOGICAL *VIGÍAS*: INTERGENERATIONAL PRACTICES OF PLACEMAKING

From 2016 to 2017, the Youth Peace Provokers (Jóvenes Provocadores de Paz, abbreviated JOPPAZ) carried out a river-mapping project of the Palenquillo River—the main body of water that runs from the peaks of the Alta Montaña to the Caribbean Sea. The river-mapping process emerged from a wider collaboration between Sembrandopaz and a coalition of youth from Montes de María and formed part of a co-constructed "Holistic Plan for a Dignified Life of Solidarity for the Youth of Montes de María" (Plan Holístico de Vida Digna y Solidaria para la Juventud de Montes de María). The plan espoused three interlocking dimensions: Ethical-social relations; spiritual, aesthetic, and artistic practices; and sustainability[7]—all under the banner of integral reparations that guarantee nonrepetition of violence under the Victim's Law.[8] Within the plan are two underlying claims: First, that youth are key actors in the implementation of the peace accords and, second, that sustainable peace can only emerge through a commitment to nonviolence that situates humans within a wider web of ecological relations. Throughout the retreat, the youth placed intergenerational and environmental practices of caretaking at the center of their claims to peace and dignified life. At the end of the retreat, they decided on a name for themselves: Ecological *Vigías*.

Prior to mapping the waterways of the Palenquillo, the Ecological Vigías and the Sembrandopaz team identified each community that the river passes. For a month, the youth and Sembrandopaz *acompañantes* facilitated conversations in these communities, presented their proposal, asked for feedback, and created a network of community allies. Traditional healers, members of women's committees, and religious leaders joined the youth at different points of the Palenquillo to accompany the mapping process. The *aliados* helped the youth identify native flora and fauna as well as the histories, memories, place names, *décimas* (songs), stories, and legends held within the river. In this way, the youth developed the river-mapping process as an intergenerational exercise of *memoria viva* (living memory).

"My name is Miguel. I am from the Alta Montaña. I am part of the *Jóvenes Provocadores de Paz* and I am one of the Ecological *Vigías*." Miguel stood before a group of older, Afro-Colombian campesino farmers with a small recorder in his hand. The men formed a circle in the middle of the Palenquillo River, bracing their bodies against the river's steady current. "We have been walking this river for the last fifteen days," Miguel continued, "we are seeking your support as allies, those who live here, those who know this area. We ask that you accompany us, that you point out different points of the arroyo, places where there is sedimentation, erosion, where there are swimming holes, that you tell us histories, myths, stories." Miguel turned the recorder to the community's *curandero* (healer): "Where there is water, there is mystery," the elder began, pausing to look out across the body of water. "In the past, they used to say that there was something mysterious in the river, that there was a *bruja* [sorceress] who bathed here, a *mojana* [water spirit].[9] She had a gourd made of gold. I believe that we have the very best river in Colombia." Miguel and the two other youth nodded in agreement. "You see," another elder interjected, leaning in toward the recorder in Miguel's hand, "for us, avocado farmers, this river has always been life."

As we moved slowly through the veins of the Alta Montaña, the Ecological Vigías took careful, handwritten notes, marking place names, stories, poems, and the presence of flora and fauna. Mango, banana, and old-growth trees lined the banks of the river. The rays of the morning sunshine streamed through the gaps in the forest. As we walked, the elders pointed out medicinal plants and identified community landmarks that held the history of the campesino struggle for land. With the support of the allies, the youth also documented the names of large farms that elite landowners continue to occupy today. Every ten meters, they measured the depth of the water and wrote detailed descriptions about the clarity of the water and the strength of the river's current. We noted when the rock beds beneath our feet turned to sand and tracked the integrity of the banks of the river. At one point, we glimpsed the slight rustling of trees in the canopy above: a troop of howler monkeys moved quickly, quietly, high above us. We craned our necks, looking upward into the expansive canopy as we counted each life. The youth rested their hands on each other's shoulders, caring not only for their steps, but for one another, taking in the nearly imperceptible movements of life overhead and underfoot.

The mapping process began from the head of the river, a subterranean source located in a large bat cave that spills over into a deep pool known as "Blue Watering Hole," which community members say never dries up, not even during the worst droughts. No one dares to swim in the endless depths of the pool's water that not only holds the source of the Palenquillo but also living spirits and ancient memories. From Blue Watering Hole, the youth spent several weeks traveling across the most remote—and densely forested—areas of the Alta Montaña toward the lowlands. They marked dramatic changes in the land, river, and lifescape of their territory, deepening their understanding of the intersections between the political, social, and environmental histories that shape everyday life in the campo. When they finished mapping the Palenquillo, the youth returned to their communities to present what they had learned and offer suggestions for how to care for the precious body of water.

In a coauthored essay the youth published titled "To Know Our Territory Is to Build Peace," they explain the significance of the river-mapping process. "To know the river is to know our history, memory, and enchanted places," the essay begins,

> In the first week, when we walked from the head of the river, we passed clear waterfalls, deep swimming holes, and an immense number of plant species. We saw four troops of the *mico titi* [cotton-top tamarin monkey], a species that is emblematic of the Montaña but who, today, is endangered. It gives us pride to know that we still have a pure river, rich in trees, water, and animals. . . . Everything is connected: the river, the trees, the soil, the plants and animals, human life. We need each other to survive. . . . We lived the river through our bodies: we saw it with our eyes, we felt it, we stepped in it, we bathed in its rich pools. We also lived its pain, the contamination, the

erosion, the felling of trees. . . . We know our history, our memory, and we
have a tool that we can use to do consciousness-raising among ourselves—to
insist that we must care for what is ours, that we can no longer think only of
today, but of the future where our children will live. (Vigías Ecológicas 2016)

Through the retrieval of place names, the history of the campesino struggle for territory, and attention to the multiple lives that sustain and are sustained by the Palenquillo, the youth learned to sense the river's joy, pain,
desire, and love with their bodies. As Leanne Betasamosake Simpson (2014)
outlines, embodied movement through places that hold social, political, and
historical meaning facilitate "learning with and from" the land (14). Land
education, Wildcat and colleagues (2014) explain, derives from a framework
of relationality that understands the territory "as a system of social relations
and ethical practices" (ii). The recitation of place names like "Blue Watering
Hole," "Treasure," "Avocado," and "Bat Cave" made present—and alive—the
multiple lives and histories anchored in the land, allowing young people to
deepen their sense of belonging and commitment to the territory. Indeed, the
land-based pedagogies that shaped the river-mapping process facilitated the
creation of what bell hooks (2009) has called a "culture of place," central to
the work of social healing in the wake of dispossession.

In the Alta Montaña, youth are not merely passive recipients of their
elders' knowledge—nor are they located solely in a distant and abstract
future.[10] Instead, they form a vital part of the campesino movement as political actors, working to regenerate the social and ecological relations that
breathe life into their *entorno* (lifeworld).[11] River mapping created a process
of emplacement for young people living in the aftermath of forced displacement. "The land is the real teacher," writes Robin Wall Kimmerer (2013),
"paying attention is a form of reciprocity with the living world" (223). Intergenerational land education positions campesinos as caretakers of the land,
with intimate knowledge born from multiple generations of working with
the land. Indeed, members of JOPPAZ insist that locating oneself (*ubicarse*)
and establishing a *sentido de pertenencia* (sense of belonging) form the foundation of territorial peacebuilding. In Spanish, *ubicarse*, "locating oneself," is
also synonymous with rootedness: to become rooted (*arraigarse*), to remain
and abide (*permanecer*), to meet (*encontrarse*). *Ubicarse* reflects the process of

positioning oneself within the wider accommodations of the world—central to how youth envision and enact dignified return. The physical movement through place, embodied in the work of river mapping, enables youth to make deep claims to territory and self in the midst of violence. In this way, the critical retrieval of ancestral histories embedded within the territory gives rise to campesino futurity.

"In the middle of [the armed conflict] my family displaced. I was born in a *barrio popular* (working-class neighborhood),"[12] Miguel explained as we walked through the shallow stream that led to his *bahareque* home, nestled in the valley of the Alta Montaña. "I grew up with a lot of gangs, a lot of drugs. When one is raised in an environment where there are always gang fights, this is tough. . . . I don't think any of those *pela'os* [kids] that grew up with me there are alive today," he paused as we both reflected on the violent fates that met so many of his young friends from the barrio. "Thank God my parents left with me because if not," he lingered on the thought as his voice grew quiet, "well, who knows where I would be."

Miguel's life history lays bare the uneven forms of violence leveled against campesino youth across the physical locations of rural *veredas* and urban barrios—without collapsing the distinction between the two. The violence that Miguel experienced as a child growing up in an urban barrio destabilizes homogenous accounts of the city as a place of equal opportunity. Instead, he locates the gap (*brecha*) between the campo/city within a wider set of political relations. Critical attention to who can participate in decision-making processes, who is deemed capable of—and permitted to "speak," and who has access to education, employment, and health care exposes the structural inequalities that—although manifest in distinct ways—move across the porous borders that separate rural and urban contexts.

"I was 15 when my parents decided to return to the Montaña," Miguel continued, "this was tragic, it was difficult. I had never lived 100% in the campo and the situation in the city and the countryside are very different." Even after returning to the campo, Miguel struggled to find a *sentido de pertencia* (sense of belonging), an experience he describes as "tragic." The armed conflict not only displaced Miguel and his family from their land but also dispossessed Miguel of his identity as a campesino. "When I was in the city, I was one of the ones who would say: 'Look at those people from the mountains, look at those who live in the *monte*,'" he explained, reflecting on the ways he had internalized the racist tropes leveled against campesinos. "But now I am the one who has returned here, now I am the one that is being *señalado* [stigmatized]."[13]

Although Miguel first experienced the campo as "tragic" and lacking the amenities of the city, his participation in the everyday place-making practices of JOPPAZ and the Peaceful Process transformed his relationship with the campo. "One lives in the territory but doesn't even know it," he explained. For Miguel, "knowing the territory," required more than simply residing in the campo; participation in intergenerational peacebuilding processes, like mapping the Palenquillo, entailed embodied movement across the vast landscape of the Alta Montaña, the critical retrieval of the ancestral histories held within the territory, and sociopolitical formation. "In these youth processes, one realizes how people are living," Miguel explained, "and this opens one's thoughts and gives one ideals—that, *here*," he tapped his finger on the table for emphasis, "this is the path, that *here*, this is one's journey, to help your people. This is what animates me now to continue in the struggle." He paused, looking out across the arroyo. "Before, I wanted to leave for the city. I said, 'well, now I've finished studying, I'm going to get out of this *monte*,' but my thoughts changed when I entered the youth process. I always say that the Montaña has opened its arms and has taken me in, in a beautiful way. I didn't expect it, but thank God, the Montaña has taken me in, in a beautiful way."

The subtle changes in the names that Miguel attaches to the "Montaña" reflect the profound shifts that have taken place in his relationship with the campo. Recalling his life before joining JOPPAZ, Miguel refers to the Alta Montaña as a distant place, reiterating his desire to "get out of *this monte*." The use of the term "*este* (this)" inscribes personal distance and lack of connection, while *monte* further indexes disdain by referring to not only mountainous terrain, but, in local parlance, to weeds and invasive plants. The term "monte" also became synonymous with the war—the bush where people had to hide during armed confrontations. Across Colombia, "monte" indexes violence, the physical location of armed combat.[14]

As Miguel's narrative unfolds, the referents change to reflect the intimate relationship of care he has cultivated with the Montaña as living and sentient. The *Mountain* embraced him, welcomed him in, and gave him a sense of belonging. He sees the Montaña not for what it lacks but for all the life and beauty it has extended to him. As he outlines how processes of "knowing the territory" rekindled his love for the campo, the attachment markers shift from "*this (este) monte*" to "the *Montaña*" to "*my* Montaña."

Miguel's life history challenges the deficiency narratives that frame prevailing discourses of the gap between rural and urban communities, which reinforce imaginaries of the campo as empty, apprehended only through absence. Like Miguel, leaders across Montes de María contest the representation of the territory as an empty and backward place. Yet, these damage-centered (Tuck 2009) imaginaries continue to guide external interventions aimed at closing the gap in the postaccord context. In an essay, JOPPAZ coordinator Jocabeth Canoles critiques the ways in which the state invokes the discourse of the urban/rural gap to justify extractivism in the name of peace and development. "The state measures development in the accumulation of capital," writes Jocabeth,

> which is why the campo is seen as "poor" and less developed. This is an imaginary rooted in modern society. From this standpoint, an imaginary of the gap between the campo and the city also emerges, one that has created a hierarchy where the city governs the countryside, where governability is concentrated in the city. . . . I have experienced the indifference between these two sectors of the population here in my beloved Colombia, where there is a development model that continues to mark differences between sectors rather than transform this reality. . . . The Final Accord guarantees us "educational coverage, quality, and relevance" to promote "the permanence of young men and women in the campo." For this reason, we are fighting for the peace accords to be realized in a concrete way, implemented from the territories. But, to talk about the commitment to close the gap poses a challenge: How does the government understand the gap between these sectors? What does it mean to close the gap? How do we "transform the campo" without losing the essence of the campo? This is a fundamental challenge that I believe must begin in the transformation of our concepts, of how we understand difference. We are also capable of implementing the accords in our communities, carrying out what is written on paper to the real lives of youth in our communities where we share the beauty and abundance of the

campo, our love for the campo, and our great desire for youth to remain in the campo, with the guarantee of dignified life.

As Jocabeth makes clear, transformative peace does not require further development projects that threaten to erase the "essence" of the campo but instead a radical shift in relations of power and forms of governance. The social construction of the territory as an empty space, defined by *absence*, renders external interventions and prescriptive solutions inevitable in ways that undermine the *riqueza* (wealth) found in grassroots communities throughout Montes de María. When Miguel and Jocabeth invoke the "gap," therefore, they do so as a critique of the structural inequalities that continue to naturalize violence against campesinos across urban and rural contexts. In contrast to the language of deficiency, campesino narratives repeatedly reclaim the territory as a space of *vida* (life), *riqueza* (wealth), *bendición* (blessing), and *abundancia* (abundance). These discourses operate within what Eve Tuck (2009) calls a "desire-based framework," capable of lifting out the multiple and complexly textured experiences of life fully lived in the face of oppression.

In a context where repeated cycles of forced displacement have produced fragmented, rather than sedimented, histories and traditions, intergenerational processes of living memory (*memoria viva*) are vital for the construction of a collective horizon.[15] The dialectic between memory and *proyección* (projection) found in the life histories of young people like Miguel reveal how subjectivities are produced within and through intergenerational relations of solidarity. "This identity, this *sentido de pertenencia* [sense of belonging] for our region and for ourselves, we must create." Miguel looked out across the Palenquillo before concluding, "In the beginning, we called ourselves campesinos. But then afterward they called us 'the displaced,' and after that 'the victims' and now they call us 'survivors.' We have not asked to be called any of these three things, neither displaced, nor victims, nor survivors. This is not who we are. We are campesinos. This is what we must struggle for, to reclaim our identity."

KEEPING VIGIL: THE TIMES OF LIVING MEMORY

In the 91 accords that the Alta Montaña signed with the state in 2013, social leaders demanded a process of historical memory as a form of reparations. For nearly a year, they negotiated the terms and conditions for a locally driven memory process, supported by the National Center for Historical Memory (CNMH). Although the researchers who worked with CNMH espoused deep commitments to community-based research, they faced institutional barriers as they sought to implement the participatory measures. In particular, legal protocols required that they hire external administrative operators for the logistics, severely restricting possibilities for participatory research. "The challenge was logistical," Val, a researcher from CNMH explained,

> How to carry out the research in the very places that people were talking about, in their *espacios cotidianos* [everyday spaces] and not in hotels, which make people feel uncomfortable. . . . We have this challenge with the logistical operator, which is a legal entity. The logistics for hotels and food and transportation are made from the outside, by someone who is contracted to make arrangements from afar, who does not know the territory. For an outsider to make calls and convene people who have lived all of their lives in the midst of armed conflict, that is an issue of security, which requires trust.

Far removed from the daily life of the territory, the logistical operators (*operadores*) manage, impose, and orchestrate technical projects from distant offices located in capital cities across Colombia. The use of hotel conference rooms rather than communal spaces, food catered and shipped in from outside the territory rather than *criollo* (traditional) meals, and detached communication practices all reduce the affective and political dimensions of social memory—including the recollection of intimate experiences of war, loss, fear, and violation—to technical matters of logistics. For Val, the legal-administrative logics that shape state practices, embodied in the figure of the logistical operator, posed the greatest barrier to CNMH's ability to support a truly participatory process.

"The challenge we faced," Val reflected, "was how to carry out the process, not through the logic of a logistical operator, but through the logic of the region." In response, Sembrandopaz offered their administrative time.

As a legally recognized organization, Sembrandopaz had the capacity to take on the role of receiving, distributing, and accounting for budgets as an alternative to the logistical operator. Sembrandopaz also successfully advocated for fair compensation for the local researchers who dedicated their expertise and time to carry out the community-based process. "As an organization Sembrandopaz facilitated the logistics, but from within the logics of the community," Val explained,

> They provided a sense of how to carry out the process, through the logic of accompaniment, which is not visible in the way facilitation is, but they oriented us, and we realized that this logic is what permits the creation of the dialogues that they have opened, that maybe they are not the ones directly doing it or facilitating it, but they are the ones who have created the spaces for it. Sembrandopaz sets this tone. The memory process reflects this approach, which does not say "you have to do it like this and this" but asks, instead, "how can we contribute to this, how can we promote this?"

Val positions the logic of accompaniment over and against the logic of the *operador*, highlighting how these fundamentally different ways of relating shape the quality of participation. Val's reflection further exposes the false binary between the political and the technical. The logic of accompaniment informed how Sembrandopaz approached technical decisions in ways that expanded and deepened community participation. Notably, Sembrandopaz also extended their accompaniment to CNMH, orienting them to the logics of the community.

Sembrandopaz's accompaniment model rarely places the *acompañantes* in front, "doing" or "facilitating." Instead, accompaniment is a practice that derives from an ethics of attention—the careful and intentional ability to notice and amplify the desires, knowledge, and social processes that exist in grassroots communities. While accompaniment allows Sembrandopaz to co-construct agendas *within* the logics of the community, this same proximity simultaneously limits the organization's ability to make their work legible to international donors. The paradox of proximity that Sembrandopaz faces raises critical questions about the ways in which funding structures reinforce the extractive practices of *fotos y firmas* in the guise of monitoring and evaluation. The experience also reveals concrete and alternative possibilities for participatory peacebuilding that emerge when organizations recognize the deeply political dimensions of technical decision-making.

The logic of accompaniment also operates with distinct temporalities from that of the logistical operator. "The permanence that Sembrandopaz has in the territory allows them to coexist with this logic," Val explained:

> Larisa, who was accompanying the Alta Montaña during this time through the dynamic in which Sembrandopaz works, had developed very close relationships and trust with the communities in ways that I, as an outsider, could not. And this permits them to co-construct together, to build a form of collective agency so that the agenda of Sembrandopaz is deeply connected to the desires expressed by the communities. Someone who is immersed in the territory for a long time also merges with the logic of the community.

For Val, Larisa, who served as the liaison between the Alta Montaña and CNMH, embodied Sembrandopaz's approach to accompaniment as a permanent practice of presence. For over a year, I witnessed Larisa fill her evenings and early mornings with individual phone calls to community members who participated in the memory process. Rather than treat decisions about food, space, and logistical elements of the memory process as isolated and bounded technical matters, Larisa placed the Alta Montaña's wider, community process of reconciliation at the center of seemingly mundane details. In contrast to the logistical operator, Larisa ensured that the community members identified the *espacios cotidianos* (everyday spaces) where they wanted to gather for each interview and focus group conversation, attending carefully to the significant sites of memory as well as the spatial dimensions of trust-building. Rather than cater food from outside restaurants, she coordinated food preparation with the women's committee to ensure that meals were harvested and prepared within the host community in ways that contributed to the campesino economy. While often framed as logistical, the nightly calls that Larisa made reflected campesino relational practices, creating a space for community members to prepare for—and debrief—the memory process. Guided by the logic of accompaniment and attentive to the expressed desires of campesinos in the Alta Montaña, Larisa's approach to technical logistics deepened trust and laid the necessary groundwork for estranged communities to listen to the multiple—and competing—truths and silences that inevitably emerged over the course of the memory process.

"Those conversations, which sometimes lasted four, six hours where the whole community gathered and had the time to share, tell stories," Larisa sat across from me in the Sembrandopaz house, her vibrant red earrings swayed back and forth as she reflected on the memory process, "well, most of that won't make it into the book, but those were spaces of change, of *memoria*, and that process will always stay in the community whether it makes it into the book or not." Larisa did not merely collect data for a book project but, instead, understood each aspect of the memory process as part of the collective struggle to build territorial peace. In co-constructing the process from the ground up, Larisa approached administrative decisions as an equally important part of peacebuilding in the Alta Montaña. The times that guided Larisa's approach to accompaniment radically reconfigured how she understood technical and logistical decisions, offering a stark contrast to technocratic interventions guided by *prisa*.

In 2018, CNMH published *Un bosque de memoria viva: Desde la Alta Montaña de El Carmen de Bolívar* (Forest of Living Memory: From the Alta Montaña of El Carmen de Bolívar). "We have created a very important and also nuanced work from different points of view, because what we are doing is a work of art. It is not telling what happened here in a linear way, but in a literary way," Dionisio Alarcón, who served as one of the book's main writers, explained. "I have read memory books in other places where the story is told in a way that is, let's say, flat. This happened, and then this happened, in a way that I would call linear, this happened on this date and so on. . . . We are not academics, many of us are not educated, but all that we have done has great literary value." Dionisio interrogates the limitations of "flat" accounts that frame lived experiences of war within linear timelines, constructed through the distant gaze of academic experts. For Dionisio, linear narratives that segment the experience of armed conflict into clear pre- and post- boxes erase the polyvocal experiences that people have and wish to tell about their experiences with the war. To frame historical accounts within ordered chronologies also gives primacy and power to the armed conflict, occluding the histories of collective *resistencia* and solidarity that shape how people organize, survive, and tend relations of love in the midst of armed conflict (Bolten 2014). In contrast, Dionisio argues that literary techniques, which draw on the aesthetic practices of campesino storytelling, offer a more nuanced account of the lived experiences of war. Kimmerer (2013) echoes Dionisio's critique, arguing that those who understand traditional stories as myths listen through "linear time" (207). The privileging of chronological time reduces story to "a recounting of the long-ago past (207)." In contrast, Kimmerer argues that "circular time" situates stories as "both history and prophecy, stories for a time yet to come. If time is turning circle," Kimmerer writes, "there is place where history and prophecy converge" (207). Indeed, hearing stories through circular time imbues the present moment with ancestral memories and future desires.

"We worked on the subject of the armed conflict because it forms part of our memories," Elmer Arrieta Herrera, one of the youth photographers, elaborated. "But we also wanted to make it known that, yes, we suffered, but *here* in the territory, *here* in the high zone of El Carmen de Bolívar, we are happy, our communities live with joy," he paused to make sure I understood the significance of the shift they made in their approach to the memory process. "You see," he continued,

> we returned to our territory without state accompaniment, without support, and we are working to recuperate our traditions, to demonstrate that campesinos are people who work, to show the culture, how campesinos survive. This is what we want to show, to make visible. And we did this, yes, through the subject of the conflict, but what we are *really* showing is the joy of the people, *the desire* to overcome hardship, the work of community processes and leaders in their search for peace for the region.

Desire, joy, and love—not suffering—animate and sustain the collective defense of life and territory in the Alta Montaña. "This is what we want to show, to make visible," Elmer asserts.

In *Wisdom Sits in Places*, Keith Basso (1996) draws on collaborative research with Western Apache elders to outline how "sensing of place" and "sensing of self" are co-constitutive processes that make up the "most basic dimensions" of what it means to be human (54). Place-making is never done in isolation, but rather forged intersubjectively, continually woven into the fabric of social life and anchored in the land. Social leaders' insistence on carrying out a *living* rather than *historical* memory process echoes the critiques that Western Apache elders leveled against historical accounts of Cibecue that relied only on linear time. As Basso outlines, privileging chronological, rather than spatial and relational, markers renders history flat, distant, inanimate—and, therefore, unrecognizable (Basso 1996). Place names, in contrast, connect the Western Apache to the ancestors, alive and present in the landscapes they call home. The invocation of place-name narratives forms part of an ethical and imaginative process, central to the construction of subjectivities. "It is in this interior landscape," Basso (1996) writes, "the landscape of the moral imagination—that most deeply influences their vital sense of place, and also, I believe, their unshakable sense of self" (86).

Basso realizes the significance of place names through his own failure of understanding. After a long day of working with his Western Apache colleagues on a mapping project, he mispronounces one of the place names. Rather than dedicate time to learn the correct pronunciation, Basso flippantly declares that his pronunciation does not matter because he had already recorded the place name for the project. Deeply offended, Apache elder Charles Henry expresses his dismay to another colleague: "It's matter. . . . What he's doing isn't right. It's not good. He seems to be in a *hurry*. Why is he in a *hurry*? It's disrespectful. . . . Tell him he's repeating the speech of our ancestors!" (10, emphasis mine). As Basso works to repair the harm done by placing the project over the collective process, he repeatedly foregrounds slowness as a mode of relating to place—a form of attention that contributes to his own process of becoming "alive to the world" (106). In the "slow moving week" that follows, Charles Henry guides Basso through the landscape of living memory (15). As they "walk slowly . . . lost in thought and the deepness of time," Basso comes to recognize the histories and lives made *present* and animate through the ancestral speech of place names (15). At "Snakes Water," Charles Henry brings a barren spring to life—now flowing with cold, refreshing, and abundant water. Place names, Basso comes to the realize, "enlarge awareness of the present" (32). In this way, sensing place and sensing self are also bound up with sensing time.

"Sometimes memory is written, and archived, and left there and this becomes history," Naún reflected when I asked him why he prefers the term *memoria viva* (living memory) to historical memory.

The difference with living memory is that we, the young people, can tell
our story, our past, how it was in ancestral times, so that we young people
have this present in daily life [*vida cotidiana*], so that our memory is told
and reflected in how we live daily. This is where memory becomes *vigente*
[active, powerful], always evolving, and *siempre caminando* [always walking].
To make living memory is to share and live in the *cotidianidad* [everyday], to
carry with you the message of what it means and has meant to be Campesino, to be Afrodescendant, to be Indigenous.

WAKEFULNESS: ON LEARNING TO SEE THE OCEAN

Plastic white chairs filled the open-air meeting room as an unlikely crowd of
people gathered to celebrate the anniversary of Sembrandopaz. Social leaders
from across Montes de María sat interspersed with state bureaucrats, INGO
workers, directors of private foundations, academics, religious leaders, and international representatives from the United States, Canada, and Switzerland.
Ricardo opened the celebration with a *cuentico*—a short story. "This is a story
about a young fish and old fish," he began, a gleam in his eye as he removed
his black and white striped *vueltiao* hat,

> The young fish said to the older fish,
> "I have a concern, and I wonder if you can help me."
> And the old fish replied, "Yes, of course!"
> "Well, it has really been worrying me," the young fish explained.
> "Tell me, my young friend," the old fish replied,
> "It's just *so* profound, this question that I have," the young fish hesitated,
> "Just tell me," the old fish encouraged.
> And so, the young fish, building confidence, finally asked the old fish:
> "Where is the ocean?"
> Startled, the old fish looked at her young companion and responded,
> "Well, my young fish, this here all around us, is the ocean."
> And the young fish, confused, replied, "No, it can't be, this is just water."

Ricardo allowed for a moment of silence before continuing:

> Sometimes it is difficult to locate ourselves [*ubicarse*], to understand where
> we are. We speak about peace as if it is far away from us—and sometimes

we even invite foreign academics and other experts to come and talk about peace, rather than clarifying where we are. And sometimes, this makes it so that communities begin to think that they do not know what it is they do know. And so, it is good that we are here together, to clarify this with one another.

The story of the young fish and the old fish illuminates the paradox of proximity that social leaders face in postaccord Colombia, where peace is consistently framed as something external to the territory. Handshakes across a negotiating table, the signing of a peace accord, pronouncements of the end of war, and the spectacular interventions of experts contribute to a fleeting and abstract experience of peace, far removed from the rhythms of the campo. Like the young fish, those who live in the territory begin to internalize a narrow vision of peace as limited only to an elite and distant reality, unable to see their own knowledge of peacebuilding as valuable, or even as such. There is an ocean of knowledge, lessons learned, and ongoing community processes of peacebuilding in Colombia. Yet, it is the very ordinariness—the day in and day out work of building peace—that renders grassroots processes imperceptible, making some see mere water where there is, in fact, an abundant ocean. For Nixon (2011), shifting the "balance of visibility both in the urgent present and over the long haul" requires collective mobilization against "the forces of temporal inattention that compound injustices of class, gender, race, and region" (30). To transcend the challenge of visibility, in other words, requires alternative ways of inhabiting time.

Slowing down, understood as a practice of presence and mode of attention, imbues everyday moments and experiences with rich, social meaning. River mapping offers a concrete example of how intergenerational processes of learning from the land resurface *memorias vivas* (living memories) that reside in places, deepening peoples' sense of rootedness and belonging in ways that disrupt the forces of slow violence. Likewise, regenerating forest ecologies from soils marred by environmental and political violence emerges from a permanent commitment to imagine, care, and tend life in the aftermath of war. As both an act of reclamation and practice of hope, tree planting draws on the wellspring of ancestral memories to cultivate imagined futures of dignified life within the present moment. The practices of slow peace that I have traced throughout this chapter, such as accompaniment, river mapping, living memory, and tree planting embody an ethics of attention—the cultivation of dispositions wakeful to life in the face of violence. In giving primacy to the *cotidianidad* (everyday), the daily and patient process of building peace slowly nurtures the capacity to feel, see, and grow the tree of a world *otherwise*, held within the seed.

CODA

"MY WHOLE LIFE, SINCE I was a young boy, I have struggled for this land," Domingo Deavila Buelvas, a social leader in the Alta Montaña, reflected as we followed the narrow, forested footpath that led through his farm. As a young boy, Domingo accompanied his father to campesino organizing meetings led by the ANUC. After establishing "Blessed Land" through a collective land recuperation action, the community petitioned the state for land titles decades ago. However, the heightened presence of armed actors in the region and sluggish bureaucratic procedures allowed the state to circumvent the land formalization process. Over the course of several decades, the institutions charged with administering property rights repeatedly changed, resulting in a perpetually delayed process that has left the community in a protracted state of waiting. Today, as one of the elected representatives of the community, Domingo splits his time between farming and negotiating with the Land Restitution Unit in an effort to finalize the community's most recent legal claim, filed in 2005. "I won't stop until we get the titles. I'll fight for the land until the day I die." The soft sound of the foliage beneath our feet filled the air as we walked. "This has been my life's dream."

I had accompanied Jocabeth and Naún to Domingo's community for a meeting with the youth committee as part of their planning process for the annual Cacicazgo Ecológico (ecological pageant). Domingo guided us through the community, pointing out significant places of memory and re-calling the soccer tournaments, fiestas, and celebrations that he had partic-ipated in as a young boy with youth from neighboring communities before the armed groups had entered the region. A mix of surprise and delight filled Jocabeth's voice as she made direct, personal connections to the individuals in Domingo's stories. While "Blessed Land" is located relatively close to Jo-cabeth's home, this was her first visit to the community. The military accom-paniment that guaranteed the safe return of Jocabeth's community coincided with an increase in selective assassinations, armed confrontations, and arbi-trary detentions in Domingo's community. These dynamics fortified *barreras invisibles* (invisible walls) across the Montaña, despite historical, familial, and social ties that had previously connected the communities. The highly con-tradictory experiences of the armed conflict, embodied and lived by people like Jocabeth and Domingo, trouble singular accounts of the armed conflict that delineate a clear before, during, and after. For some, the joy of return coincided with a sharp spike in violence for others. Collective identity in the Alta Montaña, therefore, is not created through a cohesive, linear narrative of the armed conflict, but rather forged through deep, affective ties to the campo. Love and desire for the campo, rather than a singular experience of the war, shape the "structures of feeling" that animate and sustain the col-lective defense of territory and life in the Alta Montaña (Williams 1977, 128).

Domingo has farmed and cared for the land his entire life. Unlike many farms in the region, Domingo's home remains forested with young avocado trees—alongside mango, papaya, and caracolí trees. As direct violence sub-sided in the region, his community began planting avocado trees that have proved resistant to the *Phytophthora cinnamomi* fungus. Using the natural shade from the forested land, Domingo also cultivates subsistence crops like cacao, yucca, squash, plantains, and ñame. Domingo picked a star-shaped pod from a small bush, handing me the seeds inside. "*Sachi inchi*," he said, laughing at his awkward pronunciation of the unfamiliar name. "Ricardo gave me some seeds from Sembrandopaz and I planted them here," he ex-plained, recounting the seed saving and exchange programs that Sembran-dopaz has hosted in recent years with campesinos across Montes de María. "I don't know about this *sachi*," he laughed again, "but I will plant anything. This is what I love."

As we continued to walk the hillsides of his farm, Domingo listed the different classes of mango (*puerco, azucar, corazon*) and avocado (*lorena, criollo, brasilia*), gleaning one from each tree so that we could taste the subtle differences in flavor and texture. With three half-eaten avocados in one hand and two mangos in the other, I struggled to identify the differences between them, receiving playful jabs from Domingo, Naún, and Jocabeth who laughed at my unrefined palate while we meandered through the forested landscape of Domingo's farm. The dense shade and cool air of the forest offered a refuge from the midday sun. Birdsong and the distinctive cry of a nearby donkey filled the air.

"This is giving me *recuerdos criollos* [organic memories]," Jocabeth said, transported to the avocado forests of her childhood. "Imagine it! All of the communities in the Montaña used to be like this. This is what you would see, forest everywhere." Along the coast of Colombia, the term *criollo* refers to heirloom plants and organically raised livestock. Campesinos use *criollo* as a marker of quality to index the healthier, fresher, and more flavorful food born from traditional campesino farming practices over and against produce from genetically modified seeds. Jocabeth's invocation of *criollo* also gestures toward the ways memories live in places (Basso 1996). The smells, tastes, sounds, and sensorial experiences of walking through the avocado forest transported Jocabeth to her childhood, revealing how places and landscapes evoke *sentipensamientos* (feeling-thoughts) that make present past lives, worlds, and relations (Escobar 2020; Fals Borda 1986).[1]

As we waited for homemade *pasteles* to cook—each carefully wrapped in banana leaves and placed on an open fire—the evening tradition of *echando cuentos* (swapping stories) began. Domingo pointed down over the hill, gesturing in the direction of Jocabeth's community as he recounted the military invasions that led to a series of selective assassinations in his own community. "Here," he explained, "there was no massacre, but there were more than forty people assassinated," he paused, allowing for a moment of silence. "We would be here for a long time if I named them one by one." Domingo carried many of the dead over his shoulders and in hammocks to the urban center to register their deaths and ensure proper burials. In recalling each life, each individual killed during the armed conflict, he offered a subtle critique of the ways in which the state and international community have focused their attention disproportionately on massacres as the primary sites of the armed conflict. The accumulated deaths of over forty civilians too often remain outside the dominant narratives—and reports—used to tally the cost of war.

Domingo continued to detail his experiences, recalling the day he found and carried the body of a young boy dressed in guerrilla fatigues. He described the weight of the body, the guttural wails of the family, the way that the bullet wound pierced the small body, caked in dry blood that remained conspicuously absent from the fatigues themselves. "False positive" is the label tagged on the bodies of over 6,400 civilians killed by the state in order to fulfill military quotas—another performance at the expense of campesino life used to demonstrate that the military was "winning the war" (JEP 2021). The *sentipensamientos* that Domingo evoked as he walked us through the geography of his living memory humanized each of the six thousand individual lives and relations torn asunder by this systematic tactic of state violence. The immense weight of the lie and the irrevocable loss incurred by the state's violent practice settled in around us. We sat together in silence, taking in the memories held within the land, alive and present for those willing to hear, listen, and re/member.

After dinner, Domingo led us down to a grove of pear trees, where we watched the sunset. "This is what people in the city don't understand," Jocabeth reflected, taking a bite of the ripe pear that Domingo had just handed to her, "the campo is *una bendición*—it's a blessing to live in the campo." Jocabeth finished the pear and lay back onto the soft foliage as Domingo gently lowered himself to the ground from the tree. He smiled and nodded emphatically in agreement, "I would never give up my campo for the city. Never." He took a bite of a pear, juice dripping down the side of his hand. And then, echoing Jocabeth, he repeated, "the campo is a blessing."

Domingo and Jocabeth's critical reclamation of the campo as a blessing exemplifies the findings from this ethnographic study: Social leaders in Montes de María understand peace as embedded within their daily practices of caretaking territorial relations that allow abundant life to flourish in the midst of violence. Far away from public view, gestures of reconciliation occur in the slower registers of ordinary life in the campo. As we walked Domingo's land—which he has fought for, cultivated, and tended over the course of his life—memories surfaced, creating a space for the kind of "Witnessing 2.0" that Deborah Thomas (2019) calls for as "a practice of *recognition* and *love* that destabilizes the boundaries between self and other, knowing and feeling, complicity and accountability" (2). For Thomas, bearing witness through "deep recognition" operates with dynamic and open-ended temporalities that emerge from the "quotidian practice of watching, listening, and feeling that is relational and profoundly intersubjective" (19). Domingo and Jocabeth wove the threads of their communities together, not through a symbolic act or a capacity-building workshop focused thematically on reconciliation, nor by collapsing their distinct experiences of the armed conflict into a single narrative. Instead, a process of healing emerged through their shared commitment to the daily labor of peacebuilding, environmental caretaking, and community organizing. *Recuerdos criollos* (organic memories) surfaced as we journeyed through the geographies of the campo, allowing trust to deepen in ways that transgressed the invisible barriers of community, generation, and gender.

The temporalities of slow peace cultivate an acute capacity to notice extraordinary moments of hope wrapped in the daily rhythms of ordinary life in the campo. A visit to a community, the subtle gestures during a story, the silence that accompanies the shared recognition of loss and grief, and a day spent reveling in the abundant pleasures of the campo are intimately tied to political processes of reconciliation and movement-building—yet too often remain invisible to the untrained, distant, and distracted eye. Slow peace gives primacy to the *cotidianidad* (everyday), where living memories are held and sharing can take place across generations, social location, and lived experience. Peacebuilding, within this framework, is not limited to universal prescriptions and timelines, but is instead understood as a dynamic, plural, and ongoing social process—emergent in everyday life.

Feel the Grass Grow offers a significant critique of international peacebuilding and development projects that objectify peace as a finite and linear project—something to "have," "achieve," or "bring" to war-torn regions like Montes de María. Throughout this book, I have argued that technocratic peace interventions are not merely counterproductive but enact profound harm in the name of peace. Drawing on ethnographic research, I have lifted out the temporal and structural conditions that perpetuate—and normalize—routine intervention practices that undermine local agency and political participation. I have also directed analytic attention to campesino peacebuilding practices found across Montes de María in order to identify the extant possibilities for building a more just and liberatory peace. In the pages that follow, I want to offer three central themes around which the ethnographic findings from this study coalesce—with implications for the policy and practice of international peacebuilding.

First, the social critiques, ethnographic encounters, and narratives found throughout this book indicate that more emancipatory approaches to peace-building require a fundamental shift from projects to processes. Such a move entails greater support for movement-building and community organizing as central to the work of peacebuilding. This shift also demands careful exam-ination of the harmful effects that the excessive—and pervasive—reporting culture found within the field of international peacebuilding has enacted on local communities and grassroots social movements working to build peace in the wake of violence. Rather than respond to community desires, cul-tural practices, and extant peacebuilding processes, the persistent reliance on logframes, monitoring and evaluation procedures, and short-term projects framed around measurable outcomes are too often designed to meet state and donor demands in ways that reduce peace to paper. The truncated and narrow frameworks that emerge from these common, technocratic approaches to peace carry grave consequences for those working at the epicenters of violent conflict. In particular, social leaders call into question the false binary that technocratic frameworks create between "the political" and "the technical," foregrounding the ways in which logistical, budgetary, and administrative decision-making processes are inherently political—shot through with and productive of uneven power relations.

I advocate for a critical anthropology of peacebuilding that understands peace as a historical, socioecological, and political process. Such an approach focuses our attention on relations of power, systemic inequalities, and the historical and material conditions that drive violent conflict. Doing so also demands that those of us who work within the field of international peace-building recognize our own complicity in perpetuating structures of inequal-ity and harm. We need to reckon with the detrimental effects that locating logistical, budgetary, and administrative decisions outside of particular his-torical, cultural, and political contexts has on local communities and relations. I have highlighted the accompaniment work of Sembrandopaz as an alternative model for reimagining technical decisions as deeply embedded in wider sociopolitical processes. Sembrandopaz offers insight into how attention to power and process—even for the most mundane administrative and budgetary details—can open transformative possibilities for participatory peacebuilding. The permanent and relational commitment and ethics found in Sembrandopaz's approach to accompaniment not only calls into question the efficacy and effects of short-term and project-based interventions, but also underscores the *temporal* shift that a move from technical *projects* to social *processes* demands.

Second, and relatedly, the findings from this book suggest that decolonial peace praxis requires critical attunement to "the times" of peace. The temporalities of "emergency time" that guide peace interventions erode the relations of care and love at the center of campesino practices of survival, *resistencia*, and socioecological approaches to peacebuilding (Ticktin 2011). At the same time, the external imposition of peace projects, designed far from the reaches of everyday life in the campo, contribute to repeated cycles of failed interventions, emblematic of "waiting time" (Auyero 2012). I contend that "emergency time" and "waiting time" are co-constitutive of the temporal regime of *prisa*, which undergirds prevailing approaches to international peace interventions.

The temporal contestations that I have traced throughout the previous chapters help to unveil the historical processes, constellations of power, and everyday practices that naturalize harmful intervention practices as an inevitable good within the field of international peacebuilding. Interventions carried out with *prisa* circumscribe what—and who—is seen and heard on the global stage of international peacebuilding. As the flood of postconflict funding flowed into the capital city of Bogotá, reconfiguring "peace" as the latest fad in the donor-state-university-NGO nexus, community peacebuilders faced a paradox of proximity: Their everyday practices of peacebuilding fell outside the narrow optics of the spectacles of peace produced in Colombia's "historic moment." The challenge of (in)visibility is not abstract, but an imminent and embodied threat to life for grassroots peacebuilders. In particular, I have argued that the clear delineation of roles between experts and victims found within the "theatrics of peace" not only obscures grassroots peacebuilding processes but also contributes to the criminalization of social leaders who advocate for more political and transformative approaches to peace. Over the course of writing this book, I found myself continuously increasing the death tally of social leaders in Colombia from two hundred to nearly five hundred. The grave challenges facing social leaders who continue to advocate for peace in the face of bodily harm raise critical questions about the sociotemporal practices and discourses that render certain lives invisible—and therefore disposable—in the era of *posconflicto* (postconflict).

Drawing on the narratives, social critiques, and everyday practices of grassroots leaders in Montes de María, this ethnography advances a grounded theory of slow peace. When social leaders underscore the need to build peace "without hurry or haste," they are not advocating for the continuation of sluggish bureaucratic practices that perpetually defer implementation. Nor are they suggesting that the state is *cumpliendo rápido* (fulfilling their obligations quickly). Instead, to build *paz sin prisa* (slow peace) requires a fundamental shift in power relations that shape the quality of encounter, attention to place and history, and forms of relating that imbue dignity and respect into the most mundane practices—the *ways things are done*. In other words, I argue that the campesino call to slowness is a call for greater attention to everyday practices that deepen mutual relationships of *cuidado*—care and intention. There is a profound urgency in the call to slow down, take notice, and tend territorial relations of care and solidarity in the wake of violence.

Slow peace extends the concept of positive peace to offer a relational framework for peacebuilding as a multispecies, multigenerational, and permanent social process for liberation. For those who have lived through the most intimate consequences of the war in Colombia, peace is not something you sign, but rather part of an active and collective process to create dignified life in the midst and aftermath of violence. As social leaders across Montes de María assert, the peace accords did not begin with the formal negotiations between political elites in Havana but rather emerged from a multigenerational and intercultural struggle to build emancipatory peace "from and for the territory." In giving primacy to everyday life in the campo as the wellspring for peace, slowing down reconfigures the accords' territorial focus to include the systemic changes that a just and liberatory peace demands of the *institucionalidad*.

Third, I have advocated for increased attention to the socioecological relations and histories that shape war and peace. For social leaders in Montes de María, violence and peace are experienced and understood as more-than-human. Multispecies approaches to peacebuilding offer a framework capable of responding to political and environmental violence as interlocking processes. Analyzing the armed conflict through the lens of the avocado forest reveals the ways in which approaches to peace that remove humans from the wider, ecological webs of which they are part render certain lives invisible— with grave consequences for territorial peacebuilding. Multispecies analytic frameworks offer a capacious understanding of peace—one that more accurately reflects campesino ontological experiences of war and approaches to collective healing in the wake of armed conflict. As Indigenous scholars have rightly noted, one of the most devastating effects of dispossession is the loss of "the transmission of knowledge about the forms of governance, ethics, and philosophies that arise from relationship on the land" (Simpson 2014; Wildcat et al. 2014, ii). The daily work of caretaking social and ecological landscapes marred by violence through intergenerational and intercultural approaches to collective organizing enables campesinos to make deep claims to land, identity, and futures in their pursuit of dignified permanence in the territory.

By traversing the multigenerational ecologies of peacebuilding that have fundamentally shaped Montes de María, I have sought to unearth the *riqueza*—the wealth of experiences and abundant wisdom—held within the territory. In the face of severe threats to life, campesinos buried books, carefully guarded community archives, and collectively organized large-scale, nonviolent movements built on the pedagogy of *aprender haciendo* (learning by doing). Despite systematic attempts to eradicate and divide their collective processes, they have continuously sought to retrieve and sustain intercultural spaces for dialogue where people dare to speak—finding strength and collective power in working across difference. In particular, I have highlighted the Espacio Regional's approach to coalition-building and sustained dialogue as exemplifying what it means to, in the words of Roxani Krystalli (2019a), "hold multiple truths in one embrace" (176). The Espacio Regional's approach to intercultural dialogue offers insight into the practices, ethics, and possibilities for creating more pluralistic approaches to peacebuilding.

Social leaders' temporal attunement to the dynamics of both violence and peace found throughout this book reflects what Anand Pandian (2019) has called an "affirmative spirit of critique" that emerges from "collaboration with potentials already in the world, rather than by stepping aside and pointing out what is absent yet ought to be present" (118–19). Read in the context of social leaders' lives and grounded in their collective struggle for territorial liberation, the call to build *paz sin prisa* (slow peace) offers "a means of tending an open horizon" (Pandian 2019, 118). As Zoe Todd (2016c) incisively notes, the word "tend" includes the valences of refusal, care, vulnerability, and attention. Social leaders' steadfast commitment to tending the potentials that *exist* in the campo, yet which remain largely unseen, reveals the prefigurative politics that guide the practices of slow peace, "infused with existential generosity, with care for what is and its promise of becoming otherwise" (Pandian 2019, 119). Slow peace emerges from the tenacious and collective struggle for dignified life as those living in the midst of violence create spaces to *convivir ampliamente*, live together widely.

In Montes de María, there is a traditional saying: "*Despacio, porque hay prisa*—Slow down, because there is hurry." Slowing down shifts how people relate to one another and inhabit the world, deepening attention to the multiple lives and emergent potentialities found close to the ground. Hope springs forth through the daily and patient work of cultivating peace in the campo. The shared commitment to permanently tend territorial relations of care and solidarity in Montes de María opens possibilities for creating a radically different world and polity. To "feel the grass grow" reconfigures the temporal and relational orientation of peacebuilding, opening an expansive present where the seeds of a world *otherwise* are seen, felt, and nurtured. By becoming attuned to nearly imperceptible processes of organic growth that persist in the wake of violence, the practices of slow peace bring campesino futures of dignified life into being.

The story of Montes de María is not one that can be reduced to the violence social leaders have endured, but rather one of fierce *resistencia* and a persistent commitment to the collective defense of life and territory. Despite plebiscites, floods of *chalecos* (vests), hostile political regimes, and ongoing threats to life and livelihoods, social leaders in Montes de María remain steadfast in their daily work to build peace "from and for the territory." Youth continue to map rivers and waterways that give sustenance to their territory; communities previously divided as a result of the armed conflict gather together for soccer tournaments on weekends; Sembrandopaz continues to plant trees, regenerating forests from barren hillsides; and members of the Espacio Regional have sustained their monthly dialogue process in the midst of heightened political insecurity and a global pandemic, finding creative ways to assemble in order to reflect and respond to emerging and renewed forms of violence. For social leaders in Montes de María, threats to peace are not new. Against the elements that threaten to destroy what they have cultivated across centuries of collective struggle, social leaders continue to guard and nurture the seeds of peace held within the territory.

Under the right-wing administration of former president Iván Duque, a series of grave setbacks for the national peace process, which threatened to shred (*hacer trizas*) the peace accords, filled the headlines of newspapers across Colombia.[2] As the coronavirus pandemic halted international travel, I sent an email to Ricardo expressing concern and inquiring into the situation in Montes de María. "None of this is new," he responded, "it neither surprises me nor makes me despair. The accords are not the FARC's or the government's, they are the pueblo's, the community's, they are ours. We must be strategic and courageous and find a way to reclaim them, to prevent this from turning into hopelessness." Ricardo framed the email with a question— inviting me into the praxis of slow peace: "How do you think we can materialize this future that continues to arrive sooner than what we believe?" At the end of the email, Ricardo returned to an essay that he had composed years earlier—penned the evening that the government and the FARC-EP first signed the peace accords, a moment filled with hopeful anticipation and open possibility. He titled the essay, "Looking Towards the Future with Hope" (Esquivia 2016). The wisdom of Ricardo's essay—born from a life lived waging peace—remains as relevant now as it did on that historic eve years ago. In the spirit of campesino organizing, I offer his words as a way to conclude with an open-ended invitation for collective reflection in solidarity with social leaders at the forefront of building peace in Colombia:

> We, the people, from the grassroots, full of joy and hope, with our hand on
> the plough and our feet firmly grounded on the land, look forward with ex-

pectation and moderated enthusiasm. To look forward illuminates the large challenges and obstacles along the path towards the horizon of justice, peace, and reconciliation. We do not want to think only with the enthusiasm and joy of this intoxicating moment. . . . The elite leaders, who have appropriated the establishment and the State, have not yet arrived at an agreement . . . their reactions are unpredictable and can contribute to hidden violence. . . . Administrative corruption is galloping and the clientelist and electoral industries continue to have great power. All of this is aggravated by social injustice, inequality, land grabbing, racism, and a great addiction to violence that invites us to be cautious. Popular wisdom says that "whoever sleeps on the ground never falls from the bed." With our feet firmly planted on the ground, we welcome these agreements—and, embodying faith and hope, we continue to cultivate peace in our region as we have done throughout these many years.

NOTES

TO DEFEND LIFE

1. *Vereda* is sometimes translated as "hamlet" or "village." I have chosen to translate it as "rural community" in order to avoid using terms that inadvertently reinforce pervasive tropes of campesinos as backward and not modern. *Comunidad* and *vereda* are also used interchangeably in Montes de María.

2. Jorge uses the colloquial term "ajá" to reference the death of the avocado forest.

3. In Colombian Spanish, *resistencia* has multiple valences. The term can mean both "resistance" and "resilience" and is often used in ways that include both terms as mutually reinforcing processes.

4. Catherine Bolten (2012a) distinguishes between the facts of events and the truth of peoples' narratives in Sierra Leone. The stories people choose to tell offer insight into how they make sense of life in the wake of war. Bolten contends that social memory, understood as a process of remembering and forgetting, is "more about the present than the past" (24).

5. The full *décima* was later published in the historical memory book. See Pérez ([2014] 2018), 143.

6. For additional ethnographic approaches to the study of peace, see also Millar (2018).

7. The connections to slow food and slow living movements are not abstract; throughout my research in Montes de María, campesino social leaders hosted several guest lecturers and organized forums that explicitly focused on the slow food movement.

8. I am especially indebted to María Lucía Zapata who helped me to articulate the multiple meanings attached to "prisa," which significantly shaped the development of the theory of slow peace.

9. Here, I am drawing on Judith Butler's (2005) reformulation of responsibility as a *"responsiveness* to" others that emerges from recognition of interdependencies, and which offers an alternative to paternalistic notions of responsibility as "responsibility *for*" others (88, emphasis mine).

10. Within the interdisciplinary field of peace and conflict studies, scholars have increasingly called for greater inclusion of local peacebuilding efforts within national peace processes (Firchow 2018; Kroeker 2020; Lederach 1997; Mac Ginty 2021; Mac Ginty and Richmond 2013; Richmond 2018; Tom 2017).

11. Muir (2004) writes that whereas "multi-sited" research "recognizes the many locations of culture," multi-locale research "requires field study in many locations" (187).

12. Deborah Thomas (2019) similarly writes about the affective register of *doubt* as "a diffuse sense of uncertainty" that "produces technologies of misrecognition, the result of obfuscation, denial, and the maintenance of public secrets" (20).

13. For more fine-grained analyses of the relationship between violence and environments, see also Peluso and Watts (2001).

14. In her research in Peru, Kimberly Theidon (2009) has similarly reflected on how "the words 'theory' and 'belief' are inscribed within an imbalance of power" that render invisible the "sophisticated theories Quechua speakers have elaborated about violence and its effects, about social life and their struggles to rebuild it" (9).

15. For other examples on naming as a practice of citation, see Hoover (2017); Sara Shneiderman (2021), "Collapsing Distance: Recognition, Relation, and the Power of Naming in Ethnographic Research," in "Rethinking Pseudonyms in Ethnography," edited by Carole McGranahan and Erica Weiss, *American Ethnologist* website, December 13, 2021, https://americanethnologist.org/features/collections/rethinking-pseudonyms -in-ethnography/collapsing-distance-recognition-relation-and-the-power-of-naming-in -ethnographic-research.

16. For an excellent discussion about the social fragmentation and dispossessions enacted through Colombia's multicultural politics and the counterproposals that social leaders from Montes de María have generated, which focus on building intercultural spaces for the campesino economy, see Rodríguez (2021).

17. "What does it look like, entail, and mean," Sharpe (2016) asks, "to attend to, care for, comfort, and defend, those already dead, those dying, and those living lives consigned to the possibility of always-imminent death, life lived in the presence of death" (38).

CHAPTER 1

1. Historian Eduardo Porras (2014) writes that "a complex and diverse population created Montes de María . . . which, in turn, fostered an intercultural ethos, not only because of the different ethnic origins of its protagonists but also because of the long process of coexistence and *mestizaje* . . . that led to the formation of . . . marginal living spaces, located outside of the control of the civil, military and religious authorities of the time, known since that time as *rochelas*" (340).

2. For additional ethnographic material on *interculturalidad* as part of a political project, see Gow (2008).

3. To overcome the gendered binaries embedded within Spanish words that correspond to masculine and feminine markers, I use "x" rather than "o" or "a"—as in Latinx instead of Latino or Latina.

4. The National Center for Historical Memory (CNMH 2014) asserts that the hacienda system formed the foundation of clientelism in Colombia (27). As the authors detail, beginning in the 1970s, "traditional clientelism" transformed into "*modern clientelism*" as children of elite landowners sought opportunities in the cities. Urbanization reinforced the centralist state system and contributed to the third wave of "*armed clientelism*" beginning in the late 1980s, whereby elites financed armed organizations to maintain political and territorial control (27–28).

5. I use the term "land recuperation" rather than "land invasion" to remain consistent with the oral histories of campesinos in Montes de María. The preference in terminology underscores the ancestral right to land in a context of dispossession.

6. For a comprehensive study of this period, see Guzmán Campos, Fals Borda, and Umaña Luna (1964). See also Palacios (2006).

7. Pérez (2010) cites article 30 of the Constitution (later established as article 58 in the 1991 constitution) as the legal framework that informed the Campesino Mandate, which guarantees acquired rights to land (43).

8. Joanne Rappaport's (2021) *Cowards Don't Make History* offers a detailed look into the history of PAR—a required read for those interested in the methodology.

9. For detailed studies of the role that women played in the campesino movement, see Grupo de Memoria Histórica (2011), and Wills (2007).

10. For more on the state's discursive use of "national security" to criminalize grassroots mobilization, see Ramírez (2011).

11. In other words, they are still registered by the state through open case files, leaving them vulnerable to state violence and incarceration.

12. For a detailed study of the M-19, see Grabe Loewenhertz (2017). The prologue, written by Humberto de la Calle, a chief negotiator of the 2016 accords, explicitly notes the influence that past peace agreements played in the 2016 accords.

13. Kiran Asher's (2009) *Black and Green: Afro-Colombians, Development, and Nature in the Pacific Lowlands* offers a textured ethnographic account of Black social movement organizing, experience, and advocacy following the passage of Law 70 in Colombia's Pacific coast.

14. National accounts report 56 massacres in the region. However, a local study by the *Corporación Desarrollo Solidario* places the number of massacres over 100. Although the discrepancy may seem high, one of the largest massacres to take place in Montes de María did not receive formal recognition until 2018. The "invisible massacre" of campesinos from Guáimaros and El Tapón, San Juan Nepomucena in August 2002 reflects the "invisibility" of political violence in the region (Gutiérrez Torres et al. 2018).

15. Although massacres have received the most attention from media outlets, between 1990 and 2002 the Human Rights Observatory documented over one thousand homicides (Porras Mendoza 2014, 367).

16. In their report, *Everything Passed before Our Eyes: The Genocide of the Unión Patriótica*, CNMH (2018b) documented a total of 4,153 people "assassinated or disap-

peared or kidnapped" as a result of their participation in the UP party (108). The wide-scale pattern of assassinations against the UP has led many to refer to these acts as "political genocide" (Tate 2015, 90; Cepeda Castro 2006).

17. Winifred Tate (2015) found that "by 2011, more than 120 former members of Congress—approximately one third—had come under investigation for paramilitary ties" (225).

18. See also Ojeda et al. (2015), 107–19.

19. In a report by the Center for International Policy, Isacson and Poe (2009) found that "between 2000 and 2007, the Clinton and Bush administrations provided Colombia with $5.4 billion in assistance, 80.5 percent of it for the security forces."

20. "False positive" refers to a military practice used during the armed conflict whereby soldiers killed civilians and then dressed them in guerrilla fatigues to fulfill quotas aimed at showing that the state was "winning the war."

21. "*Ajá*" infers the attempted assassination of Alejandro's father.

22. The FARC-EP increasingly used land mines as a tactic of war beginning in the 2000s. There are 112 documented casualties from land mines in El Carmen alone—the majority of whom were soldiers in the Colombian Armed Forces (PNUD 2010, 45–46).

23. Here, I am drawing on Kimberly Theidon's (2013) ethnographic concept of "intimate enemies."

24. For more on arts-based approaches to community healing, explore the work of the Mampuján Mujeres Tejiendo Sueños y Sabores de Paz: Ruiz Hernández (2013).

25. After the military forcibly displaced Ricardo Esquivia in the 1980s for his work as a human rights lawyer with the ANUC, he founded Justapaz (Justpeace) in Bogotá. Justapaz accompanies community leaders in conflict-affected regions across Colombia, documenting human rights violations and engaging in policy and advocacy work for peace at the national and international level. In Montes de María, Justapaz accompanied religious leaders who had begun providing sanctuary to people in their churches in direct opposition to the armed actors operating in the region (Esquivia Ballestas 2009; Hunter-Bowman 2018).

26. The approach to building peace emerged in direct collaboration with John Paul Lederach (1997), who similarly advocated for creating an infrastructure for strategic peacebuilding in *Building Peace: Sustainable Reconciliation in Divided Societies.*

27. Over one thousand homicides attributed to the paramilitaries were documented during the demobilization period, with no state response (Ronderos 2014).

28. Between 2002 and 2009, the municipality of Toluviejo alone registered eleven cases of false positives (PNUD 2010, 20).

29. One of the primary alliances that spearheaded the expansion of *teca* (teak trees), with the support of USAID, later came under intense legal scrutiny for participation in the dispossession of campesinos from their land (La Silla Vacía 2016).

30. By 2017, the Murgas-owned company, Oleoflores S.A. had over 11,000 hectares of palm oil plantations in Montes de María (Rutas 2017). Across Colombia, Oleoflores S.A. owns 50,000 hectares of palm oil plantations with ties to multinational corporations that operate the palm oil industry across the world.

31. In 2012 alone, WOLA (Washington Office on Latin America) reported that the municipalities with the highest levels of palm oil reported eleven new rape cases in a period of two months, reflecting the clear use of sexual violence as a tactic of displacement (Isacson, January 30, 2012).

CHAPTER 2

1. For a deeper look into Angelina's life history, see González Jiménez (2021).

2. The poem has since been published under the modified title, "The Feeling of a People" in *Un bosque de memoria viva, desde la Alta Montaña de el Carmen de Bolívar.* CNMH (2018a), 403

3. Campesinos often describe the military's strategy for territorial control as one that sought to "remove the water from the fish." Angelina expands that imagery to unearth the dual destruction of forced displacement—not only do campesinos choke without the campo, the campo also dries up without the care of campesinos.

4. Zoe Todd (2016b) reminds us, "what many an Indigenous thinker around the world could have told you for millennia: the climate is a common organizing force!" (8).

5. Initially named the Peaceful Movement of the Alta Montaña, organizers changed the name to the Peaceful Process when the movement ran for political office in municipal elections in 2015.

6. For Thomas (2019), deep recognition moves beyond legal frameworks that produce a binary between victims and perpetrators. "In creating a field of intersubjective recognition through dialogue, the relating of narratives is a form of Witnessing 2.0," writes Thomas, "whose purpose is not merely to document tragedy, suffering, and abuse for an audience elsewhere but is geared toward materializing a transformation in the very relation between narrator and audience" (216).

7. The 2011 Victim's Law 1448 forms the state's legal framework for the transitional justice legislation passed prior to the signing of the 2016 peace accords. Thus, the collective reparations process in the Alta Montaña began several years before implementation of the national peace accords.

8. Campesinos recount how years later, on a visit to the Alta Montaña, García wept when he realized the extent of the destruction the fungus caused.

9. García explained that past subsidies had come through an alliance with the Rural Capital Incentive, channeled through the Ministry of Agriculture's Financial Fund with support from intermediary financiers. From: Archivo propio del Proceso Pacífico de Reconciliación e Integración de la Alta Montaña, 15–16. April 2013.

10. Indigenous women leaders in southern Colombia similarly identify themselves as the "*renacientes*—reborn." In their historical memory book, *Pasto Women in the Struggle for Land Recuperation*, they write: "In this spiral, the events, characters, things and places of the past are ahead of those of us who live now. Everything that has already happened is present again in the lives of us, the *renacientes* [reborn], in the stories that our elders tell us . . . and in the daily struggle of indigenous life" (CNMH 2021, 45–46).

11. The coordinating committee of the Peaceful Process as well as Sembrandopaz encouraged the youth to have equal gender representation during their first meetings.

While external encouragement laid the groundwork for women's inclusion, the establishment of the gender equity policy in the constitution emerged from the youth leaders who ratified the policy during the first general assembly.

12. *Corroncha* is a derogatory term used to characterize campesinos as backward and premodern.

13. Writing about the colonial violence enacted against the Indigenous territories of Guachucal and Cumbal in southern Colombia, Indigenous women leaders similarly describe the violence committed against Indigenous communities and lands as leaving a "heaviness," which continues to live in places (CNMH 2021, 23).

14. As Ruiz Serna (2015) writes, "by holding that the forest is an animated place and that animals' will can be manipulated, peasants are not merely imputing a breath of life on their material world. Rather, they are recognizing a set of ontological premises that are shared by humans and animals: their behavior is often intentional" (86).

15. In his definition of a "relational ontology," Escobar (2015) writes that "things and beings are their relations, they do not exist prior to them" (18).

16. Naún uses the singular rather than plural conjugation (*es*), further underscoring his understanding of identity and territory as *one*.

17. *Reinados de belleza*—beauty pageants—are a favorite cultural event in Colombia. The term *reinado* also means empire or reign and is rooted in Spanish colonial rule.

18. Onwehonwe scholar Taiaiake Alfred (2005) has also argued that intergenerational sharing is vital for Indigenous resurgence. I am grateful for conversations with Justin de Leon, who helped me to make the connection between Alfred's focus on intergenerational relationships and those found in the Alta Montaña.

19. The poem has since been published in *Un bosque de memoria viva, desde la Alta Montaña de el Carmen de Bolívar* (CNMH 2018, 183).

CHAPTER 3

1. While much of the literature within the field of International Relations has focused on state formation through warfare, Fattal (2018) contends that "state making in Colombia was tied not only to waging war but also to the attempts to achieve a state of affairs that might resemble peace" (7). In *Forgotten Peace: Reform, Violence, and the Making of Contemporary Colombia*, Robert A. Karl (2017) similarly offers a deep, historical account of Colombian state formation through peace negotiations, reforms, and demobilization campaigns.

2. *Mesa*—"table"—is used to describe negotiating tables, formal meetings, and the "monitoring committees" or "working groups" developed to oversee the implementation of war reparations.

3. Charles Tilly (2008) defines "contentious performances" as consisting of "individual actions and interactions" that "compound into repertoires, each characterizing some set of political relations" (201). While repertoires of performances are patterned and recurrent, contentious performances are also dynamic and can change across time as actors learn, adapt, and innovate over the course of iterative interactions (4).

4. For a more detailed discussion of the state's discursive circulation of *hacer presencia* (making a presence), see McFee (2020). "Given the real and imagined historic absence that made the conflict possible to begin with," Erin McFee writes, *"making a presence carries with it a corrective connotation.* Approached in this way, understanding its use(s) and significance(s) can provide meaningful insight into state-making in war-to-peace transitions."

5. Despite the "local turn" in international peacebuilding, local stakeholders are rarely included in the design of the programs, let alone hired to lead and manage projects (Hughes, Öjendal, and Schierenbeck 2015; Mac Ginty 2015; Richmond 2012). As Roger Mac Ginty (2015) writes, "while projects may have a local face, and be enacted by local personnel in local communities, the real power may come from donors and administrators in New York, London, Geneva or elsewhere. Given that there is rarely a fundamental shift in power relations, it is prudent to label much of the local turn as shallow" (846).

6. James Ferguson (1994) has provocatively argued that international development is an "anti-politics machine" that draws on an "interpretive grid" built around identifying social and economic deficiencies in order to legitimize external technical interventions, despite the counterproductive and harmful results that those projects have on the local communities that they purport to improve (xiii).

7. Catherine Bolten (2012b) has shown how international humanitarian organizations and donors imposed the script of "sensitization" on survivors of the Sierra Leonean civil war as part of the postaccord reintegration process. Civilians declared themselves "sensitized" to the former combatants responsible for the violence they endured in order to make themselves legible within the international community's framework of healing and reconciliation. However, as Bolten uncovers, many people continued to express profound distrust and resentment toward the former combatants in everyday, community spaces. As a result, former combatants seeking to reintegrate into community life experienced increased forms of social marginalization.

8. Kimberly Theidon (2013) outlines how Indigenous women in Peru repeatedly foregrounded narratives of courage, bravery, and agency in their accounts of the civil war. However, the Peruvian Truth and Reconciliation Commission repeatedly silenced these narratives, erasing womens' agentive acts of survival in order to render them "helpless" victims, deemed worthy of justice.

9. For a detailed study of the ways "absence" has been deployed by multiple actors in the Colombian context—and the profound social and political effects that the discursive circulation of absence has for state formation and violence—see Ballvé (2020).

10. In other words, the right-wing ideology of former president Álvaro Uribe permeated state institutions at national and local levels.

11. Here, the bureaucrat is referring to the state-paramilitary nexus exemplified in the *parapolítica* scandal discussed in chapter 1, which drove practices that sought to erase state-sponsored violence from official, public records.

12. Here, *oferta* means offer or program. *Oferta* is also the term used to refer to "discount," "deal," or "bargain" and is rooted in market logics.

13. For another example of a state-led citizens fair in a different region of Colombia, see McFee (2020).

CHAPTER 4

1. Collective actions are not isolated, spontaneous, or single events but rather emerge from "life experiences, deliberate organizing, and concerted episodes of claim making" (Tilly 2008, 8). For Tilly, attention to social movements engaged in continuous processes of interaction, learning, and invention provides key insights into how claims are made collectively through performances.

2. "Los Cultivadores de Ñame Que Se Volvieron Youtubers," www.youtube.com/watch?v=oPiwuQvaapU&app=desktop.

3. Kristina Lyons (2020) similarly notes how individuals' "mere presence on the attendance lists . . . fulfills the prior consultation requirement [*consulta previa*] that oil and mining companies are legally bound to engage in with ethnic groups and other collectively owned territories" before carrying out extractive projects (160).

4. A traditional, campesino home made with reeds and mud.

5. William's use of the phrase "eating ñame with ñame" indicates the severe poverty and hunger that stems from the overproduction of a monoculture crop.

6. Through ethnographic research in the Department of the Guajira in Colombia, Pablo Jaramillo (2012) similarly found that the state's everyday bureaucratic practices have resulted in an affective experience of reparations as a "situation of permanent waiting" (44).

7. *Apretada* is often used to describe a "tight," "busy," or "packed" schedule, used to explain one's inability to make room for additional meetings as a result of a hectic schedule.

8. Elizabeth Povinelli (2011) writes compellingly about how econometric models perpetuate a culture of impunity by reducing the structural and institutional processes that produce social suffering to individual calculations: "The social is practiced as nothing more than an aggregate of individuated risk calculators working according to mathematically predictable econometric models. I am not in you. You are not in me. We are merely playing the same game of chance, whose truth lies not here and not between us, but there and then in who wins and who loses. And I am killing no one. We are each only responsible for ourselves" (183).

9. Oliver Richmond (2011) outlines how the political economic structures that drive liberal peacebuilding have exacerbated inequality in postaccord contexts across the world: "In fifteen out of twenty-three cases . . . increased wealth circulates mainly amongst the few, meaning a general peace dividend is marginal for most of the population. . . . This is partly a result of the nature of the liberal peace, especially given NGO business, and the political elites it creates. Indeed, the data on these cases suggest that inequality tends to be worse in relation to HDI and UN backed cases of peacebuilding. . . . Most stability often associated with UN involvement allows more foreign direct investment, which enables a very rich class to emerge. This exacerbates inequality" (35).

10. The "professional class" refers to those with formal training and university degrees.

Professionals could be consultants, state bureaucrats, or contract workers who are positioned as the "technical experts" of projects.

11. In *Economies of Abandonment*, Elizabeth Povinelli (2011) illuminates how bureaucratic practices such as "proliferating and changing program names; redirecting previous or unspent or promised budgetary allowances; and closing programs" make "the actual distribution of wealth" difficult to track (57).

CHAPTER 5

1. Teo Ballvé has outlined how the paramilitaries, in collaboration with private sector companies, also deployed the discourse of "sustainable development" to mask their past and ongoing participation in processes of land dispossession in Urabá, Colombia (2013).

2. For a compelling discussion of the term *institucionalidad*, see Roxani Krystalli, "Being Seen Like a State: Transitional Justice Bureaucrats and Victimhood in Colombia," *Current Anthropology*, forthcoming. As a former state official explained to Krystalli in an interview, "the *institucionalidad* is more than institutions. It is more abstract than any single entity. It is a gigantic ghost of the Colombian state" (quoted on p. 42, footnote 18).

3. Gwen Burnyeat similarly found that the Office of the High Commissioner for Peace espoused an explicitly "rational" and "nonpolitical" approach to peace as a key strategy of their pedagogy campaign following the signing of the peace accords (2021). For more on how global discourses of "the technical" work to suppress grassroots organizing against extractive violence, see Li (2015).

4. Like many accounts of the war that I have heard across the Alta Montaña, Naún did not specify which guerrilla group. The constant movement of multiple, armed actors across the territory—and the chaos that their presence generated—often blurred the distinction between armed groups for those "caught in between" warring factions.

5. Alex Fattal's ethnographic study underscores the fact that the government's individual demobilization program accounts for nearly double the number of former FARC combatants that disarmed following the signing of the peace accords (2019, xiii). Naún offers further insight into how these unaccounted for individuals disarmed and demobilized *outside* of formal government programs with the support of existing community structures of conflict resolution and local reintegration practices.

6. Elsewhere, I have written about Western perceptions of circling around as a form of stagnation, rather than a practice that deepens social healing (Lederach and Lederach 2010).

CHAPTER 6

1. In Spanish, the Espacio Regional describes their work as: "*Re-encuentros entre iguales en desencuentro y diálogos improbables entre desiguales.*" For more, see https://espacioregional.wordpress.com/.

2. Within the field of peace studies, scholars have long argued that lasting peace requires forging horizontal connections across multiple social sectors as well as creating vertical alliances that include the state and international organizations. See Lederach (1997); Philpott and Powers (2010); Schirch (2005); Ricigliano (2012).

3. For more on sustained dialogue, see Saunders (2011).

4. Filmmaker Reina Gossett (2011) articulates a clear understanding of abolitionism rooted in prefigurative praxis, writing, "it is not enough to just be urgent and in opposition to state violence but uncritically practice it through exclusion, alienation, sexism, ableism, transphobia, and homophobia and a racist politic of policing authenticity. . . . I wanted the work I did to prefigure the world or communities I wanted to live in" (329).

5. For a more detailed look at the political theologies that have shaped grassroots peace activism in Montes de María, see Hunter-Bowman (2018, 2022).

6. Mery Rodriguez (2012) writes against the assumption that peace comes *after* a negotiated settlement or cease fire. She contends, instead, that peacebuilding became one of "the only means for surviving or fulfilling basic human needs" for grassroots communities during the armed conflict (69).

7. In *Doing Democracy: The MAP Model for Organizing Social Movements*, Bill Moyer (2001) similarly identifies the importance of celebrating small, incremental successes for movements seeking long-term change. George Lakey (2017) also outlines the need to connect campaigns to movements in the ongoing work of building a "movement of movements."

8. "Cachaco" and "Paisa" are colloquial terms for people from the cities of Bogotá and Medellín, or more generally the interior of the country. Cachacolandia and Paisalandia is a play on words that combines terms for those from the interior of the country with Disneyland, gesturing toward the experience of the theatrics of peace enacted by external actors from the capital cities.

9. In *The Force of Nonviolence*, Judith Butler (2020) also locates vulnerability as a site of resistance. Centering interdependency as the grounds for ethical, nonviolent action, Butler writes: "Vulnerability traverses and conditions social relations, and without that insight we stand little chance of realizing the sort of substantive equality that is desired. Vulnerability ought not to be identified exclusively with passivity; it makes sense only in light of an embodied set of social relations, including practices of resistance" (192). For Butler, "these social relations can serve as a ground for thinking about the broader global obligations we bear toward one another" (200).

CHAPTER 7

1. In an ethnography, Natalia Quiceno Toro (2016) contends that the concept of *vivir sabroso* (living deliciously) connects "therapeutic, kinship, and spiritual" dimensions of social movement organizing found among Afro Colombian and Indigenous social leaders in the Colombian Pacific. The term came to prominence in the national lexicon as a result of vice president Francia Márquez's electoral campaign in 2022.

2. The ambiguity surrounding the assassination made it difficult to classify it as either an act of political violence or a homicide.

3. Over the course of my fieldwork, Sembrandopaz hosted dozens of delegations, including representatives from the Washington Office on Latin America, Mennonite Central Committee, United States Institute of Peace, the Swiss Embassy, the UN, Universidad de Javeriana, CINEP, and peace and human rights defenders from Peru, Nicaragua, Honduras, and South Africa to Montes de María.

4. David Gow (2008) similarly distinguishes between the ongoing, political framework afforded by the "life plan" and short-term projects put forward through international "development plans" in his ethnographic research with Indigenous communities in southwest Colombia.

5. Ann Mische (2009) writes: "hope is both constituted and constitutive; it provides the emotional substratum . . . of the dialectic between the old and the new, between the reproduction and the transformation of social structures as these figure in thinking and acting individuals" (294).

6. In *Thinking, Fast and Slow*, Daniel Kahneman (2011) outlines a binary model for cognitive processing: "Fast thinking" includes daily habits that result in "automatic" responses ("system 1"), while "slow thinking" ("system 2") includes deliberative processing (13). The habitual and iterative practices of slow peace outlined in this chapter trouble Kahneman's binary to offer a conceptualization of slowness as a mode of experience and form of relating to the world that cultivates what Tsing (2011) calls an "open yet focused attention" (10). Tim Ingold (2011) has similarly sought to "correct the widespread misapprehension that the training of the body through repetitive exercise . . . leads to a progressive loss of conscious awareness" (60). Anthropological studies consistently show how the cultivation of skills necessary for the crafts of weaving, pottery, and woodworking are "anything but automatic" (61). Ingold argues that enskillment is "rhythmically responsive to ever-changing environmental conditions. In this responsiveness there lies a form of awareness that does not so much retreat as grow in intensity with the fluency of action" (61).

7. The plan includes both *sostenible* and *sustentable*, which are translated interchangeably in English as "sustainable." However, Sembrandopaz distinguishes between the two terms. Ricardo offered the following reflection during a team meeting: "some talk about sustainability [*sostenibilidad*] but *sostenibilidad* focuses only on the economic aspect. *Sustentabilidad* has an ethic of the environment and of nonviolence." For Ricardo, *sustentabilidad* is closely related to *buen vivir* (good living), which he explains as "a concept that emerges from Latin America that implies living together in an integral way."

8. The youth argue that obligatory military service violates their right to "nonrepetition" of violence guaranteed in the Victim's Law. For young men, the *libreta militar*—a military ID card that demonstrates completion of service—is a prerequisite for higher education and lawful employment. While military service is purportedly obligatory for all Colombians, families with financial means can pay a one-time "quota" to obtain the ID card, producing a deep disparity between those conscripted into the military and those who can pay their way out of conscripted service.

9. *La mojana* is a shapeshifting water spirit, sometimes known as the Mother of Water.

10. Siobhan McEvoy-Levy (2012) argues against shallow forms of intergenerational sharing that position youth merely as "recipients or beneficiaries of knowledge of the past and not initially as the authors or creators of history" (26–27).

11. In *Wasáse: Indigenous Pathways of Action and Freedom*, Alfred (2005) positions youth as key actors in resurgent political action, writing that "regeneration means we will reference ourselves differently, both from the ways we did traditionally and under colonial dominion" (34).

12. "Popular neighborhood" refers to settlements on the urban margins.

13. *Señalado* often refers to being falsely stigmatized and targeted for assassination.

14. Kimberly Theidon (2007) writes about how demobilized combatants in Colombia talk about "the monte" as synonymous with the violence and suffering wrought by war (77).

15. Here I am engaging with Arjun Appadurai (2004) who has called for greater inquiry into "how collective horizons are shaped . . . and how they constitute the basis for collective aspirations" (61). While he does not entirely dismiss the dialogical relationship between past memories and future aspirations, Appadurai places emphasis on "sedimented traditions" in his conception of the past (84).

CODA

1. Arturo Escobar (2020), drawing on Orlando Fals Borda, uses *sentipensamientos* as the correlative noun to *sentipensar* (feeling-thinking), which he describes as "a way of knowing that does not separate thinking from feeling, reason from emotion, knowledge from caring" (xxxv).

2. For a comprehensive report that details the trajectory of implementation over the first five years, see Echavarría et al. (2022).

REFERENCES

Abitbol Piñeiro, Pablo. 2010. "Hacia una política pública participativa de memoria histórica en los Montes de María." *Economía & Región* 12 (1): 133–55.

———. 2016. *Columnas para la paz*. Cartagena, Colombia: Universidad Tecnológica de Bolívar.

Ackerly, Brooke, and Jacqui True. 2008. "Reflexivity in Practice: Power and Ethics in Feminist Research on International Relations." *International Studies Review* 10 (4): 693–707.

"Acta Mesa de Agricultura, Aguacate, Vivienda y Tierras." 2013. El Carmen de Bolívar: Archivo propio del Proceso Pacífico de Reconciliación e Integración de la Alta Montaña.

Adams, Laura L. 2010. *The Spectacular State: Culture and National Identity in Uzbekistan*. Durham, NC: Duke University Press.

Adams, Laura L., and Assel Rustemova. 2009. "Mass Spectacle and Styles of Governmentality in Kazakhstan and Uzbekistan." *Europe-Asia Studies* 61 (7): 1249–76.

Ahmed, Sara. 2006. *Queer Phenomenology: Orientations, Objects, Others*. Durham, NC: Duke University Press.

———. 2017. *Living a Feminist Life*. Durham, NC: Duke University Press.

Alarcón, Dionisio. 2018. "Verano." In *Un bosque de memoria viva, desde la Alta Montaña de el Carmen de Bolívar*, edited by CNMH, 183. Bogotá: National Center for Historical Memory.

Alarcón, Dionisio, Hernando González, and Glenda Jaraba. 2018. "Quitarse el paraguas para sentir la lluvia: Una lección para la academia desde la Alta Montaña." *Economía y Región* 11 (2): 331–38.

Alfred, Taiaiake. 2005. *Wasáse: Indigenous Pathways of Action and Freedom*. Toronto: University of Toronto Press.

Alto Comisionado para la Paz República de Colombia. 2016. "Acuerdo final para la terminación del conflicto y la construcción de una paz estable y duradera." Oficina del Alto Comisionado para la Paz.

Appadurai, Arjun. 2004. "The Capacity to Aspire: Culture and the Terms of Recognition." In *Culture and Public Action*, edited by Vijayendra Rao and Michael Walton, 59–84. Stanford, CA: Stanford University Press.

———. 2013. *The Future as Cultural Fact: Essays on the Global Condition*. New York: Verso.

Asher, Kiran. 2009. *Black and Green: Afro-Colombians, Development, and Nature in the Pacific Lowlands*. Durham, NC: Duke University Press.

Austin, J. L. 1962. *How to Do Things with Words*. Oxford: Oxford University Press.

Autesserre, Séverine. 2014. *Peaceland: Conflict Resolution and the Everyday Politics of International Intervention*. New York: Cambridge University Press.

Auyero, Javier. 2012. *Patients of the State: The Politics of Waiting in Argentina*. Durham, NC: Duke University Press.

Ballvé, Teo. 2013. "Grassroots Masquerades: Development, Paramilitaries, and Land Laundering in Colombia." *Geoforum* 50: 62–75.

———. 2020. *The Frontier Effect: State Formation and Violence in Colombia*. Ithaca, NY: Cornell University Press.

Barreto Henriquez, Miguel. 2016. *Laboratorios de paz en territorios de violencia(s)*. Bogotá: Fundación Universidad de Bogotá.

Basso, Keith. 1996. *Wisdom Sits in Places: Landscape and Language among the Western Apache*. Albuquerque: University of New Mexico Press.

Berents, Helen, and Siobhan McEvoy-Levy. 2015. "Theorising Youth and Everyday Peace(Building)." *Peacebuilding* 3 (2): 115–25.

Berg, Maggie, and Barbara K. Seeber. 2016. *The Slow Professor: Challenging the Culture of Speed in the Academy*. Toronto: University of Toronto Press.

Berry, Maya J., Claudia Chávez Arguelles, Shanya Cordis, Sarah Ihmoud, and Elizabeth Velásquez Estrada. 2017. "Toward a Fugitive Anthropology: Gender, Race, and Violence in the Field." *Cultural Anthropology* 32 (4): 537–65.

Bolten, Catherine. 2012a. *I Did It to Save My Life: Love and Survival in Sierra Leone*. Berkeley: University of California Press.

———. 2012b. "'We Have Been Sensitized': Ex-Combatants, Marginalization, and Youth in Postwar Sierra Leone." *American Anthropologist* 114 (3): 496–508.

———. 2014. "The Memories They Want: Autobiography in the Chaos of Sierra Leone." *Ethnologie Française* 44 (3): 429.

———. 2019. *Serious Youth in Sierra Leone: An Ethnography of Performance and Global Connection*. Oxford: Oxford University Press.

Boulding, Elise. 1990. *Building a Global Civic Culture: Education for an Independent World*. Syracuse, NY: Syracuse University Press.

Boulding, Kenneth. 1978. *Stable Peace*. Austin: University of Texas Press.

Bouvier, Virginia Marie, ed. 2009. *Colombia: Building Peace in a Time of War*. Washington, DC: United States Institute of Peace.

Burnyeat, Gwen. 2018. *Chocolate, Politics, and Peace-Building: An Ethnography of the Peace Community of San José de Apartadó, Colombia*. Cham, Switzerland: Palgrave Macmillan.

———. 2021. "Government Peace Pedagogy in Colombia." *Anthropology News*, April 13, 2021. www.anthropology-news.org/articles/government-peace-pedagogy-in-colombia/.

Butler, Judith. 2005. *Giving an Account of Oneself*. New York: Fordham University Press.

———. 2015. *Notes toward a Performative Theory of Assembly*. Cambridge, MA: Harvard University Press.

———. 2020. *The Force of Nonviolence: An Ethico-Political Bind*. New York: Verso.

Cadena, Marisol de la. 2010. "Indigenous Cosmopolitics in the Andes: Conceptual Reflections beyond 'Politics.'" *Cultural Anthropology* 25 (2): 334–70.

———. 2015. *Earth Beings: Ecologies of Practice across Andean Worlds*. Durham, NC: Duke University Press.

Caro Tapia, Duván. 2021. "Los árboles y su rol en la construcción de la memoria histórica en los Montes de María." In *Montes de María: Un territorio en disputa*, edited by Diana Ojeda Ojeda, Catalina Quiroga Manrique, and Diana Vallejo Bernal, 82–95. Bogotá: Pontificia Universidad Javeriana.

Castaneda, Dory. 2012. "The European Union in Colombia: Learning How to Be a Peace Actor." *Paris Papers*, vol. 3. Paris: Institut de Recherche Stratégique de l'Ecole Militaire 3.

Cepeda Castro, Iván. 2006. "Genocidio político: El caso de la Unión Patriótica en Colombia." *Revista CEJIL* 1 (2): 101–12.

CNMH. 2011. Mujeres y guerra: Víctimas y resistentes en el Caribe Colombiano. Bogotá: Taurus.

———. 2014. La tierra en disputa: Memorias de despojo y resistencia campesina en la costa Caribe: Resumen. Bogotá: Centro Nacional de Memoria Histórica.

———. 2015. Aniquilar la diferencia: Lesbianas, gays, bisexuales y transgeneristas en el marco del conflicto armado colombiano. Bogotá: CNMH; UARIV; USAID; OIM.

———. 2018a. *Un bosque de memoria viva, desde la Alta Montaña de El Carmen de Bolívar*. Informe del Centro Nacional de Memoria Histórica y del Proceso Pacífico de Reconciliación e Integración de La Alta Montaña de El Carmen de Bolívar. Bogotá: Centro Nacional de Memoria Histórica.

———. 2018b. *Todo pasó frente a nuestros ojos: El genocidio de la Unión Patriótica, 1984–2002*. Bogotá: Centro Nacional de Memoria Histórica.

———. 2021. Mujeres pastos en la lucha por la recuperación de tierras: Resguardos de Guachucal y Cumbal. Bogotá: Centro Nacional de Memoria Histórica.

Cohn, Carol. 2013. "Woman and Wars: Toward a Conceptual Framework." In *Women and Wars*, edited by Carol Cohn, 1–35. Malden, MA: Polity Press.

Corntassel, Jeff. 2012. "Re-envisioning Resurgence: Indigenous Pathways to Decolonization and Sustainable Self-Determination." *Decolonization: Indigeneity, Education, and Society* 1 (1): 86–101.

Coronado Delgado, Sergio, and Kristina Dietz. 2013. "Controlando territorios, reestruc-turando relaciones socio-ecológicas: La globalización de agrocombustibles y sus efec-tos locales, el caso de Montes de María en Colombia." *Iberamericana* 13 (49): 93–115.

Cortright, David. 2009. *Gandhi and Beyond: Nonviolence for a New Political Age.* 2nd ed. Boulder, CO: Paradigm.

Coulthard, Glen Sean. 2014. *Red Skin, White Masks: Rejecting the Colonial Politics of Rec-ognition.* Minneapolis: University of Minnesota Press.

Cox, Aimee Meredith. 2015. *Shapeshifters: Black Girls and the Choreography of Citizenship.* Durham, NC: Duke University Press.

Crapanzano, Vincent. 2003. "Reflections on Hope as a Category of Social and Psycholog-ical Analysis." *Cultural Anthropology* 18 (1): 3–32.

Crenshaw, Kimberlé. 1991. "Mapping the Margins: Intersectionality, Identity Politics, and Violence against Women of Color." *Stanford Law Review* 43 (6): 1241–99.

Cronon, William, ed. 1996. *Uncommon Ground: Rethinking the Human Place in Nature.* New York: W. W. Norton.

Cross Riddle, Karie. 2017. "Structural Violence, Intersectionality, and Justpeace: Evalu-ating Women's Peacebuilding Agency in Manipur, India." *Hypatia* 32 (3): 574–92.

CSPP (Comité de Solidaridad con los Presos Políticos). 2020. "Solo preguntan por mi nombre: Detenciones arbitrarias y masivas en Montes de María." Bogotá: CSPP.

Daigle, Michelle. 2018. "Resurging through Kishiichiwan: The Spatial Politics of Indige-nous Water Relations." *Decolonization: Indigeneity, Education, and Society* 7 (1): 159–72.

D'Alisa, Giacomo, Federico Demaria, and Giorgos Kallis, eds. 2015. *Degrowth: A Vocab-ulary for a New Era.* New York: Routledge.

Daniels Puello, Amaranto, and Alfonso Múnera. 2011. "Los Montes de María: Entre la modernidad tardía y el colapso del estado." Cartagena, Colombia: University of Cart-agena.

Das, Veena. 2007. *Life and Words: Violence and the Descent into the Ordinary.* Berkeley: University of California Press.

Dave, Naisargi N. 2018. "What It Feels Like to Be Free: The Tense of Justice." *Cultural Anthropology Correspondences*, June 29, 2018. https://culanth.org/fieldsights/what-it-feels-like-to-be-free-the-tense-of-justice.

Davis, Angela Y. 2005. *Abolition Democracy: Beyond Prison, Torture, and Empire.* New York: Seven Stories Press.

———. 2016. *Freedom Is a Constant Struggle: Ferguson, Palestine, and the Foundations of a Movement.* Chicago: Haymarket Books.

De Leon, Justin. October 1, 2019. "Resurgent Visual Sovereignty: Film and Native Rep-resentation." Paper presented at the Kroc Institute for International Peace Studies. University of Notre Dame, Indiana.

———. 2020. "Relationship and Responsibility: Indigeneity in the IR Classroom." In *Teaching International Relations in a Time of Disruption*, edited by Heather Smith and David Hornsby, 75–88. Cham Switzerland: Palgrave McMillan.

De los Ríos, Edwin, Carmen Andrea Becerra Becerra, and Fabian Enrique Oyaga Martinez. 2012. *Montes de María: Entre la consolidación del territorio y el acaparamiento de tierras*. Bogotá: ILSA.

Department of the Environment and Heritage Australian Government. 2004. "Phytophthora Dieback." www.awe.gov.au/biosecurity-trade/invasive-species/diseases-fungi-and-para sites/phytophthora-cinnamomi-disease.

Descola, Philippe. 2013. *The Ecology of Others*. Chicago: Prickly Paradigm Press.

Dest, Anthony. 2020. " 'Disenchanted with the State': Confronting the Limits of Neoliberal Multiculturalism in Colombia." *Latin American and Caribbean Ethnic Studies* 15 (4): 368–90.

Diamond, Alex. 2019. "Will Megaprojects Destroy Colombia's Peace Process?" *NACLA* 5, August 2019. https://nacla.org/news/2020/03/03/will-megaprojects-destroy-colombia %E2%80%99s-peace-process.

Distler, Werner, Elena B. Stavrevska, and Birte Vogel, eds. 2019. *Economies of Peace*. New York: Routledge.

Duarte, Carlos. 2016. *Desencuentros territoriales: Caracterización de los conflictos en las regions de la altillanura, Putumayo y Montes de María*. Bogotá: Instituto Colombiano de Antropología e Historia.

Dwyer, Leslie. 2010. "Building a Monument: Intimate Politics of 'Reconciliation' in Post-1965 Bali." In *Transitional Justice: Global Mechanisms and Local Realities after Genocide and Mass Violence*, edited by Alexander Laban Hinton, 137–57. New Brunswick, NJ: Rutgers University Press.

Echavarría Álvarez, Josefina. 2019. "Pedagogías para la reconciliación: Prácticas artísticas para hacer las paces en Colombia." *Convergencia Revista de Ciencias Sociales* 27: 1–30.

Echavarría Álvarez, Josefina, et al. 2022. *Five Years after the Signing of the Colombian Final Agreement: Reflections from Implementation Monitoring*. Notre Dame, IN: Kroc Institute for International Peace Studies/Keough School of Global Affairs. https://doi .org/10.7274/0z708w35p43.

"El cultivo del aguacate: Corazón de la Alta Montaña." 2017. El Carmen de Bolívar: Proceso Pacífico de Reconciliación e Integración la Alta Montaña and Sembrandopaz.

Enloe, Cynthia. 1990. *Bananas, Beaches, and Bases: Making Feminist Sense of International Politics*. Berkeley: University of California Press.

———. 2004. *The Curious Feminist: Searching for Women in a New Age of Empire*. Berkeley: University of California Press.

———. 2013. *Seriously! Investigating Crashes and Crises as If Women Mattered*. Berkeley: University of California Press.

Escobar, Arturo. 1995. *Encountering Development: The Making and Unmaking of the Third World*. Princeton, NJ: Princeton University Press.

———. 2008. *Territories of Difference: Place, Movements, Life, Redes*. Durham, NC: Duke University Press.

———. 2015. "Thinking-Feeling with the Earth: Territorial Struggles and the Ontological Dimension of the Epistemologies of the South." *Revista de Antropología Iberoamericana* 11 (1): 11–32.

———. 2020. *Pluriversal Politics: The Real and the Possible.* Durham, NC: Duke University Press.

Espacio Regional de Construcción de Paz de Los Montes de María. June 2020. "Collective Proposal for a Community Policy of Security Guarantees for Life and Territorial Protection."

Esquivia Ballestas, Ricardo. 2009. "The Local Community as a Creative Space for Transformation: The View from Montes de María." In *Colombia: Building Peace in a Time of War,* edited by Virginia Bouvier, 295–311. Washington, DC: United States Institute of Peace.

———. 2016. "Looking Towards the Future with Hope." Sincelejo, Colombia: Sembrandopaz. September.

Fajardo, Darío. 2014. *Las guerras de la agricultura Colombiana, 1980–2010.* Bogotá: ILSA.

Fals Borda, Orlando. 1986. *Historia doble de La Costa: Tomo IV, Retorno a la tierra.* Bogotá: Carlos Valencia Editores.

Fattal, Alexander L. 2018. *Guerrilla Marketing: Counterinsurgency and Capitalism in Colombia.* Chicago: University of Chicago Press.

Ferguson, James. 1994. *The Anti-Politics Machine: Development, Depoliticization, and Bureaucratic Power in Lesotho.* Minneapolis: University of Minnesota Press.

Firchow, Pamina. 2018. *Reclaiming Everyday Peace: Local Voices in Measurement and Evaluation after War.* Cambridge: Cambridge University Press.

Flaherty, Michael G. 1999. *A Watched Pot: How We Experience Time.* New York: New York University Press.

Foucault, Michel. 2003. *Society Must Be Defended: Lectures at the Collège de France, 1975–76.* New York: Picador.

Freire, Paulo. (1970) 2005. Pedagogy of the Oppressed. 30th anniversary ed. New York: Continuum International Publishing Group.

———. 1994. *Pedagogy of Hope.* New York: Continuum Publishing.

Fuentes, Agustín. 2010. "Naturalcultural Encounters in Bali: Monkeys, Temples, Tourists, and Ethnoprimatology." *Cultural Anthropology* 25 (4): 600–624.

Galtung, Johan. 1969. "Violence, Peace, and Peace Research." *Journal of Peace Research* 6 (3): 167–91.

Gandhi, Mahatma. 1948. *Gandhi's Autobiography: The Story of My Experiments with Truth.* Washington, DC: Public Affairs Press.

García Durán, Mauricio. 2006. *Movimiento por la paz en Colombia, 1978–2003.* Bogotá: CINEP.

García Durán, Mauricio, Vera Grabe Loewenherz, and Otty Patiño Hormaza. 2008. *The M-19's Journey from Armed Struggle to Democratic Politics.* Berghof Transitions Series No. 1. Berlin: Berghof Research Center for Constructive Conflict Management.

García-Godos, Jemima, and Knut Andreas O. Lid. 2010. "Transitional Justice and Victims' Rights before the End of a Conflict: The Unusual Case of Colombia." *Journal of Latin American Studies* 42 (3): 487–516.

García Reyes, Paola, and Jenniffer Vargas Reina. 2014. "Land Transactions and Violent

Conflict: A Review of the Cases of Turbo, Antioquia and El Carmen de Bolívar, Bolívar." *Análisis Político* 82: 22–44.

Gaviria Betancur, Paula. 2011. *Región y reconciliación: Claves de política pública desde lo local.* Bogotá: Fundación Social; Editora Géminis.

Geertz, Clifford. 1980. *Negara: The Theatre State in Nineteenth-Century Bali.* Princeton, NJ: Princeton University Press.

Gill, Lesley. 2016. *A Century of Violence in a Red City: Popular Struggle, Counterinsurgency, and Human Rights in Colombia.* Durham, NC: Duke University Press.

González Jiménez, Angelina Isabel. 2018. "The Feeling of a People." In *Un bosque de memoria viva, desde la Alta Montaña de el Carmen de Bolívar,* edited by CNMH, 403. Bogotá: National Center for Historical Memory.

———. 2021. *Mis vivencias campesinas.* Madrid: MaquiWarmi.

Gossett, Reina. 2011. "Abolitionist Imaginings: A Conversation with Bo Brown, Reina Gossett, and Dylan Rodriguez." In *Captive Genders: Trans Embodiment and the Prison Industrial Complex.* Oakland, CA: AK Press.

Gossett, Reina, and Dean Spade. 2014. "Prison Abolition and Prefiguring the World You Want to Live In." Barnard Center for Research on Women: https://bcrw.barnard.edu /videos/reina-gossett-dean-spade-part-1-prison-abolition-prefiguring-the-world-you -want-to-live-in/.

Gow, David. 2008. *Countering Development: Indigenous Modernity and the Moral Imagination.* Durham, NC: Duke University Press.

Grabe Loewenherz, Vera. 2017. *La paz como revolución: M-19.* Bogotá: Taller de Edición Rocca Historia.

Grupo de Memoria Histórica. 2011. *Mujeres que hacen historia: Tierra, cuerpo y política en el Caribe Colombiano.* Bogotá: CNRR—Grupo de Memoria Histórica.

Guha, Ramachandra. 1989. "Radical American Environmentalism and Wilderness Preservation: A Third World Critique." *Environmental Ethics* 2: 71–83.

Gupta, Akhil. 2012. *Red Tape: Bureaucracy, Structural Violence, and Poverty in India.* Durham, NC: Duke University Press.

Gutiérrez Sanín, Francisco. 2020. "Fumigaciones, incumplimientos, coaliciones y resistencias." *Estudios Sociojurídicas* 22 (2): 471–507.

Gutiérrez Torres, Carolina, Alejandro Jiménez Ospina, and Irina Junieles Acosta. 2018. *Los Guáimaros y El Tapón: La masacre invisible.* Bogotá: Dejusticia.

Guzmán Campos, Germán, Orlando Fals Borda, and Eduardo Umaña Luna. 1964. *La violencia en Colombia: Tomo I and II.* Bogotá: Ediciones Tercer Mundo.

Hale, Charles R. 2006. *Más que un Indio: Racial Ambivalence and Neoliberal Multiculturalism in Guatemala.* Santa Fe, NM: School of American Research Press.

Hale, Charles, ed. 2008. *Engaging Contradictions: Theory, Politics, and Methods of Activist Scholarship.* Berkeley: University of California Press.

Hale, Charles, and Lynn Stephen, eds. 2013. *Otros Saberes: Collaborative Research on Indigenous and Afro-Descendant Cultural Politics.* Santa Fe, NM: School for Advanced Research Press.

Hall, Budd, and Rajesh Tandon. 2018. "From Action Research to Knowledge Democracy: Cartagena, 1977–2017." *Revista Colombiana de Sociología* 41 (1): 227–36.

Hall, Stuart. 1997. "Old and New Identities, Old and New Ethnicities." In *Culture, Globalization, and the World-System: Contemporary Conditions for the Representation of Identity*, edited by Anthony D. King, 41–68. Minneapolis: University of Minnesota Press.

Hallward, Maia Carter, and Julie M. Norman, eds. 2015. *Understanding Nonviolence.* Cambridge: Polity Press.

Hallward, Maia, Juan Masullo, and Cécile Mouly. 2017. "Civil Resistance in Armed Conflict: Leveraging Nonviolent Action to Navigate War, Oppose Violence, and Confront Oppression." *Journal of Peacebuilding and Development* 12 (3): 1–9.

Haraway, Donna. 1988. *Situated Knowledges: The Science Question in Feminism and the Privilege of Partial Perspective. Feminist Studies* 14 (3): 575–99.

——. 2016. *Staying with the Trouble: Making Kin in the Chthulucene.* Durham, NC: Duke University Press.

Harrison, Faye V., ed. 1991. *Decolonizing Anthropology: Moving Further Toward an Anthropology for Liberation.* Washington, DC: Association for Black Anthropologists, American Anthropological Association.

Harvey, David. 1994. "The Social Construction of Space and Time: A Relational Theory." *Geographical Review of Japan, Series B* 67 (2): 126–35.

——. 2005. *A Brief History of Neoliberalism.* Oxford: Oxford University Press.

Hatala, Andrew R., Darrien Morton, Chinyere Njeze, Kelley Bird-Naytowhow, and Tamara Pearl. 2019. "Re-imagining *miyo-wicehtowin*: Human-Nature Relations, Land-Making, and Wellness among Indigenous Youth in a Canadian Urban Context." *Social Science and Medicine* 230: 122–30.

Hernández Delgado, Esperanza. 2012. Intervenir antes que anochezca: Mediaciones, intermediaciones y diplomacias noviolentas de base social en el conflicto armado Colombiano. Bogotá: IEP-UNAB.

Hickel, Jason. 2019. "Degrowth: A Theory of Radical Abundance." *Real World Economics Review* 87: 54–68.

Hill Collins, Patricia. 2019. *Intersectionality as Critical Social Theory.* Durham, NC: Duke University Press.

Hinton, Alexander Laban. 2018. *The Justice Façade: Trials of Transition in Cambodia.* Oxford: Oxford University Press.

Hinton, Alexander Laban, ed. 2010. *Transitional Justice: Global Mechanisms and Local Realities after Genocide and Mass Violence.* New Brunswick, NJ: Rutgers University Press.

Honoré, Carl. 2005. *In Praise of Slowness: Challenging the Cult of Speed.* New York: HarperOne.

hooks, bell. 2009. *Belonging: A Culture of Place.* New York: Routledge.

Hoover, Elizabeth. 2017. *The River Is in Us: Fighting Toxics in a Mohawk Community.* Minneapolis: University of Minnesota Press.

Howland, Todd. 2017. "Esperamos que muy pronto el defensor Jorge Montes sea liberado y reparado." *Semana*, June 13, 2017.

Hughes, Caroline, Joakim Öjendal, and Isabell Schierenbeck. 2015. "The Struggle versus the Song—The Local Turn in Peacebuilding: An Introduction." *Third World Quarterly* 36 (5): 817–24.

Hunter-Bowman, Janna. 2018. "Constructive Agents under Duress: Alternatives to the Structural, Political, and Agential Inadequacies of Past Theologies of Nonviolent Peacebuilding Efforts." *Journal of the Society of Christian Ethics* 38 (2): 149–68.

———. 2022. *Witnessing Peace: Becoming Agents under Duress in Colombia*. London: Routledge.

Hurston, Zora Neale. (1942) 1996. *Dust Tracks on a Road: A Memoir*. New York: Harper-Collins.

ICA (Instituto Colombiano Agropecuario). 2009. "ICA impulsa plan para erradicar 6000 árboles de aguacate en Montes de María." www.ica.gov.co/Noticias/Agricola/2009/ICA-impulsa-plan-para-erradicar-6000-arboles-de-ag.aspx.

Igoe, James. 2010. "The Spectacle of Nature in the Global Economy of Appearances: Anthropological Engagements with the Spectacular Mediations of Transnational Conservation." *Critique of Anthropology* 30 (3): 375–97.

Imanishi, Kinji. (1941) 2002. *A Japanese View of Nature: The World of Living Things*. Translated by Pamela J. Asquith, Heita Kawakatsu, Shusuke Yagi, and Hiroyuki Takasaki. New York: Routledge.

Indepaz. 2021. "Líderes sociales, Defensores de DDHH y firmantes de acuerdo asesinados en 2021." www.indepaz.org.

Ingold, Tim. 2000. *The Perception of Environment*. New York: Routledge.

———. 2011. *Being Alive: Essays on Movement, Knowledge, and Description*. New York: Routledge.

Isacson, Adam. December 2012. "Consolidating 'Consolidation.'" Washington, DC: Washington Office on Latin America. www.wola.org/files/Consolidating_Consolidation.pdf.

———. January 30, 2012. "'Consolidation,' Land Restitution, and Rising Tensions in Montes de María." CCAI-Colombia, Washington Office on Latin America.

Isacson, Adam, and Abigail Poe. 2009. "After Plan Colombia: Evaluating 'Integrated Action,' the Next Phase of U.S. Assistance." Washington, DC: International Policy Report. www.kolko.net/downloads/Center_for_intl_policy_After_Plan_Colombia.pdf.

Jaramillo, Pablo. 2012. "Deuda, desesperación y reparaciones inconclusas en La Guajira, Colombia." *Antípoda: Revista de Antropología y Arqueología* 14: 41–65.

Jaramillo, Sergio. 2013. "La Paz Territorial." Bogotá: Alto Comisionado Para La Paz.

JEP (Jurisdicción Especial para la Paz). 2021. "La JEP hace pública la estrategia de priorización dentro del Caso 03 conocido como el de falsos positivos." Comunicado 019, 2021: www.jep.gov.co/Sala-de-Prensa/Paginas/La-JEP-hace-p%C3%BAblica-la-estrategia-de-priorizaci%C3%B3n-dentro-del-Caso-03,-conocido-como-el-de-falsos-positivos.aspx.

Jiménez Ahumada, Rosa. 2004. "Desarrollo y paz en los Montes de María: Una propuesta desde la región." In *Dimensiones territoriales de La Guerra y La Paz*, 503–18. Bogotá: Universidad Nacional de Colombia.

Johnson, Symone. 2019. "Making, Holding, and Guarding as Spatial Politics of Healing." *Anthropology News*, March 27, 2019. www.anthropologynews.org/articles/making -holding-and-guarding-as-spatial-politics-of-healing/.

Junieles Acosta, Irina. 2017. "Relatos de víctimas de detenciones arbitrarias." *El Especta- dor*, September 26, 2017, Colombia 2020 edition. https://colombia2020.elespectador. com/verdad-y-memoria/relatos-de-victimas-de-detenciones-arbitrarias.

Junieles Acosta, Irina, Cheryl Morris, Angélica María Cuevas Guarnizo, Carolina Mila Torres, and Hobeth Martinez. March 21, 2019. *Que nos llamen inocentes: Testimonios de detenciones arbitrarias desde El Carmen de Bolívar*. Bogotá: Dejusticia.

Kaba, Mariame. 2018. "Hope Is a Discipline." *Beyond Prisons*, January 5, 2018. www.be yondprisons.com/home/hope-is-a-discipline-feat-mariame-kaba.

———. 2021. *We Do This 'Til We Free Us: Abolitionist Organizing and Transforming Jus- tice*. Chicago: Haymarket Books.

Kahneman, Daniel. 2011. *Thinking, Fast and Slow*. New York: Farrar, Straus and Giroux.

Kallis, Giorgos, Susan Paulson, Giacoma D'Alisa, and Frederico Demaria. 2020. *The Case for Degrowth*. Medford, MA: Polity Press.

Kaplan, Oliver Ross. 2017. *Resisting War: How Communities Protect Themselves*. New York: Cambridge University Press.

Karl, Robert A. 2017. *Forgotten Peace: Reform, Violence, and the Making of Contemporary Colombia*. Oakland: University of California Press.

Kimmerer, Robin Wall. 2013. *Braiding Sweetgrass: Indigenous Wisdom, Scientific Knowl- edge, and the Teachings of Plants*. Minneapolis: Milkweed Editions.

King, Martin Luther. 1963. "Letter from Birmingham Jail." *Ebony* (August 1963): 23–32. https://kinginstitute.stanford.edu/encyclopedia/letter-birmingham-jail.

Kirksey, Eben. 2012. *Freedom in Entangled Worlds: West Papua and the Architecture of Global Power*. Durham, NC: Duke University Press.

Kirskey, Eben, and Stephen Helmreich. 2010. "The Emergence of Multispecies Ethnog- raphy." *Cultural Anthropology* 25 (4): 545–76.

Kleist, Nauja, and Stef Jansen. 2016. "Introduction: Hope over Time—Crisis, Immobil- ity, and Future-Making." *History and Anthropology* 27 (4): 373–92.

Koepnick, Lutz P. 2014. *On Slowness: Toward an Aesthetic of the Contemporary*. New York: Columbia University Press.

Kohn, Eduardo. 2013. *How Forests Think: Toward an Anthropology beyond the Human*. Berkeley: University of California Press.

Koopman, Sara. 2012. "Making Space for Peace: International Protective Accompani- ment in Colombia (2007–2009)." PhD diss., University of British Columbia.

Kroeker, Wendy. 2020. *Multidimensional Peacebuilding: Local Actors in the Philippine Context*. Lanham, MD: Lexington Books.

Krystalli, Roxani. 2019a. "Narrating Violence: Feminist Dilemmas and Approaches." In *Handbook on Gender and Violence*, edited by Laura J. Shepherd, 173–88. Cheltenham, UK: Edward Elgar.

———. 2019b. "'We Are Not Good Victims': Hierarchies of Suffering and the Politics of

Victimhood in Colombia." PhD diss., Fletcher School for International Diplomacy, Tufts University.

———. 2020. "Attendance Sheets and Bureaucracies of Victimhood in Colombia." *Political and Legal Anthropology Review Emergent Conversation 10*, November 24, 2020. https://polarjournal.org/2020/11/24/attendance-sheets-and-bureaucracies-of -victimhood-in-colombia/.

Krystalli, Roxani, and Philipp Schulz. 2022. "Taking Love and Care Seriously: An Emergent Research Agenda for Remaking Worlds in the Wake of Violence." *International Studies Review* 24 (1): 1–25.

La Silla Vacía. 2016. "Argos pierde una batalla en Montes de María," April 2016. https://lasillavacia.com/historia/argos-pierde-una-batalla-en-montes-de-mar%C3%ADa-55399.

Lakey, George. August 4, 2017. "A Manual for the New Era of Activist." *Yes Magazine:* www.yesmagazine.org/democracy/2017/08/04/a-manual-for-the-new-era-of-activist.

Lederach, Angela J. 2017. "'The Campesino Was Born for the Campo': A Multispecies Approach to Territorial Peace in Colombia." *American Anthropologist* 119 (4): 589–602.

———. 2019. "Youth Provoking Peace: An Intersectional Approach to Territorial Peacebuilding in Colombia." *Peacebuilding* 8 (2): 198–217.

———. 2020. "'Each Word Is Powerful': Writing and the Ethics of Representation in Peace and Conflict Fieldwork." *The Palgrave Companion to Peace and Conflict Fieldwork*, edited by Roddy Brett, Roger Mac Ginty, and Birte Vogel, 455–70. London: Palgrave Macmillan.

Lederach, John Paul. 1997. *Building Peace: Sustainable Reconciliation in Divided Societies.* Washington, DC: United States Institute of Peace.

———. 1999. *The Journey Toward Reconciliation.* Scottdale, PA.: Herald Press.

———. 2003. *The Little Book of Conflict Transformation.* Intercourse, PA: Good Books.

———. 2005. *The Moral Imagination: The Art and Soul of Building Peace.* Oxford: Oxford University Press.

———. 2016. "Con un acuerdo de paz, Colombia abre una nueva era de posibilidades: Se requerirán nuevas capacidades." *Oficina del Alto Comisionado para La Paz* (blog). 2016. www.altocomisionadoparalapaz.gov.co/Prensa/Paginas/2016/noviembre/Pioneros-en-la-construccion-de-paz-desde-la-regiones.aspx.

Lederach, John Paul, and Angela J. Lederach. 2010. *When Blood and Bones Cry Out: Journeys through the Soundscape of Healing and Reconciliation.* Oxford: Oxford University Press.

Li, Fabiana. 2015. *Unearthing Conflict: Corporate Mining, Activism, and Expertise in Peru.* Durham, NC: Duke University Press.

Li, Tania Murray. 2007. *The Will to Improve: Governmentality, Development, and the Practice of Politics.* Durham, NC: Duke University Press.

Lichterman, Paul. 1999. "Talking Identity in the Public Sphere: Broad Visions and Small Spaces in Sexual Identity Politics." *Theory and Society* 28 (1): 101–41.

Livingston, Julie. 2019. *Self-Devouring Growth: A Planetary Parable as Told from Southern Africa.* Durham, NC: Duke University Press.

Lombard, Louisa. 2016. *State of Rebellion: Violence and Intervention in the Central African Republic*. London: Zed Books.

Lugones, Maria. 2010. "Toward a Decolonial Feminism." *Hypatia: A Journal of Feminist Philosophy* 25 (4): 742–59.

Lyons, Kristina. 2014. "Soil Science, Development, and the 'Elusive Nature' of Colombia's Amazonian Plains." *Journal of Latin American and Caribbean Anthropology* 19 (2): 212–36.

———. 2016. "Decomposition as Life Politics: Soils, Selva, and Small Farmers under the Gun of the U.S.-Colombian War on Drugs." *Cultural Anthropology* 31 (1): 56–81.

———. 2020. *Vital Decomposition: Soil Practitioners and Life Politics*. Durham, NC: Duke University Press.

Lyons, Kristina, Lina B. Pinto-García, and Daniel Ruiz Serna. 2019. "Presentación: Conflicto y paz en Colombia, más allá de lo humano." *Maguaré* 33 (2): 15–22.

Mac Ginty, Roger. 2011. *International Peacebuilding and Local Resistance: Hybrid Forms of Peace*. New York: Palgrave Macmillan.

———. 2015. "Where Is the Local? Critical Localism and Peacebuilding." *Third World Quarterly* 36 (5): 840–56.

———. 2018. "The Limits of Technocracy and Local Encounters: The European Union and Peacebuilding." *Contemporary Security Policy* 39 (1): 166–79.

———. 2021. *Everyday Peace: How So-Called Ordinary People Can Disrupt Violent Conflict*. Oxford: Oxford University Press.

Mac Ginty, Roger, and Oliver Richmond. 2013. "The Local Turn in Peace Building: A Critical Agenda for Peace." *Third World Quarterly* 34 (5): 763–83.

Mahmood, Cynthia Keppley. 2008. "Anthropology from the Bones: A Memoir of Fieldwork, Survival, and Commitment." *Anthropology and Humanism* 33 (1–2): 1–11.

Mahmood, Saba. 2005. *Politics of Piety: The Islamic Revival and the Feminist Subject*. Princeton, NJ: Princeton University Press.

Mahony, Liam, and Luis Enrique Eguren. 1997. *Unarmed Bodyguards: International Accompaniment for the Protection of Human Rights*. West Hartford, CT: Kumarian Press.

Malkki, Liisa H. 2015. *The Need to Help: The Domestic Arts of International Humanitarianism*. Durham, NC: Duke University Press.

Maring, Clayton. 2016. "Simple Miracles: Ricardo Esquivia Ballestas." In *Peacemakers in Action: Profiles in Religious Peacebuilding, Volume II*, edited by Joyce S. Dubensky, 186–237. Tanenbaum Center for Interreligious Understanding. New York: Cambridge University Press.

Marshall, Katherine. 2011. "Blessed be the Peacemakers: Mourning Dekha Ibrahim Abdi. *Faith in Action: Berkley Center for Religion, Peace, and World Affairs*. July 21, 2011. https://berkleycenter.georgetown.edu/posts/blessed-be-the-peacemakers-mourning-dekha-ibrahim-abdi.

Mason, Ann. 2003. "Colombia's Democratic Security Agenda: Public Order in the Security Tripod." *Security Dialogue* 34 (4): 391–409.

Masullo, Juan. 2015. "The Power of Staying Put: Nonviolent Resistance against Armed Groups in Colombia." ICNC Monograph Series. Washington, DC: International

Center on Nonviolent Conflict. www.nonviolent-conflict.org/wp-content/uploads/2016/01/The-Power-of-Staying-Put.pdf.

McCoy, Kate, Eve Tuck, and Marcia McKenzie. 2016. *Land Education: Rethinking Pedagogies of Place from Indigenous, Postcolonial, and Decolonizing Perspectives*. New York: Routledge.

McEvoy-Levy, Siobhan. 2012. "Youth Spaces in Haunted Places: Placemaking for Peacebuilding in Theory and Practice." *International Journal of Peace Studies* 17 (2): 1–32.

McFee, Erin K. 2020. "'Making a Presence': Reconciliation and the State in Colombia." *Political and Legal Anthropology Review Emergent Conversation 10*, November 24, 2020. https://polarjournal.org/2020/11/24/making-a-presence-reconciliation-and-the-state-in-colombia/.

McGranahan, Carole. 2021. "The Truths of Anonymity: Ethnographic Credibility and the Problem with Pseudonyms." In "Rethinking Pseudonyms in Ethnography," edited by Carole McGranahan and Erica Weiss, *American Ethnologist*, December 13, 2021. https://americanethnologist.org/features/collections/rethinking-pseudonyms-in-ethnography/the-truths-of-anonymity-ethnographic-credibility-and-the-problem-with-pseudonyms.

McLean, Lisa, and María Lucía Zapata Cancelado. 2015. "Peace Studies and Feminism: Debates, Linkages, and Intersections," in *Gender and Peacebuilding: All Hands Required*, edited by Maureen P. Flaherty et al., 281–98. Lanham, MD: Lexington Books.

McLeod, Allegra M. 2019. "Envisioning Abolition Democracy." *Harvard Law Review* 132: 1613–49.

Meertens, Donny. 2015. "Discursive Frictions: The Transitional Justice Paradigm, Land Restitution, and Gender in Colombia." *Papel Político* 20 (2): 353–81.

Méndez, María José. 2018. "'The River Told Me': Rethinking Intersectionality from the World of Berta Cáceres." *Capitalism Nature Socialism* 29 (1): 7–24.

Mesa de Interlocución y Concertación de los Montes de María. 2014. *En busca de la permanencia digna en el territorio*. Cartagena, Colombia: Corporación Desarrollo Solidario.

Mignolo, Walter. 2005. *The Idea of Latin America*. Malden, MA: Blackwell Publishers.

Millar, Gearoid, ed. 2018. *Ethnographic Peace Research: Approaches and Tensions*. Cham, Switzerland: Palgrave Macmillan.

Million, Dian. 2008. "Felt Theory." *American Quarterly* 60 (2): 267–72.

Mische, Ann. 2009. "Projects and Possibilities: Researching Futures in Action." *Sociological Forum* 24 (3): 694–704.

Moraga, Cherríe, and Gloria Anzaldúa. 1981. *This Bridge Called My Back: Writings by Radical Women of Color*. Watertown, MA: Persephone Press.

Mouly, Cécile, Annette Idler, and Belén Garrido. 2015. "Zones of Peace in Colombia's Borderland." *International Journal of Peace Studies* 20 (1): 51–63.

Moyer, Bill. 2001. *Doing Democracy: The MAP Model for Organizing Social Movements*. Gabriola Island, BC: New Society Publishers.

Muir, Stewart. 2004. "Not Quite at Home: Field Envy and New Age Ethnographic Dis-Ease." In *Anthropologists in the Field*, edited by Lynne Hume and Jane Mulcock, 185–99. New York: Columbia University Press.

Negrete Barrera, Víctor. 2013. *IAP: La investigación acción participativa en Córdoba*. Montería, Colombia: Publicaciones Unisinú.

Nixon, Rob. 2011. *Slow Violence and the Environmentalism of the Poor*. Cambridge, MA: Harvard University Press.

Nordstrom, Carolyn. 1995. "War on the Frontlines." In *Fieldwork under Fire: Contemporary Studies of Violence and Survival*, edited by Carolyn Nordstrom and Antonius C. G. M. Robben, 129–54. Berkeley: University of California Press.

———. 1997. *A Different Kind of War Story*. Philadelphia: University of Pennsylvania Press.

———. 1999. "Visible Wars and Invisible Girls, Shadow Industries, and the Politics of Not Knowing." *International Feminist Journal of Politics* 1 (1): 14–33.

Nussio, Enzo. 2011. "Learning from Shortcomings: The Demobilisation of Paramilitaries in Colombia." *Journal of Peacebuilding and Development* 6 (2): 88–92.

Ojeda, Diana, Pablo Guerra, Camilo Aguirre, and Henry Díaz. 2020. *Caminos condenados*. Bogotá: Laguna Libros.

Ojeda, Diana, Jennifer Petzl, Catalina Quiroga, Ana Catalina Rodríguez, and Juan Guillermo Rojas. 2015. "Paisajes del despojo cotidiano: Acaparamiento de tierra y agua en Montes de María, Colombia." *Revista de Estudios Sociales* 54: 107–19.

O'Neill, Bruce. 2017. *The Space of Boredom: Homelessness in the Slowing Global Order*. Durham, NC: Duke University Press.

Paarlberg-Kvam, Kate. 2019. "What's to Come Is More Complicated: Feminist Visions of Peace in Colombia." *International Feminist Journal of Politics* 21 (2): 194–223.

———. 2021. "Open-Pit Peace: The Power of Extractive Industries in Post-Conflict Transitions." *Peacebuilding* 9 (3): 1–22.

Palacios, Marco. 2006. *Between Legitimacy and Violence: A History of Colombia, 1875–2002*. Durham, NC: Duke University Press.

Paladini Adell, Borja. 2020. "From a Divisive Peace Agreement to a Legitimate Peace in Colombia." In *Local Legitimacy and International Peacebuilding*, edited by Oliver Richmond and Roger Mac Ginty. Edinburgh: Edinburgh University Press.

Pandian, Anand. 2019. *A Possible Anthropology: Methods for Uneasy Times*. Durham, NC: Duke University Press.

Parkins, Wendy, and Geoffrey Craig. 2006. *Slow Living*. Oxford: Berg.

Pellegrino, Silvana Valentina. 2017. "Incumplir cumpliendo: Una etnografía al papeleo del auto 005." PhD thesis, Universidad de los Andes, Colombia.

Pellegrino, Valentina. 2022. "Between the Roll of Paper and the Role of Paper: Governmental Documentation as a Mechanism for Complying Incompliantly." *Political and Legal Anthropology Review* 45 (1): 77–93.

Peluso, Nancy Lee, and Michael Watts, eds. 2001. *Violent Environments*. Ithaca, NY: Cornell University Press.

Pérez, Jesús María. 2010. Luchas campesinas y reforma agraria: Memorias de un dirigente de la ANUC en la Costa Caribe. Bogotá,: Puntoaparte Editores.

Pérez, Jorge. (2014) 2018. "Un paseo vallenato inspirado en ACOMM." In *Un bosque de memoria viva: Desde la Alta Montaña de El Carmen de Bolívar*, edited by CNMH, 143. Bogotá: Centro Nacional de Memoria Histórica.

Petrini, Carlo. 2007. *Slow Food Nation: Why Our Food Should Be Good, Clean, and Fair.* New York: Rizzoli Ex Libris.

Philpott, Daniel, and Gerard F. Powers, eds. 2010. *Strategies of Peace.* Oxford: Oxford University Press.

PNUD. 2010. "Los Montes de María: Análisis de la conflictividad." Bogotá: PNUD, Área de Paz, Desarrollo y Reconciliación.

Porras Mendoza, Eduardo. 2014. "Conflictos, violencias y resistencias en Los Montes de María." In *Territorio y conflicto en la Costa Caribe*, edited by González G. Fernán, 331–86. Bogotá: Odecofi-CINEP.

Postero, Nancy. 2017. *The Indigenous State: Race, Politics, and Performance in Plurinational Bolivia.* Oakland: University of California Press.

Povinelli, Elizabeth A. 2011. *Economies of Abandonment: Social Belonging and Endurance in Late Liberalism.* Durham, NC: Duke University Press.

Presidencia de la República—Ministerio de Defensa Nacional. 2003. "Política de Defensa y Seguridad Democrática." Presidencia de la República de Colombia.

Pugh, Michael C., Neil Cooper, and Mandy Turner. 2008. *Whose Peace? Critical Perspectives on the Political Economy of Peacebuilding.* New York: Palgrave Macmillan.

Quiceno Toro, Natalia. 2016. *Vivir Sabroso: Luchas y movimientos afroatrateños, en Bojayá, Chocó, Colombia.* Bogotá: Universidad del Rosario.

Ramírez, María Clemencia. 2011. *Between the Guerrillas and the State: The Cocalero Movement, Citizenship, and Identity in the Colombian Amazon.* Durham, NC: Duke University Press.

Rappaport, Joanne. 2021. *Cowards Don't Make History: Orlando Fals Borda and the Origins of Participatory Action Research.* Durham, NC: Duke University Press.

RCN Radio. 2017. "Exportaciones de ñame se perdieron por su envío en mal estado, según MinAgricultura." *RCN*, September 12, 2017. www.rcnradio.com/economia/exportaciones-name-se-perdieron-envio-mal-estado-segun-minagricultura.

Rey Sabogal, Camilo. 2013. "Análisis espacial de la correlación entre cultivo de palma de aceite y desplazamiento forzado en Colombia." *Cuadernos de Economía* 32 (61): 683–718.

Riaño-Alcalá, Pilar. 2006. *Dwellers of Memory: Youth and Violence in Medellín, Colombia.* New York: Routledge.

Richmond, Oliver. 2011. *A Post-Liberal Peace.* New York: Routledge.

———. 2012. "Beyond Local Ownership in the Architecture of International Peacebuilding." *Ethnopolitics* 11 (4): 354–75.

———. 2018. "Rescuing Peacebuilding? Anthropology and Peace Formation." *Global Society* 32 (2): 221–39.

Ricigliano, Robert. 2012. *Making Peace Last: A Toolbox for Sustainable Peacebuilding.* New York: Routledge.

Rifkin, Mark. 2017. *Beyond Settler Time: Temporal Sovereignty and Indigenous Self-Determination.* Durham, NC: Duke University Press.

Roberts, Neil. 2015. *Freedom as Marronage*. Chicago: University of Chicago Press.

Robles Lomeli, Jafte Dilean, and Joanne Rappaport. 2018. "Imagining Latin American Social Science from the Global South: Orlando Fals Borda and Participatory Action Research." *Latin American Research Review* 53 (3): 597–612.

Rocha, Daniel, ed. 2010. *Trazos de libertad*. Bogotá: Comisión Nacional de Reparación y Reconciliación.

Rodríguez, Ana Catalina. 2021. "Entre la lucha campesina y la afirmación de la identidad cultural en Montes de María." In *Montes de María: Un territorio en disputa*, edited by Diana Ojeda Ojeda, Catalina Quiroga Manrique, and Diana Vallejo Bernal, 40–57. Bogotá: Pontificia Universidad Javeriana.

Rodríguez, Clemencia. 2011. *Citizens' Media against Armed Conflict: Disrupting Violence in Colombia*. Minneapolis: University of Minnesota Press.

Rodriguez, Mery. 2012. "Colombia: From Grassroots to Elites—How Some Local Peace-building Initiatives Became National in Spite of Themselves." In *Local Peacebuilding and National Peace: Interaction between Grassroots and Elite Processes*, edited by Christopher Mitchell and Landon E. Hancock, 69–92. New York: Continuum.

Rojas, Diana Marcela. 2015. *El Plan Colombia: La intervención de Estados Unidos en el conflicto armado Colombiano (1998–2012)*. Bogotá: Instituto de Estudios Políticos y Relaciones Internacionales. Universidad Nacional de Colombia.

Ronderos, María Teresa. 2014. *Guerras recicladas: Una historia periodística del paramilitarismo en Colombia*. Bogotá: Penguin Random House Grupo Editorial.

Ross, Fiona. 2003. *Bearing Witness: Women and the Truth and Reconciliation Commission in South Africa*. London: Pluto.

Roux, Francisco de. 2018. *La audacia de la paz imperfecta*. Bogotá: Editorial Planeta.

———. 2020. "Nos creíamos invencibles." *Semana*, March 29, 2020.

Ruiz Hernández, Juana Alicia. 2013. *Vivensías*. Marialabaja, Colombia: US Department of Justice.

Ruiz Serna, Daniel. 2015. "Threads of Life and Death: A Photo Essay on Hunting and Fishing in Northwest Amazonia." *Visual Anthropology Review* 31 (1): 73–86.

———. 2017. "El territorio como víctima: Ontología política y las leyes de víctimas para comunidades Indígenas y Negras en Colombia." *Revista Colombiana de Antropología* 53 (2): 85–113.

Rutas del Conflicto. 2017. "Historias de acuatenientes." CNMH and Verdad Abierta. http://rutasdelconflicto.com/especiales/acuatenientes/.

Salamanca Rangel, José Manuel. 2018. "Otros Saberes, Otras Paz-Es." Paper presented at the Latin American Studies Association Congress. Barcelona, Spain.

Santos, Juan Manuel. 2016. "Discurso del Presidente Santos en la firma del Acuerdo Final de Paz." Firma del Acuerdo Final de Paz, Cartagena, Colombia.

Sarmiento Santander, Fernando, Jesús David Huertas, Julián Barajas, Laura Constanza Henao, and Marcela Fernanda Pardo. 2018. *Aprendizajes de construcción de paz en Montes de María*. Bogotá: CINEP.

Saunders, Harold. 2011. *Sustained Dialogue in Conflicts*. New York: Palgrave Macmillan.

Scheper-Hughes, Nancy, and Philippe Bourgois, eds. 2004. *Violence in War and Peace.* Malden, MA: Blackwell.

Schirch, Lisa. 2005. *The Little Book of Strategic Peacebuilding.* New York: Good Books.

Scott, James C. 1990. *Domination and the Arts of Resistance: Hidden Transcripts.* New Haven, CT: Yale University Press.

Serrano Amaya, José Fernando. 2018. *Homophobic Violence in Armed Conflict and Political Transition.* London: Palgrave Macmillan.

Serrano Amaya, José Fernando, and Adam Baird, eds. 2013. *Paz, paso a paso: Una mirada a los conflictos colombianos desde los estudios de paz.* Bogotá: Pontificia Universidad Javeriana.

Shange, Savannah. 2019. *Progressive Dystopia: Abolition, Antiblackness, and Schooling in San Francisco.* Durham, NC: Duke University Press.

Sharma, Sarah. 2013. "Critical Time." *Communication and Critical/Cultural Studies* 10 (2): 312–18.

Sharpe, Christina. 2016. *In the Wake: On Blackness and Being.* Durham, NC: Duke University Press.

Shaw, Rosalind, and Lars Waldorf. 2010. "Introduction: Localizing Transitional Justice." In *Localizing Transitional Justice: Interventions and Priorities after Mass Violence,* edited by Rosalind Shaw, Lars Waldorf, and Pierre Hazan, 3–26. Stanford, CA: Stanford University Press.

Shaw, Rosalind, Lars Waldorf, and Pierre Hazan, eds. 2010. *Localizing Transitional Justice: Interventions and Priorities after Mass Violence.* Stanford Studies in Human Rights. Stanford, CA: Stanford University Press.

Simpson, Audra. 2014. *Mohawk Interruptus: Political Life across the Borders of Settler States.* Durham, NC: Duke University Press.

Simpson, Leanne Betasamosake. 2014. "Land as Pedagogy: Nishnaabeg Intelligence and Rebellious Transformation." *Decolonization: Indigeneity, Education, and Society* 3 (3): 1–25.

Solnit, Rebecca. 2016. *Hope in the Dark: Untold Histories, Wild Possibilities.* Chicago: Haymarket Books.

Stasch, Rupert. 2011. "Ritual and Oratory Revisited: The Semiotics of Effective Action." *Annual Review of Anthropology* 40 (1): 159–74.

Strathern, Marilyn. (1991) 2005. *Partial Connections.* Lanham, MD: AltaMira Press.

Sultana, Farhana. 2007. "Reflexivity, Positionality, and Participatory Ethics: Negotiating Fieldwork Dilemmas in International Research." *ACME* 6 (3): 374–85.

Tam, Daisy. 2008. "Slow Journeys: What Does It Mean to Go Slow?" *Food* 11 (2): 207–18.

Tambiah, Stanley J. 1981. *A Performative Approach to Ritual.* London: British Academy.

Tasch, Woody. 2010. *Inquiries into the Nature of Slow Money: Investing as If Food, Farms, and Fertility Mattered.* White River Junction, VT: Chelsea Green Publishing.

Tate, Winifred. 2015. *Drugs, Thugs, and Diplomats: U.S. Policymaking in Colombia.* Stanford, CA: Stanford University Press.

Taussig, Michael. 1987. *Shamanism, Colonialism, and the Wild Man: A Study in Terror and Healing.* Chicago: University of Chicago Press.

Taylor, Sunaura. 2017. *Beasts of Burden: Animal and Disability Liberation*. New York: New Press.

Temblores, Paiis, and Indepaz. 2021. Informe de Temblores ONG, Indepaz y Paiis a la CIDH sobre la violación sistemática de la Convención Americana y los alcances juris- prudenciales de la Corte IDH con respeto al uso de la fuerza pública contra la socie- dad civil en Colombia. Colombia: Temblores ONG.

Terriquez, Veronica. 2015. "Intersectional Mobilization, Social Movement Spillover, and Queer Youth Leadership in the Immigrant Rights Movement." *Social Problems* 62 (3): 343–62.

Theidon, Kimberly. 2007. "Transitional Subjects: The Disarmament, Demobilization, and Reintegration of Former Combatants in Colombia." *International Journal of Transitional Justice* 1 (1): 66–90.

———. 2009. "The Milk of Sorrow: A Theory on the Violence of Memory." *Canadian Woman Studies* 27 (1): 8–16.

———. 2013. *Intimate Enemies: Violence and Reconciliation in Peru*. Philadelphia: Univer- sity of Pennsylvania Press.

Thomas, Deborah. 2019. *Political Life in the Wake of the Plantation: Sovereignty, Witness- ing, Repair*. Durham, NC: Duke University Press.

Ticktin, Miriam. 2011. *Casualties of Care: Immigration and the Politics of Humanitarian- ism in France*. Berkeley: University of California Press.

Tilly, Charles. 1994. "The Time of States." *Social Research* 61 (2): 269–95.

———. 2008. *Contentious Performances*. Cambridge: Cambridge University Press.

Todd, Zoe. 2016a. "From a Fishy Place: Examining Canadian State Law Applied in the Daniels Decision from the Perspective of Métis Legal Orders." *TOPIA: Canadian Journal of Cultural Studies* 36: 43–57.

———. 2016b. "An Indigenous Feminist's Take on the Ontological Turn: 'Ontology' Is Just Another Word for Colonialism." *Journal of Historical Sociology* 29 (1): 4–22.

———. 2016c. "Tenderness Manifesto." *Speculative fish-ctions*. https://zoestodd.com/2016/09/18/tending-tenderness/.

———. 2017. "Fish, Kin, and Hope: Tending to Water Violations in Amiskwaciwâska- hikan and Treaty Six Territory." *Afterall: A Journal of Art, Context, and Enquiry* 43 (1): 102–7.

———. 2019. "On Time." *Fish Philosophy*, January 5, 2019. https://fishphilosophy.org/2019/01/05/on-time-some-of-my-newer-work/.

Tom, Patrick. 2017. *Liberal Peace and Post-Conflict Peacebuilding in Africa*. London: Pal- grave Macmillan.

Tsing, Anna Lowenhaupt. 2005. *Friction: An Ethnography of Global Connection*. Prince- ton, NJ: Princeton University Press.

———. 2011. "Arts of Inclusion; or, How to Love a Mushroom." *Australian Humanities Review* 50: 5–22.

———. 2015. *The Mushroom at the End of the World: On the Possibility of Life in Capitalist Ruins*. Princeton, NJ: Princeton University Press.

Tuck, Eve. 2009. "Suspending Damage: A Letter to Communities." *Harvard Educational Review* 79 (3): 409–540.

Unidad Para la Atención y Reparación Integral de las Víctimas. 2014. *Fase de diagnóstico del daño de la comunidad campesina de la Alta Montaña de El Carmen de Bolívar.* Bogotá: Unidad Para la Atención y Reparación Integral de las Víctimas.

Valenzuela, Pedro. 1995. "Un marco analítico del proceso de terminación de conflictos violentos, con aplicación al caso colombiano." *América latina hoy: Revista de ciencias sociales*: 29–36.

———. 2009. *Neutrality in Internal Armed Conflicts: Experiences at the Grassroots Level in Colombia.* Uppsala, Sweden: Uppsala Universitet.

Vega, Jair, and Soraya Bayuelo. 2008. "Ganándole terreno al miedo: Cine y comunicación en Los Montes de María." In *Lo que le vamos quitando a la guerra: Medios ciudadanos en contextos de conflicto armado en Colombia*, edited by Clemencia Rodríguez. Bogotá: Centro de Competencia en Comunicación para América Latina.

Velásquez Estrada, R. Elizabeth. 2022. "Intersectional Justice Denied: Racist Warring Masculinity, Negative Peace, and Violence in Post-Peace Accords El Salvador." *American Anthropologist* 124 (1): 39–52.

Vigías Ecológicas. 2016. "Conocer nuestro territorio es construir paz: jóvenes Montemarianos mapean el arroyo Palenquillo." *Sembrandopaz* (blog).

Viveiros de Castro, Eduardo. 2004. "Perspectival Anthropology and the Method of Controlled Equivocation." *Tipití: Journal of the Society for the Anthropology of Lowland South America* 2 (1): 3–22.

Watts, Vanessa. 2013. "Indigenous Place-Thought and Agency amongst Humans and Non Humans (First Woman and Sky Woman Go On a European World Tour!)." *Decolonization: Indigeneity, Education, and Society* 2 (1): 20–34.

West, Paige. 2016. *Dispossession and the Environment: Rhetoric and Inequality in Papua New Guinea.* New York: Columbia University Press.

Wildcat, Matthew, Mandee McDonald, Stephanie Irlbacher-Fox, and Glen Coulthard. 2014. "Learning from the Land: Indigenous Land Based Pedagogy and Decolonization." *Decolonization: Indigeneity, Education, and Society* 3 (3): i–xv.

Williams, Becca. 2017. "Visions of Peace in the Colombian Countryside." Notre Dame, IN: University of Notre Dame.

Williams, Raymond. 1977. *Marxism and Literature.* Oxford: Oxford University Press.

Wills, María Emma. 2007. *Inclusión sin representación: La irrupción política de las mujeres en Colombia, 1970–2000.* Bogotá: Editorial Norma.

Yabrudy Vega, Javier. 2012. *El aguacate en Colombia: Estudio de caso de Los Montes de María, en el Caribe Colombiano.* Documentos de Trabajo Sobre Economía Regional Número 171. Cartagena, Colombia: Banco de la República; Centro de Estudios Económicos Regionales.

Zamosc, León. 1986. *The Agrarian Question and the Peasant Movement in Colombia: Struggles of the National Peasant Association, 1967–1981.* Cambridge: Cambridge University Press.

Zapata-Cancelado, María Lucía. 2020. "A Conflict Transformation Analysis of Local
    Peacebuilding Initiatives in the Montes de María Region of Colombia: The Case of
    Sembrandopaz." PhD thesis, Peace and Conflict Studies. University of Manitoba,
    Winnipeg.
Zigon, Jarrett. 2009. "Hope Dies Last: Two Aspects of Hope in Contemporary Moscow."
    Anthropological Theory 9 (3): 253–27.

INDEX

Page numbers in *italics* denote photographs, and endnotes are indicated by "n" followed by the endnote number.

narratives of victimhood and, 245n8;
paramilitary violence, 49; state violence and repression, 52, 82
world-building, 15, 17–18, 29, 184–90

yam crisis. *See* ñame crisis (2017)
Youth Peace Provokers. *See* JOPPAZ
    (Youth Peace Provokers of the Alta
    Montaña)

Zamosc, León, 42–43, 48
Zehr, Larisa, 1–2, 5, 22, 73, 78, 81–82,
    220–21
Zenú peoples, 40
ZRC (Campesino Reserve), 191
ZVTN (Transitory Rural Zones for Nor-
    malization), 182

The authorized representative in the EU for product safety and compliance is:
Mare Nostrum Group
B.V Doelen 72
4831 GR Breda
The Netherlands

www.ingramcontent.com/pod-product-compliance
Lightning Source LLC
Chambersburg PA
CBHW020506270326
41926CB00008B/763